LITTLE
OHIO

QUARRY BOOKS

AN IMPRINT OF

INDIANA UNIVERSITY PRESS

LITTLE
OHIO

SMALL-
TOWN
DESTINATIONS

JANE SIMON AMMESON

This book is a publication of

Quarry Books
an imprint of

INDIANA UNIVERSITY PRESS
Office of Scholarly Publishing
Herman B Wells Library 350
1320 East 10th Street
Bloomington, Indiana 47405 USA

iupress.org

This book is printed on acid-free paper.

Manufactured in China

First printing 2023

Library of Congress Cataloging-in-Publication Data

Names: Ammeson, Jane Simon, author.
Title: Little Ohio : small-town destinations / Jane Simon Ammeson.
Description: Bloomington, Indiana : Quarry Books, [2023]
Identifiers: LCCN 2022033208 (print) | LCCN 2022033209 (ebook) |
ISBN 9780253065100 (paperback) | ISBN 9780253065117 (ebook)
Subjects: LCSH: Ohio—Guidebooks.
Classification: LCC F489.3 .A46 2023 (print) | LCC F489.3 (ebook) |
DDC 917.7104—dc23/eng/20220727
LC record available at https://lccn.loc.gov/2022033208
LC ebook record available at https://lccn.loc.gov/2022033209

For my husband, John, and my children, Evan and Nia.

And to all the wonderful people at
Indiana University Press, who are the best!

Contents

Acknowledgments

Knowing that I'll always take the back roads over the highway and, when given the choice, turn onto a dirt road and leave the pavement behind, Ashley Runyon, my editor at Indiana University at the time, asked me if I'd write this book.

Why not? I thought. I had flown over and driven through Ohio many times—on my way to other places. Now I'd get to see what, if anything, I'd been missing. So I grabbed my car keys, and sunglasses, got a map, and hit the road—and learned a large life lesson: always take the back roads; make a U-turn if you passed something by, because you never know if you'll pass that way again; take time to explore; and especially, if the road is unpaved, you definitely need to go. Every turn in the road revealed a new adventure, sometimes turning the clock back to when Native Americans built ceremonial mounds and earthworks or entering Amish villages, where horse and buggies are more common than cars.

Ohio, with its immaculate farms, tidy towns, and glittering cities, once was a wilderness on the edge of America's frontier, a setting for several game-changing battles where America's fate as a new country was on the line. It is a place where people value their heritage and showcase it by maintaining the beauty of their towns, villages, and hamlets.

There are so many people to thank who introduced me to what Ohio has to offer, making it difficult to know where to start. But I'm giving it a good try here. If I inadvertently leave someone's name out, I am so sorry.

Jill Bauer, Public Relations Manager, Lake Erie Shores & Islands
Ryan Berry, Executive Director, Darke County Visitors Bureau
Tamara K. Brown, Public Relations Manager, Office of Tourism Ohio
Buxton Inn, Granville, Ohio
Golden Lamb, Lebanon, Ohio
Shannon Folts, Visitor Experience Director, Marietta, Ohio

Angela Feenerty, President, Historical Society of Mount Pleasant, Ohio

Tiffany Gerber, Executive Director, Holmes County Chamber of Commerce & Tourism Bureau

Caleigh (Oravecz) Heuring, Marketing Manager, Destination Toledo, Convention & Visitors Bureau

Scott Hutchinson, Senior Communications Manager, Warren County Convention & Visitors Bureau

Kim Krieger, Media Relations, Sauder Village

Tonja Marshall, Executive Director of Marketing & Communications, Visit Canton

Emily McKinley, Coordinator of First Impressions, Ashland Area Chamber of Commerce

Taylor Meredith, Enjoy Oxford

John and Julie Mitchell, owners, Fig & Oak, Ashland

Robert Schilling, owner of the Buxton Inn, Granville

Jared Shive, Marketing Specialist, Starks Park District

Stephanie Siegel, Executive Director, Ashtabula County Convention & Visitors Bureau

Doug Smith, Doug Smith Realty & Auction Co.

Matthew Staugler, former Executive Director, Darke County Visitors Bureau

Carol Thress, Director of Sales & Marketing, Explore Licking County

Uniontown Brewing Co.

Amy Weirick, Weirick Communications

Sophia Winegard, CTA, Account Coordinator, Weirick Communications

Karen Wintrow, Executive Director, Yellow Springs Chamber of Commerce

Last but not least, thanks to all you Buckeyes for sharing your beautiful state!

NORTHEAST
OHIO

1

Alliance

Carnations and the Civil War may seem like an odd mix, but the town of Alliance in Northeast Ohio was a hotbed of abolitionism leading up to and during the Civil War and also the place where Dr. Levi Lamborn propagated from French seedlings a scarlet carnation he named the Lamborn red. A politician as well as a doctor, Lamborn, when running against William McKinley for a congressional seat, presented his carnation to the future president of the United States. McKinley came to believe that the Lamborn boutonniere was good luck and wore one frequently. Indeed, right before he was assassinated, he removed the carnation he was wearing to give it to an admirer. Would history be different if he hadn't been so gallant?

Lamborn lost his election; McKinley, who was assassinated, lost his life. But carnations officially became the state flower, and Alliance the Carnation City.

EAT

A large menu of classic Greek dishes such as pitas, gyros, Greek salads, baklava, and rizogalo, as well as of traditional American fare like hamburgers and french fries, makes Papa Gyros the kind of place everyone will enjoy.

In business since 1940 and still family owned, Heggy's Confectionery is a combination casual breakfast eatery and candy shop using family recipes dating back a century or so.

John and Nancy Grant, in stages between 1828 and 1842, built a home later used by their daughter and son-in-law, Sarah and Ridgeway Haines, as a station on the Underground Railroad. Now the Haines House Underground Railroad Museum, the home and its mid-Victorian decor and furnishings are on display, as is the attic where freedom seekers hid as they continued their way north, farther away from slave states. Programs presented here include Underground Railroad reenactments; Christmas lamplight tours; Music of the Civil War; Hands-On History, in which children engage in nineteenth-century activities; and reenactments of documented slave narratives. The Haines House has been recognized by the National Park Service's Network to Freedom program and the Ohio Underground Railroad Association.

The 164-acre Beech Creek Botanical Garden and Nature Preserve is a must-see for nature lovers. Beyond the beautiful gardens, there are other attractions, such as the butterfly house, caterpillar nursery, Amazing Garden Plant Science Center, nature playgrounds, hiking trails, nature store, and wildlife observation deck. Events and workshops include garden symposia, guided hikes, and Christmas at Beech Creek.

Cat lovers, rejoice. Your tabby is finally getting the recognition he or she more than deserves. The 1906 bank building, designed by one of Frank Lloyd Wright's associates, is now home to the five-thousand-square-foot Feline Historical Museum. Managed by the Cat Fanciers' Association, which is also housed in the building, it's a quirky place to visit, to say the least, but for feline aficionados, it offers so much. The walls are lined with cat-centric artwork, and the museum also boasts a six-thousand-volume library of feline-related books and Best Cat awards dating back to the 1880s, including the silver collar awarded to the Best Cat in New York in 1895.

Built as a private residence for Col. William Henry Morgan in 1904 at a cost of $400,000 and now the central administration building for the Alliance Public School System, Glamorgan Castle is open for tours at specified times. The hour-long tours encompass all four floors and cover the family who built the castle, their history, and the architecture of this one-of-a-kind place.

The opposite of vast castle-like estates fit for royalty, the Troll Hole Museum could be called "Trolls Galore," as it offers the largest collection of trolls in the world, according to the Guinness Book of World Records.

For all things trolls, this is it. It all adds up to thirty thousand troll dolls and pieces of memorabilia, as well as backdrops such as waterfalls and grottoes. But there's nothing static about this collection, as more and more trolls are frequently added. In keeping with the troll theme, the Grumpy Troll Café serves, among other menu offerings, gourmet brews, gourmet candy, and waffles. Learn the history of trolls and how they went from evil mythological beings to cute-ugly children's toys. There's also an annual Troll Mania on Main, a scavenger hunt for escaped trolls hiding throughout downtown Alliance, and a gift shop.

2

Ashland

Once called Uniontown when it was founded in 1815, the name had to be changed because there was already a town by that name. Supporters of Henry Clay, a noted Kentucky politician who ran for president several times, thought Ashland, the name of his grand mansion in Lexington, was the thing for their nameless town. Indeed, some Ashlanders liked the name so much that after moving to Oregon in the mid-1800s, they founded a city there with the same name.

EAT

Having set up shop in the old Gilbert Furniture store (they kept the cool neon sign), the Uniontown Brewing Company is in the city's historic downtown. It is a family-friendly place with an eclectic menu that includes some beer-based recipes, like chicken marinated in their cream ale, flank steak marinated in their 1850 Stout, and drunken fish—India pale ale (IPA)–battered perch with lettuce, pickles, and spicy tartar sauce.

Stop by Eva's Treats and Yoder's Red Barn Ice Cream—we know those are two ice cream shops, but it wouldn't hurt to try both. That's because our theory is that calories consumed on road trips don't count.

Get java-jazzed at Downtown Perk.

Fig and Oak

PLAY

Up, up, and away—for three decades, the Ashland BalloonFest has been an extravaganza of balloons in pretty patterns, unique shapes (think Santa Claus, a red dragon, an American flag, and a giant birthday cake), and bright colors. Held the last weekend in June, it has a whole lot going on, including stage performances.

There's also the annual Ashland Chautauqua, where famous actors do first-person historical portrayals in live performances.

No matter your musical tastes, there's something for everyone in Ashland, from the Ashland Symphony Orchestra to rock and roll at the Myers Memorial Band Shell.

The Jerome Fork of the Mohican River flows through the 215-acre Audubon Wetlands Preserve, creating a diverse ecological environment to explore. Follow the 250-foot boardwalk, the only way to see the majority of the park, through a large cattail marsh or take several short trails around the park's perimeters. There are meadows, wetlands, bridges, and river channels to see.

Uniontown Brewing Company

Find your way through the corn maze and pick your own pumpkins at Honey Haven Farms. For children, there's a petting zoo and a straw maze. For all, the seasonal market overflows with produce grown on the farm.

During the holiday season, the downtown hosts a holiday parade. Other events include Heritage Days and Farm Tour and a candlelight open house and madrigal feast. Enjoy Ashland University's Festival of Lights.

Arts and entertainment options include Ashland Symphony, Ashland University Theatre, Ashland Regional Ballet, and Ashland Symphonic Youth Chorus. And as the county seat, Ashland is also home to the county fair every year.

SHOP

Originally a general store owned by George Leonhart, the Fig and Oak, a boutique selling furniture, gifts, and the latest in home goods, was also once a bank, a bar, a barbershop, a grocery store, law offices, various small businesses, and a bookstore. Many of their products are sourced from quality suppliers who give back to charities and causes. They also carry a few vintage, repurposed, and handmade items.

For artisan products and munchies, check out Grandpa's Cheesebarn and Sweeties Chocolates, which offers summer sausages, meat sticks, jarred goods, cheese spreads, and over seventy varieties of cheese. Sweet selections include buckeye bark, chocolate-covered Rice Krispies, caramel marshmallows, and a variety of fudges besides just chocolate—sea salt caramel, peanut butter, and praline pecan. Hungry? Take a break at their café.

Since 1934, Ashley's Candy and Nut Shoppe has been the place to go for hand-dipped chocolates, toffees, turtles, nut clusters, truffles, buckeyes (of course), and so much more, as well as a variety of nuts, including toffee, butter-rum, cheddar-jalapeño, and honey-roasted peanuts.

Like the old vinyl LPs, 45s, and CDs from before electronic became the thing? Then stop by Kelley's Vinyl, where you can buy, sell, or trade good clean classic rock and roll, blues, hard rock, black metal, bluegrass, country, and rockabilly.

3

Ashtabula

Oh, what a difference a century or so makes. In the 1800s, Ashtabula Harbor, located on a curve of land where the Ashtabula River meets Lake Erie, held the rather dubious honor, along with Calcutta and Shanghai, of being the roughest port in the world. Now the revitalized Bridge Street District's commercial Victorian-era buildings—which in rowdier days housed bustling bordellos and the toughest of dive bars—have been renovated and replaced with unique shops, galleries, and restaurants. But that's not all: for nature lovers, Ashtabula's city parks and beaches offer options for boating, water sports, and fishing.

STAY

Built around 1887, Michael Cahill Bed and Breakfast, listed on the National Register of Historical Places and located in the historic district of Ashtabula Harbor, has a back-in-time feeling and a killer complimentary breakfast served in the dining room, which is set with fine crystal, china, and linens. Ingredients are seasonal and locally sourced, and breakfast can include sophisticated offerings such as strawberry Belgian waffles, eggs Benedict with sherry cream sauce, fresh asparagus, ribbon-cut fresh zucchini, and cherry tomato salad tossed with five peppercorn blend, white balsamic vinegar, and sea salt.

Family owned and operated for over fifty years, the Edge-O-Town Motel, noted by the Ashtabula County Ohio Visitors Bureau as one of

Ashtabula Harbor Light

the best places to stay in Ashtabula County, is close to Lake Erie, offers quality service, and is known for its cleanliness.

EAT

Once a butcher shop owned by Thomas Rennick and his family from 1889 to 1962, the Rennick Meat Market, a farm-to-table restaurant that honors its past, features "butcher inspired American food." Seasonal appetizers include deep-fried beets, cheddar cheese curds, small plates of pierogi, and Kobe corn dogs with house-made ketchup. Entrées include braised short ribs and beef Stroganoff. And then there are, of course, a variety of cuts of meat, from rib eyes to lesser-known cuts like bavette and flat iron—both tender and tasty. Sauce choices include béarnaise, blueberry, and horseradish cream.

For southern-style barbecue, a great craft beer bar, Briquettes Smokehouse, with its awesome patio and slow-smoked meats, is the place.

Need a jolt of caffeine? Harbor Perk has just the thing: specialty coffees such as lattes and cappuccinos roasted and brewed on-site, as well as teas, smoothies, and locally made pastries.

Ashtabula Harbor

PLAY

There's a wide spectrum of creative endeavors at the Ashtabula Arts Center, which offers classes, performances, and activities in the areas of dance, theater, music, and visual arts for all ages. Part of the community for sixty years, the center offers programming for all ages and levels of artistic talents, with workshops in pottery, painting, woodworking, knitting, and screen painting.

Bridge Street Art Works, a cooperative of local artists, features creations such as steampunk jewelry, painted furniture, pottery, and home decor, as well as classes and gallery displays.

Once the home of the lightkeepers and Coast Guard chiefs, the Ashtabula Maritime and Surface Transportation Museum on Walnut Boulevard, built in 1871, displays artifacts such as vintage photos of Ashtabula during its heyday as a shipping port, paintings, navigational equipment, and tools. For those really into this kind of thing, another great feature at the museum is the world's only working scale model of a Hulett ore-unloading machine. To provide a realistic feel for how it was back then, the museum offers interactive model train layouts of the harbor around the mid-twentieth century.

Walnut Beach Park has a great sandy beach with lots of space for setting up lounge chairs and flopping open beach towels. The park also has a waterfowl pond where white mute swans as well as mallards and other ducks come to rest.

Other Walnut Park Beach amenities include a playground, volleyball courts, boccie courts, picnic tables, and a short boardwalk. Another bonus is the pretty view of Ashtabula's historic lighthouse. Open year-round, the eighteen-hole disc golf course, boat launch, bait shop, boccie court, and swimming beach are popular features at Lakeshore Park.

A stop on the Underground Railroad, the nineteenth-century Hubbard House, now a museum, tells the story of the Hubbard family, who helped escaping slaves find their way to freedom.

A small stretch of beach is accessible by trail at Saybrook Township Park.

At the pet-friendly Brant's Apple Orchard, October is the time for their fall harvest activities, with cider making, apple picking, and everything apple (they grow twenty-two varieties) that's good to eat: caramel, apple cider doughnuts, cider slushies, pies, turnovers, muffins, cooking demonstrations, hay wagon rides, and more. Check the schedule for the date of their Halloween costume contest.

SHOP

Founded in a home in 1963, Marianne's Chocolates continues to be a purveyor of handcrafted sweets, known for its best-selling dark chocolate sea salt bark, dark chocolate sea salt caramels, and kettle-fresh small-batch candies like milk chocolate turtles. Located on historic Bridge Street.

Carlisle's Home in the Harbor, a family-owned store filled with home decor and gift items, is one of many eclectic shops on Bridge Street. It features a wine of the month, gifts such as Bambino light-up picture frames, and Cherith Valley's Hot 'n Spicy yummies, like their pickled vegetables, spirited fruits, and assorted condiments. Women's brands like Mona B. offer fashions designed for the urban American woman who craves both romanticism and individuality.

Check out the unique body care products, artistic and retro clothing, jewelry, and accessories at Heartmade Boutique and Bitchy Bath Co.

4

Berlin

It doesn't take more than one guess to figure out how Berlin got its name. Founded in 1818 by John Swigert and Joseph Troyer, who had both immigrated from Berlin, Germany, Berlin, Ohio, is the oldest village in Holmes County. A school was established that year, and four years later Berlin had its own post office. The village grew quickly, attracting German and Swiss immigrants who first settled in Pennsylvania before moving farther west to take advantage of this region's lush and cheap farmland. By 1832, Berlin boasted twenty-one residential houses, two stores, two taverns, and a physician. The completion of the National Road and Zane's Trace, large enough to accommodate horse and wagons, helped boost Berlin's prosperity.

The Amish were the next wave of settlers, and as the years progressed, their numbers increased to such an extent that Berlin bills itself as "the World's Largest Amish Settlement." And for good reason: Ohio has about fifty-six thousand Amish residents.

We think of regions settled by the Amish as life in the slow lane, and that's true when traveling through the countryside. But Berlin bustles with things to do.

EAT

Boyd and Wurthmann, the oldest restaurant in town, first opened as Hummel's Market in 1938. Seven years later, Dale Boyd and Herman Wurthmann purchased and renamed the business, and the name stuck

Amish buggy

for the forty years they owned it. Two of the reasons for their success were their quality pies, made daily by Bryl Wurthmann, and the welcoming atmosphere—they created a place for regulars to meet, drink coffee, and discuss, well, whatever needed to be talked about. Word got out, and the restaurant now serves four million customers a year.

For those who can't get enough of Amish fare, Berlin Farmstead Restaurant, located in the heart of town, is well known for their pan-fried chicken, real mashed potatoes, and wide selection of desserts: think whoopie pies in such flavors as chocolate or peanut butter pumpkin, as well as classic Amish pies—shoofly, maple custard, and red raspberry cream. In all, they typically have fifteen to twenty varieties of pie daily.

We're suckers for the pie à la mode smash at Der Bake Oven, which is basically what the name implies: vanilla ice cream smashed into your choice of pie. Trust us on this one—it's good. Or order their half-moon pie filled with apple schnitz, a local favorite. It's also a great place for sandwiches, salads, soups, and breakfast.

STAY

Berlin Cottages offers luxury accommodations close to everything the historic downtown has to offer. Berlin Village Inn is within walking

Kettle corn vendor

distance of many of the town's attractions. Donna's Premier Lodging provides a choice of villas, cottages, and suites downtown, as well as cabins and chalets located in the woods one mile outside the town.

Looking for cozy? Check in at Jake and Ivy's Bed and Breakfast.

For easy access to shopping and all Berlin has to offer, as well as a pool and a free breakfast, the Comfort Inn is a good place to rest at night.

SHOP

Come prepared to shop until you drop because Berlin is a serious destination for all things shopping. Start small for quilting supplies, classes, and information at Helping Hands Quilt Shop.

Stop by the Pottery Niche, which may well be the only place in the country specializing in handmade heirloom pottery from Boleslawiec, Poland. Much of it is labeled unikat, a designation meaning "unique" and given for the style's complicated designs and use of more colors.

Or go big at Berlin Village Gift Barn, once a dairy barn but now a multilevel twenty-thousand-square-foot store offering gifts, clothing, jewelry, handbags, home decor, garden accessories, and quilts, as well as products from such premium brands as Vera Bradley and Willow Trees.

The Red Poppy is a fun boutique with an assortment of gifts and home decor.

Just a mile north of Berlin (despite its Millersburg address), take a tour at Heini's Cheese Chalet, founded by Swiss immigrant Hans Dauwalder in the 1920s. The family-owned business sends its cheeses all over the country but continues to operate as it did all those years ago, offering early-morning deliveries of old-fashioned metal cans filled with fresh milk from Amish farmers. Back in the 1970s, the family also developed their original yogurt cheese, which is a big seller, as is their delicious homemade fudge, available in such flavors as root beer float, rainbow sherbet, chocolate peanut butter, chocolate mint, chocolate nut, and peanut butter. And did we mention their unique and tasty cheese fudge? Visitors can taste before they buy, as free samples of over fifty varieties of cheese, meat, jams, and fudge are available every day. Be sure to take time to browse through the gift shop. Tours are available.

Treasure hunters and vintage lovers are sure to find what they're looking for at the twenty-six-thousand-square-foot Berlin Village Antique Mall.

So many goodies, so little time. Dating back almost sixty years, Troyer Country Market is home to Amish Wedding Foods, a small-batch, naturally made line of jar goods ranging from the typical (but yummy) apple butters, salsas, and pickles to such intriguing foods as hot pickled asparagus, brandied peaches, blue goose jam (a mixture of blueberries and gooseberries), and candied jalapeños.

5

Carrollton

Located in the heart of Appalachia, Carrollton was originally called Centreville after Peter Bohart built a two-story log tavern at the crossroads of the Steubenville to Canton and New Lisbon to Cadiz Pikes soon after immigrating in 1809. But when the county was chartered in 1832 and named after Charles Carroll, the last surviving signer of the Declaration of Independence (we hope he learned about the honor before he died the following year), Centreville was renamed Carrollton. Bohartville might have been a good choice as well because the tavern owner was not only a businessman but also a civic benefactor, donating lands for a church and cemetery, and it is there that he is buried, the spot marked by a grand monument.

EAT

Betty Kaye Bakery, famous for their brownies, which come in over twenty seasonal flavors, has been open since 1950. Since then, anyone walking into the store has been greeted with freshly baked coconut or cinnamon rolls, fruit-filled danish, and other sweet rolls.

Donna's Deli, located on the public square, features a long list of house-made soups, sandwiches, and desserts. Check out their panini, such as the Cuban panini, made from a slow-cooked shredded pork shoulder, or the Walnut Creek ham and swiss, made with pickle slices and their homemade pepper mustard on a ciabatta-style flatbread.

PLAY

The McCook House Civil War Museum, home to the Carroll County Historical Society, is a large antebellum brick house on the southwest corner of Carrollton's public square. It was built by Daniel McCook in 1837. He needed a huge house, as he and his wife had twelve children—nine boys and three girls. The family was known as the Fighting McCooks but shouldn't be confused with the more famous McCoy family of the McCoy-Hatfield feud.

Fifteen members of the McCook family focused their fighting by joining the Union army during the Civil War.

Daniel, a sixty-five-year-old major, was killed in action at the Battle of Buffington Island; his son Latimer, a physician, was wounded at Vicksburg and again during Sherman's March to the Sea; he died of complications from his battle wounds four years after the war ended. Another son, Brigadier General Robert Latimer McCook, was killed by one of John Hunt Morgan's cavalrymen near Salem, Alabama, and Brigadier General Daniel McCook Jr. was killed in action at Kennesaw Mountain. After refusing an offer of a lieutenant's commission in the regular army, Charles Morris McCook died in his father's arms at the First Battle of Bull Run.

Algonquin Mill Fall Festival

Even the among the ones who didn't die fighting for the Union cause, some of Daniel's other children didn't fare well either. Things looked good for a while for Colonel Edwin Stanton McCook, who was elected governor of the Dakota Territory until he was assassinated in office. Another son, John James McCook, a graduate of the US Naval Academy, died off the coast of South America while serving as a midshipman on the US frigate *Delaware*. One can only imagine poor Mrs. McCook receiving one letter after another telling of the loss of her beloved husband and sons.

If you're counting, there was another tribe of McCooks—the five sons of Daniel's younger brother, Dr. John McCook, who all—including John—fought in the war. But they had much better luck and all survived.

Enjoy nature at the Bluebird Farm Park, where there are trails and a walking bridge, a summer concert series at the Bluebird Amphitheater, Susie's Museum of Childhood, and a gift shop.

The Ashton House Museum, home of philanthropists John and Evelyn Ashton, showcases their life, and just down the street is the Ashton 5¢

and 10¢ Store, open for almost a century. Also called the Ashton Franklin Store, it is one of the now almost forgotten five-and-dime stores so popular for several generations. It has a myriad of goods stuffed everywhere at great prices. It was the first of many dime stores owned by the Ashtons.

The Algonquin Mill Complex is centered on the old mill built about 1826. The mill continues to function, making flours, mixes, and other products for sale. There's also the Mill Barn; listed on the National Register of Historic Places, it was the place for travelers to rest and feed their horses while the grain was being milled. Other historic buildings appear on the grounds of the complex: a one-room schoolhouse, a stagecoach inn, a doctor's office, several log cabins, a farmhouse, and more. It's a delightful collection of region homes from the past now curated by the Carroll County Historical Society.

The society also presents the annual Algonquin Mill Fall Festival every October.

6

Chagrin Falls

A scenic series of waterfalls cascade through the center of Chagrin Falls, a village of around four thousand founded in 1837. The village itself is adorable, but the name may be considered less so. Its origins are hazy, and among the choices are the fact that *chagrin* means "clear water" in the dialect of one of the Native American tribes, including the Ottawa who resided in the region. Another pinpoints a French trader named François Seguin (also Saguin), who was the first recorded European settler in what would become Cuyahoga County. Seguin established a trading post on the nearby Cuyahoga River sometime before 1742, constructing several buildings and establishing a trading partnership with the tribes living there. But wait—there's another theory. In French, the word *chagrin* means "annoyance, frustration, or vexation," and supposedly Moses Cleveland who founded—yes, you guessed it—Cleveland was severely vexed when crossing the Chagrin River because its many sandbars made the passage difficult.

Besides scenic bridges crossing the river, Chagrin Falls also has a lovely historic downtown, with architecture similar to that of New England. Shops, restaurants, and galleries are now housed in Victorian commercial, Gothic Revival, and Italianate buildings dating back to the 1800s. Take any side street, and find numerous excellently maintained century-plus homes in myriad styles, including Federal, Queen Anne, and Colonial. As small as the village is, its historic roots are such that there are three historic districts on the National Register of Historic Places

Main Street Bridge

with more than one hundred contributing structures; the historical society offers tours. Among those are Chagrin Arts, the former Harmon Barrows Harness Shop built in 1846, and Chagrin Hardware and Supply Co. on Main Street, which first opened for business in 1857.

STAY

In downtown Chagrin Falls, the Inn of Chagrin Falls, built in 1927, is a lovely place with exquisitely turned-out rooms and pretty gardens accented with restored fountains.

EAT

Enjoy the stunning views of the falls and the classic American fare at 17 River Grille.

Get a touch of France at the Paris Room, which serves such dishes as wild-caught sole with crabmeat stuffing and lemon caper cream sauce and tender boneless beef short ribs. Enjoy one of their signature drinks, like the Madam Springs Bubbly, a mix of sparkling wine with Chambord; classic sidecars; and the James "Bond" McSherry Hendricks Martini, to the accompaniment of live music.

Bell Street Park

Or go for the French country château experience—or really four themed dining areas at Cru Uncorked. With over 350 wine selections from around the globe, you can choose a wine for each course.

Try the handcrafted beer and menu items at Crooked Pecker Brewing Company, housed in a repurposed warehouse.

If you haven't yet tasted Jeni's Splendid Ice Creams, you're in luck because there's a Jeni's in Chagrin Falls. Eschewing synthetic flavorings, food colorings, off-the-shelf mixes, and such bizarre stuff as emulsifiers and stabilizers, Jeni's makes sure it's all about the ice cream. The flavors are sophisticated—like brandied banana brûlée, cognac with gingerbread, and sweet cream biscuits and peach jam.

The Original Dave's Cosmic Subs also has a store in Chagrin Falls. In business for almost a quarter of a century, this is a kind of hippie-dippie business with wholesome ingredients, intriguing names, and psychedelic colors.

PLAY

Chagrin Arts offers year-round performing arts events and gallery exhibits. Chagrin Valley Little Theatre, founded in 1930, is one of the oldest community theaters in the United States. It presents plays, musicals, youth theater education, and special events throughout the year.

River Run Park, the place for such annual local festivals as Blossom Time Carnival and Art by the Falls, stretches along the Chagrin River and offers seating areas by the largest falls and in a covered picnic area.

Behind the baseball diamond, it connects to the 298-acre Frohring Meadows, where there are two walking paths: the 0.7-mile Dragon Fly Trail and 2.8-mile Big Bluestem Trail.

Learn about local history at the Chagrin Falls Historical Society and Museum, housed in a home built in 1874.

SHOP

The Chagrin Falls Popcorn Shop, an iconic store that first opened in 1949, is known for its varieties of popcorn, including pecan almond caramel corn, Chrissy corn (sweet cranberry), sweet sriracha corn, garlic white cheddar, sweet sriracha cheese, and Cajun kettle corn. They also serve Country Parlour ice cream, a Northeast Ohio favorite, as well as Euclid Beach custard and locally roasted coffee. The brightly painted store with its old-fashioned window awnings was built in 1875 as a sales office for the mill that once stood next to it.

For home decor and interior design, there's Chestnut Hill Home, with its stylish collections of furniture, lighting, drapery, and tabletop accessories,

Chuck's Fine Wines not only has a large, curated section of wines but also ales, beers, gourmet foods, and cheese.

Emphasizing smaller lines and emerging designers, Blush Boutique carries clothing, shoes, accessories, and gifts.

The three-story Fireside Book Shop, in business for over fifty-five years, is what we all yearn for—a marvelous independent bookstore with tomes for all interests as well as gifts.

NOTABLES

Actor Tom Conway, who was known for his role as Ensign Parker in *McHale's Navy* and who was also a regular on *The Carol Burnett Show*, where he had several ongoing characters, including the Oldest Man, the Dumb Private, and Mister Tudball.

Doug Kenney, cofounder of *National Lampoon* magazine and screenwriter of such movies as *Caddyshack* and *Animal House*.

Cartoonist Bill Watterson, creator of the *Calvin and Hobbes* comic strip.

San Francisco Giants outfielder Ted Wood.

7

Charm

The road to Charm runs along fenced-in pastures where mares and their foals nuzzle between breaks to graze and past a school where a horse-drawn cart is parked outside the front door and girls in bonnets and skirts play soccer in the sports fields next door. It rises and falls as it curves past farmland and woods, branching off to even narrower lanes that lead upward through woods before opening up to panoramic views of the valley far below.

Charm itself should be a slip of a town. After all, only sixty-five people live here, all Mennonites. But it's a busy place during the day, with workers and guests visiting the restaurants, stores, and, most of all, the amazing Keim Lumber, a place for hobbyists, homeowners, home builders, construction workers, and land developers to shop. But more about that later.

STAY

Surrounded by a gently rolling landscape featuring ponds, gardens, and two gazebos, the family-owned Guggisberg Swiss Inn offers guided horseback trips, sleigh rides, and a recently opened winery on the premises. Everyone who stays in one of the inn's twenty-three rooms is treated to a hot Amish breakfast casserole each morning. All rooms face west overlooking the expansive Doughty Valley. Watch the sun set below the ridge while you sip one of their award-winning wines, such as Misty Meiner, a gewürztraminer with subtle hints of pear and a floral fragrance; pink catawba, with its perfect balance of sweet and tart; a semidry pinot noir; or one of their fruit wines—strawberry, raspberry, or cranberry.

Wander the grounds, but beware: the many horses who live at the stables wander freely and want nothing more than to be part of the crowd, often gently nudging a guest to make sure they get the attention they deserve. In the morning, the inn serves breakfast in the enclosed porch. At night, buy a bottle of the house wine and admire the stars.

Guggisberg Cheese

EAT

Authentic Austrian-Swiss food (with a little German thrown in as well) graces the menu at Chalet in the Valley. Owned by the Guggisberg family, the Chalet is known for their fondue, six types of schnitzel, Bavarian meatloaf, and award-winning grilled cheese made with—you guessed it—Guggisberg cheese.

Charm Sweet Shoppe and Pizzeria covers the bases when it comes to baked goods, whether its savory pizzas or something sweet. Charm Family Restaurant is definitely the place to go for Amish-style meals.

PLAY

Remember those horses wanting some attention at the Guggisberg Swiss Inn? During the day, they earn their keep because the inn is also home to the Amish Country Riding Stables, which offers guided horseback rides throughout the day.

SHOP

With such a large population of German, Amish, and Swiss inhabitants, Charm has to have at least one cheese store. We're recommending

Guggisberg Swiss Inn

Guggisberg Cheese, housed in a Swiss-style building. There you can watch cheesemaking and munch on samples before deciding which of the award cheeses you want to take home.

It all started when Alfred Guggisberg—a native of Switzerland who attended the Swiss Federal Molkereishulle, or Institute of Cheese, and practiced as a cheesemaker for a few years—immigrated to the US and opened his cheese factory, which is still family-owned. Guggisberg Baby Swiss was recently awarded number one cheese in America as the grand champion at the US Championship Cheese Contest. Along with first place in the Baby Swiss category, Guggisberg took first, second, and third places in the swiss category with their premium swiss. Their "Original Baby Swiss," which is patented, is one of the more than forty varieties of cheese they produce. Shop for other Swiss specialties in the store as well, like cuckoo clocks and chocolates.

Outside, enjoy the pretty Swiss-themed garden on the property.

It often seems in Amish country that the more back roads you take, the more there is discover.

Hershberger's Farm and Bakery is known for its wonderful assortment of baked goods, jarred goods, country decor and furniture, and just about everything else. The grounds also offer a petting zoo and pony rides.

The two-story Charm General Store is the place to go for ice cream on a hot day, bulk foods at great prices (a very Amish shopping experience), housewares, and deli items. Downstairs (you can get there through the stairs at the back of the store or enter through the alleyway separating the General Store from the Charm Family Restaurant) is where the Amish and Mennonites shop for those bonnets, black hats, heavy boots (good for farmwork), and plain dresses of white and pale colors (for single women and girls) and dark blue and black (for matrons). It's like walking into a cultural museum of clothing as well as a great place to pick up a straw hat for an inexpensive price.

But the really big draw in Charm—and we're talking major league—is Keim Lumber, a the fourth-generation family-owned business that opened in 1911 as a rough lumber mill with four employees. Fast-forward to the present, and Keim now encompasses a fifty-acre complex with not only the retail store but also offices, a warehouse, and millwork production space totaling with more than seven hundred thousand square feet. Keim employs nearly five hundred employees.

But even more than that, it's beautiful (yes, I know we're talking about a huge hardware store, but it truly is), with cherrywood staircases, railings, balustrades, and cozy sitting nooks. Unlike any other hardware store we've been in, there's a place to dine. That would be the aptly named Carpenter Café. Keim is so popular that it's on the itinerary of many bus tours. It is indeed a wonder even if you've never held a hammer. Stocked with everything you could think of, Keim has an entire area dedicated to fascinating tree trunks (those who are handy use them to make tables) and such exotic woods as Chakte kok, padauk, katalox, and purpleheart, which are sourced from such places as Africa, Indonesia, South America, the Pacific Rim, and Central America.

Beside the large parking lot, Keim also has hitching posts for Amish and Mennonite shoppers.

8

Conneaut

Conneaut, tucked away on the shores of Lake Erie, is located at the mouth of Conneaut Creek on an old Indian trail in the very farthest corner of Northeast Ohio. As far as the name goes, its origins are somewhat mysterious, so take your pick of the options out there. Is it from the Seneca word meaning "standing stone," "place of many fish," or "place where snow lies in spring"? If that's not confusing enough, Conneaut has had various American names since its founding. It first was known as Port Independence, then Salem, and later Lakeville. How any of those morphed into Conneaut is unknown. But one thing that's for sure—Conneaut, with its seven miles of Lake Erie shoreline, is a popular summertime destination.

Moses Cleveland arrived here on July 4, 1796, along with a group of fifty men, women, and children. He and most of the group didn't stay long, and it's an easy guess where he ended up. But James Kingsbury stayed, along with his pregnant wife, three children, and a nephew. Then business called him back to New Hampshire, and circumstances—a fever, a dead horse, lots of snowstorms—kept him from returning until Christmas Eve, when he found his wife almost dead of starvation. Stories diverge here: the baby either died before he was able to return home or perished shortly afterward. The bottom line is that this baby was the first White child born in the Western Reserve of northern Ohio. The Kingsburys moved on, but the new settlement did OK without them, and in 1833 Conneaut—or whatever it was called then—had a meetinghouse, several shops and stores, a printing house, and two taverns.

STAY

Off the beaten path, Buccia Vineyards is a winery producing cool-climate, handcrafted, artisanal wines; a lovely setting to sample wines; and a bed and breakfast.

Described in an early history of Ashtabula County as "one of the more attractive homes in Ashtabula County," the three-story Grandpa's Castles Bed and Breakfast, completed in 1898, is an architectural delight of burnished wood, graceful staircase, turret, and wraparound porch. Amenities include luxurious accommodations with private baths, a salt-water heated pool, and a dry sauna.

Built in the early 1800s, the Centennial Inn Bed and Breakfast was once the home of Dr. John Venen, Conneaut's first medical doctor. The inn is a perfect balance of history and modern amenities.

EAT

Established in 1952, the White Turkey Drive-In is the real deal, a bebop, carhop kind of place. If you're wondering about the name, well, founders Eddie and Marge Tuttle also raised White Holland turkeys. Using the meat from their birds, Marge created their famed shredded turkey sandwich, and the couple decided to name the restaurant in honor of the breed. As for the sandwich, it's still made from Marge's recipe and remains a best seller today.

Located in the historic port area just one block from Lake Erie and the marina, Biscotti's Restaurant offers Italian cuisine, such as Italian wedding soup; chicken florentine alfredo; langostinos diablo; veal dishes such as piccata, parmesan, and florentine; and some Lake Erie specialties, such as pan-fried perch and grilled salmon.

Housed in a century-old church, Heavenly Creamery makes over 150 flavors of small-batch premium custards and sorbets.

Open from 4:00 a.m. to 3:00 p.m., Angela's Café is a casual eatery with good food and friendly service—the kind of place where you can get stacks of pancakes, corned beef hash, and french toast. There's also outdoor dining.

Fun and casual, Sparky's Place is the kind of restaurant with a scratch kitchen, making sausage and other items on site. Look for such specials as their jalapeño popper burger, made with fresh ground beef, jalapeño cheddar cream cheese, thick-cut bacon, sliced jalapeños, cheddar crisps,

Conneaut Township Park

pickles, and red onions, or the Salty's jalapeño-cheddar sausage on a bun, topped with sautéed onions and jalapeños, bacon, shredded cheddar, their homemade queso, and brown mustard.

PLAY

Perch and Pilsner is typically a Labor Day weekend event celebrated on the shores of Lake Erie at the nearly sixty-acre Conneaut Township Park. Enjoy such festival highlights as shows by the Chippewa Lake Water Ski Show Team, the state's only competitive water ski show team, live entertainment, and lots of food vendors selling such fair necessities as corn dogs, kettle corn, gyros, elephant ears, beer, and wine. And because this is a perch fest with a perch fishing tournament, there are also perch sandwiches.

Often overlooked—though it shouldn't be—the lovely stretch of sand along Lake Erie in Conneaut Township Park has much to offer: wide beaches, a historic lighthouse, a boardwalk, a pavilion, and concessions. And from Memorial Day through September, the Lighthouse Cruisers offer Cruise-Ins for classic car enthusiasts starting at 6:00 p.m. and going until dusk. You don't have to own a classic vehicle to enjoy the food and music while looking at the cars and, most likely, a stunning sunset.

Conneaut Historical Railroad Museum, housed in the 1900 New York Central Station, is filled with treasures from the railroad days, including an 1866 stock certificate of the Red River Line (NYC); artifacts from the Ashtabula Bridge Disaster of 1876; displays of lanterns, timetables, passes, and old photos; steam locomotives; freight cars; and other railroad equipment. The museum also has one of the last Nickel Plate Berkshires as well as a wooden caboose from the Bessemer Railroad.

World War II historians will like seeing the exhibits at the North Coast D-Day WWII History Museum, but more than that, the museum is supported by D-Day Ohio, the largest D-Day reenactment in the US. Held annually at Township Park, the free event is an educational reenactment of the World War II European theater of operations and the D-Day Normandy invasion. Thousands of reenactors remain in costume—and in role—throughout the three-day event, allowing visitors to move from camp to camp, getting each participant's view of the battle.

The 2,236,800-acre Lake Erie American Viticulture Area (AVA) stretches along the south shore of Lake Erie through the states of Ohio, Pennsylvania, and New York. It's a prime grape-growing area, and Conneaut is home to several wineries, including the well-established Markko Vineyard, which opened in 1969 and pioneered the raising of European vinifera grapes in the area, creating two vinifera-chardonnay and riesling varietals.

Tastings at Tarsitano Winery are by appointment only, but they're worth the trip. Owner Ken Tarsitano is a vineyard consultant and lecturer who has spent more than two decades in the wine and grape industry.

Located on the Lake Erie shore, the Conneaut Arts Center is the place for community events, programs, and art classes.

Conneaut Creek is one of four Ohio-designated Wild and Scenic Rivers, those defined as having outstanding natural, cultural, and recreational values, located in Ashtabula County. That's a lot considering that there are only fifteen Wild and Scenic Rivers in the entire state. The 43.9-mile river, which is stocked with steelhead, musky, tiger musky, and walleye, meanders through northwestern Pennsylvania and Northeast Ohio. Harbor Yak rents canoes and kayaks.

9

Dover

I f dandelions are your thing, think Dover in Tuscarawas County, home
of the annual Dandelion May Fest, held at the beginning of May each
year. Where else can you sip dandelion sangria, compete in a dandelion-
picking contest, make your own dandelion jelly, and shop for such products as dandelion soap, jewelry, and pottery? To take the dandelion theme
even further, vendors are on hand to sell sausage, bread, gravy, lasagna,
and whatever else someone has come up with—all made with dandelions
as an ingredient.

Nestled in the foothills of the Appalachian Mountains, Dover is on
the Tuscarawas River, and beyond dandelions, there's plenty to see and
do in this adorable town.

STAY

The Crowe's Nest Bed and Breakfast, a grand Victorian built in 1881, offers an experience that's a step back in time with modern-day amenities.

EAT

We dare you to stop at just one at Dough Co. Doughnuts and Coffee. It's
a hard choice, but here are the options: cream sticks filled with caramel,
chocolate, maple, and more; cake or yeast doughnuts; turnovers; and meat
and cheese filled kolaches—pepperoni and swiss, sausage and American,
and bacon and swiss.

Breitenbach Wine Cellars

Ernest Warther Museum and Gardens

The former Oak Grove School (District 6), built in 1886, is a quaint old-fashioned school topped with a belfry and bell for calling kids to class. Now, it's the School House Winery, and it has a deck overlooking a green expanse of lawn and garden with a pond and fountain. The setting is perfect for sampling wine and indulging in their menu offerings, such as pizza, appetizers, and subs.

Other eating options include Mindy's Diner, open for breakfast and lunch, located in the historic downtown. Check out their daily specials.

PLAY

Breitenbach Wine Cellars introduced the Dandelion May Fest more than twenty-six years ago. But they first introduced dandelions into their wine even longer ago than that and now make a dandelion sangria, selling

Dover Dam

hundreds of gallons during the festival. For those who hate the weeds—at least when they're dotting your lawn—take a hint from the festival and host your own dandelion-picking contest like they do here. Located in Der Marktplatz, they also make wines from grapes, fruit, and berries. Enjoy wood-fired pizzas and salads either indoors or out on the patio at their Breitenbach Café.

The seventeen-room Reeves Victorian Home and Carriage House Museum (and that's not including the third-floor ballroom) has been completely restored and is filled with the Reeves family's original furniture and memorabilia, all arranged as they would have been when the family lived there more than a century ago. Behind the home, check out the vehicles—ranging from a carriage used by the family in 1892, a family sleigh, a restored doctor's buggy from when physicians made house calls, and a very rare 1922 electric car.

Celebrate Dover's history during their annual Canal Festival held on Memorial Day weekend.

A fascinating third- and fourth-generation family-owned museum, the Ernest Warther Museum and Gardens are built around the original location of Ernest and Frieda Warther's home, Ernest's original work-shop, and the first museum that opened in the backyard in 1936. The museum's exhibitions include American Indian artifacts and arrowheads as well as Ernest's amazing hand carvings, which showcase the history of the steam engine.

SHOP

Started as a co-op in 1933 by farmers, Broad Run Cheesehouse has evolved over the years. Now, there's a gift shop and a curtain and lace shop, as well as their Swiss Heritage Winery, offering a wide range of wines from sweet to dry and made with both grapes and other fruits. Both their cheeses and wines are made on the premises and garner awards.

Silver Moon Winery makes and sells more than forty styles of wine—sweet, dry, bold reds, and crisp whites, as well as dessert wines. Sip and enjoy in the lovely tasting room or outside during warm weather.

NOTABLE

Playwright, director, and actor Elliott Nugent was born in Dover in 1899.

Rear Admiral Herald F. Stout, born in Dover, served in World War II and Korea. The USS *Stout* was named after him. He is buried in Dover Burial Park.

William Clarke Quantrill, a Confederate guerrilla leader during the American Civil War, was born in Dover in 1837 and is buried at Dover's Fourth Street Cemetery.

10

Geneva

Ashtabula County, part of the Lake Erie AVA in the heart of the Grand River Valley, has a seemingly endless number of wineries, and the majority are within a ten-mile-square area encompassing Geneva, Geneva-on-the-Lake, and Harpersfield. So pull out the map and get ready to explore Northeast Ohio wine country.

But let's start with a little history before you go. First settled in 1805 and named after Geneva, New York, Geneva interestingly wasn't incorporated as a city until 1958. It's located close to Lake Erie and also to Geneva-on-the-Lake, so it's easy to get the two confused. But while Geneva-on-the-Lake is actually on the beach, Geneva has more wineries. So it evens out.

STAY

Maddie's Place is a one-bedroom duplex that comfortably sleeps four in downtown Geneva. It's within walking distance of several of the local wineries, shopping centers, and restaurants. The beach and other attractions are just a short drive away.

Warner-Concord Farms is a luxury bed and breakfast and horse farm set on 130 acres and conveniently located close to many area wineries.

The one-room Moonshine Manor Cabin (don't you just love the name!) at Sawdust Camp provides a luxury glamping experience. Located near the Sawdust Preserve, which is part of the Natural History Museum of Cleveland, it's just uphill from a creek and the perfect place to spot

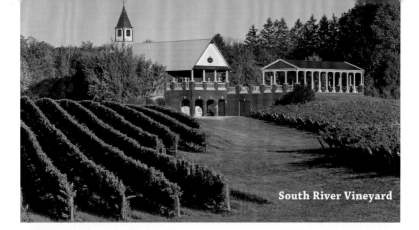

South River Vineyard

Geneva State Park

wildlife. It sleeps four very snugly, and there's a firepit, a porch, a cast iron cookstove for heat, kitchenware, hammock hooks, and an Amish-built outhouse.

EAT

Order a glass of sweet pea dandelion, pink delight, or blackberry wine and enjoy a shrimp, chicken, or prime rib dinner at the Virant Family Winery, where they've been making wine for three generations.

Parrots galore! Harvest spice wine! Great food for lunch, dinner, and Sunday brunch! You can't beat this unique combination at Deer's Leap Winery. Their wines are a culmination of six generations of wine making, and the winery is home to Robert Bostwick, the international award-winning winemaker with more than thirty-five years of experience in making wine.

The Italian-centric menu at the Ferrante Winery and Ristorante also offers vegetarian options and hosts experiences such as live music, off-site wine tastings, and Ohio Wine Producers events.

PLAY

Barrels and Bridges Tours not only offer wine tours, including one visiting four of the county's nineteen covered bridges, but also fun day trips, such as their Middlefield Amish Experience, Chardon antiquing, and outlet mall shopping, as well as educational tours of wineries.

You can't miss the red barn—a big giveaway that you're at the Red Eagle Distillery. It's the type of place that produces award-winning spirits using locally sourced ingredients.

A casual place that attracts a diverse crowd, the Winery at Spring Hill has a nice selection of menu items, wines to taste, and, for fun, cabernet sauvignon slushies.

Geneva has three covered bridges—the double-spanned 228-foot Harpersfield Bridge, built in 1868 and listed on the National Register of Historic Places, is the third-longest in the state. Located in Harpersfield Covered Bridge Metropark, it is one of only sixteen drivable covered bridges in the state. The longest single-span bridge in the state, Mechanicsville Road Covered Bridge, spans the Grand River. Built in 1866, it is believed to be the oldest covered bridge in the state, and like the Harpersfield Bridge, it is one of only sixteen drivable covered bridges in Ohio.

Sample the fruits of the vineyard at the family-owned Hundley Cellars, surrounded by acres of grapes, woods, and fields. The view can be enjoyed from both inside the lodge-like setting with its fireplaces going to keep toasty on a winter's day and outside on the decks on a pretty spring, summer, or fall day.

A stop on the Vines and Wines Wine Trail, the Old Mill Winery is housed in an adorable 1860s mill, one of the oldest buildings in Geneva. Besides a full menu, there are gluten-free offerings and a kids' menu. It's open year-round, so you can enjoy the live music, tastings outdoors in warm weather, and the overall historic atmosphere.

At the third-generation Kosicek Vineyards, founded in 1929 by the Slovenian grandfather of one of the owners, the wine list includes locally grown offerings and those produced at the winery, and the menu features local cuisine. There's an emphasis on pairing local foods with their wines.

South River Vineyard is an estate winery located in a church at least a century old with vistas of Grand River Valley's many vineyards. The 1892 church was moved from another location, but in honor of the building's history, its original pews, interior door, wainscoting, flooring, and some of the stained-glass windows remain.

A couple more wineries to put on your list: M Cellars and Laurello Vineyards.

Geneva State Park

Take a break from wine and visit the 698-acre Geneva State Park which stretches along the Lake Erie shores and offers accessibility to Lake Erie's central basin with a six-lane boat ramp and marina with temporary slips and charter fishing boats.

SHOP

Offering one of the largest gift shops in the area and housed in a century-old home, Catherine's Christmas has, you guessed it, lots of holiday finds all year-round.

Earth's Natural Treasures sells health foods, healing stones and crystals, lotions, clothing, lucky bamboo, and works by regional artists.

For vintage goods, check out the great selections at Broadway Antiques.

11

Geneva-on-the-Lake

Back when the region was all water, prairie, sand, swale, woods, and ponds, three gents with names that would be recognized even today as captains of industry—John D. Rockefeller, Harvey Firestone, and Henry Ford—came here to fish and hunt.

But even before that, in the early 1800s, lumber, lime kilns, sawmills, and shipbuilding were activities in the region. Monstrous-sized sturgeons swam close to shore, and wildlife abounded. Soon after the Sturgeon Point House, located on the water, opened, catering to travelers and tradesmen wanting to fish and hunt. After the Civil War, Cullen Spencer and Edwin Pratt turned land they called Sturgeon Point into a playground with a horse-powered carousel and then later campgrounds, cabins, a dance hall, and tourist cabins. By 1869, Geneva-on-the-Lake (nicknamed GOTL) had become a destination, and so it continues today.

STAY

No matter what you want in a place to stay, Lakehouse Inn has you covered. A restaurant, winery, spa, and bed and breakfast, the inn is located right on the southern shore of Lake Erie.

Call it a triple run at the Crosswinds Grille—enjoy a glass of wine as the sun sets, stay for dinner, and spend the night.

Built in the 1880s, Eagle Cliff Inn is a lovely bed and breakfast listed on the National Register of Historic Places. The owners also have charming cottages with private courtyards. All can enjoy the water views from the large wraparound porch.

EAT

In business since 1938, Madsen Donuts knows their doughnuts, but don't count them out when it comes to breakfast, lunch, and dinner as well.

For local wines, wine slushies, and more than twenty artisan beers on tap, as well as their popular tea beers and appetizers, burgers, and other good grub from the grill, check out Goblin Wine and Ale House

Open for over seventy-five years, Mary's Kitchen is a friendly family-style place serving breakfast, lunch, and dinner with such classic lakeside menu items as their lake perch dinner and spicy garlic langostinos, as well as landlubber-type foods like homestyle meatloaf and smokehouse chicken.

The Sandy Chanty Seafood Restaurant lives up to its name with lots of delicious dishes, such as salmon

Eddie's Grill

stuffed with crab patty, covered in lobster sauce; conch fritters; lobster lasagna; and mussels and cockles on potatoes.

PLAY

You don't have to stay at the Lodge at Geneva-on-the-Lake to take advantage of the Ohio Wine Shuttle, a year-round shuttle offering trips to a variety of wineries. Trips last up to five hours, depending on what you choose. Oh, and just for more fun, the Lodge is home to Lake Erie Canopy Tours, so check out their zip-line options.

Best Coast Water Sports rents Jet Skis, WaveRunners, Sea-Doos, stand-up paddleboards (SUP), and kayaks and offers temporary boater licenses and SUP lessons.

Water-sport rentals like kayaks and paddleboards are also available at North Coast Outpost at Breakwater Beach in the Geneva State Park, Geneva-on-the-Lake West Site.

Old Firehouse Winery

GOTL's "Strip" is a section of State Route 531 that has long drawn visitors because of its multitude of arcades, restaurants, and parks. Places to eat include Eddie's Grill, a longtime favorite that opened in 1950 as Richardson Root Beer and Hotdog Stand. The Old Firehouse Winery has outdoor dining with great views of Lake Erie, a full-service menu, dancing, and an old-fashioned Ferris wheel that is open in the evening for rides. Its name, #5 Old Eli, refers to its status as the fifth model made from the original patent of George Ferris, whose Ferris wheel was introduced in Chicago at the 1893 World's Columbian Exposition. This one was built in 1956 and functioned as a ride at a now-closed amusement park before being rescued and refurbished by the winery, which claims to be the only winery with a Ferris wheel. They're probably right.

For artisan brews, check out GOTL Brewing Company, a restaurant with a full-service bar and outdoor dining with views of Lake Erie.

SHOP

Frank's Toybox is a buy, sell, and trade place specializing in motorcycle memorabilia, vintage items like old signs and ads, petroliana (items related to gas stations and the oil business), furniture, and you name it. Frank, the owner of the Toybox, is called "the original American picker."

The Gift Shop at the Lodge offers a wide arrangement of items—apparel, regional wines and foods, jewelry, gift baskets (great at holiday time), works by local authors and artists, and Northeast Ohio memorabilia.

L. Taylor Glass Studio is a home studio featuring finished glass art, glass art supplies, and classes in stained glass, fused glass, beach glass, and wire wrapping.

NOTABLE

Ransom E. Olds, founder of Oldsmobile, was born and raised in Geneva-on-the-Lake.

12

Hanoverton

A tiny hamlet with a population under five hundred, Hanoverton, founded in 1813 by a Quaker abolitionist, once bustled as a midway point on the Sandy and Beaver Canal, which stretched 73.5 miles from the Ohio River at Smith's Ferry to the Ohio and Erie Canal at Bolivar. At

Spread Eagle Tavern

Spread Eagle Tavern

the height of its canal days, Hanoverton had two thousand residents. The twenty-three-acre Hanoverton Canal Town District boasts thirty brick and frame homes built in a canal-era architecture style between 1817 and 1874, many of them little changed since then.

Hanoverton was also a stop on the Underground Railroad, and an underground passage still connects George Sloan's Brick Row with the home of his brother-in-law Dr. James Robertson just across the street, which had a secret room on the second floor accessible only by the window. When the all clear was given at night, a canal boat took the freedom seekers to the next station on the Underground Railroad, with the ultimate destination being Canada, where slavery was illegal.

STAY

Whether it's true or not isn't documented, but local lore has it that Abraham Lincoln stopped at the Spread Eagle Tavern, as did two other presidents of the United States, William McKinley and James Garfield.

The three-story tavern, built in 1837, is considered one of the area's best examples of Federal architecture. Its design, including eleven rooms, fluted columns, and intricately carved mantels on the twelve fireplaces, comes from the pattern books of Asher Benjamin, an American architect and author whose books were designed to elevate American architecture. There's also a functioning tavern tunnel dating back to the Underground Railroad days.

Restored, the Spread Eagle is a destination of itself, and its location on Plymouth Street along with ten other historical designated buildings adds to the attraction. You can dine and stay at the inn or next door at the Hanover House, an old saltbox building built in 1820 that once served as a justice of the peace office. There's even more early nineteenth-century ambience to be had at Gaver's Rathskeller, with its twelve-foot-high vaulted ceiling and stone walls in the tavern's basement.

13

Jefferson

Founded by Postmaster General Gideon Granger in 1803, Jefferson, centrally located in Ashtabula County, serves as the county seat. Home to abolitionists who were active in the Underground Railroad, the downtown is dominated by the county courthouse built in 1851 after the first one dating back to 1811 burned down. Legend has it that the fire resulted when a caretaker, who was stoking the fires to keep the courthouse warm, partook of too much libation at the tavern across the street and, unfortunately, fell asleep.

STAY

Once a farmhouse built in 1848, the lovely Herb Garden now serves not only as a bed and breakfast but also as a cooking school offering private classes with such themes as soup for supper, best meals using thyme, and herb dishes. Many of the ingredients for their healthy but delicious breakfasts and for the classes come from the inn's gardens.

EAT

Open since 1941, the Jefferson Diner serves breakfast, lunch, and dinner. It's definitely a homey place with good food at reasonable prices. Expect fare such as country-fried steak, burgers, beef liver, fried chicken, meatloaf, house-made soups, pies, cinnamon rolls, and strawberry shortcake.

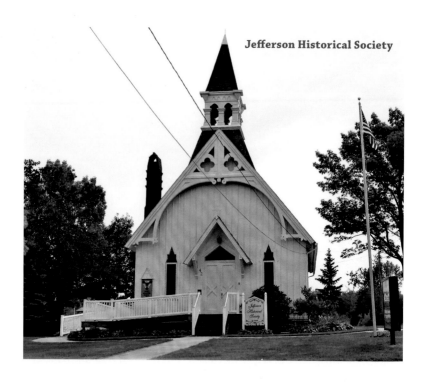

The sixty-five-acre Emerine Estates Winery features 100 percent all-natural greenhouse-grown dry and sweet wines for sipping, a menu with appetizers, burgers grilled to order, and sandwiches, and for dessert they offer Wineshake, a creamy frozen wine dessert in such flavors as caramel apple, blackberry, and chocolate raspberry. Enjoy on their outdoor patio or inside.

"Drink Coffee and Do Good" is the tagline at Wall Street Coffee Company, which features specialty coffee and tea drinks, including their house specialties—lavender white mocha and maple macchiato. There are also smoothies and milkshakes, loaded bagels, and creative salads.

PLAY

Downtown Jefferson is the center of the Ashtabula County Covered Bridge Festival, held the second weekend in October. Here visitors can partake of a pancake breakfast, watch a parade, and meander among numerous vendors selling food, crafts, and antiques. You can also pick up a driving map for a self-guided tour of the nineteen covered bridges in the county.

How many venues say they're one of a kind or the only one in the world when of course that's not true? We're here to tell you that the Victorian Perambulator Museum is indeed all that. In the fifteen rooms of collections, you'll find wicker baby and doll carriages, including one shaped like an Italian gondola, as well as a pram that once belonged to Queen Elizabeth and her sister, Princess Margaret, and that was pulled by miniature horses. Ah, it's good to be queen. Other exhibits showcase unique toys, some dating back to the nineteenth century, including rocking horses, rare dolls, paintings, and, well, you just have to go there.

The Jefferson Depot Village is a living history village presenting life as it was back in the 1800s. Costumed interpreters explain the history of such buildings as the Lake Shore and Michigan Southern Railroad Station, Church in the Wildwood, church barn, one-room schoolhouse, and more. Annual events include the Strawberry Festival and Craft Bazaar held on the third weekend of June, the Early America Alive 1890 reenactment on the second Saturday and Sunday in July, and the Old-Fashioned Williamsburg Christmas on the first Saturday in December.

Netcher Road Covered Bridge

Be sure to make your way to the Giddings Law Office Museum. A prominent abolitionist, attorney, and politician, Joshua Reed Giddings moved to Jefferson in 1806, when he was eleven. Though he had no formal education, he read voraciously when not doing chores on his father's farm, and he passed the bar in 1821. His law office, built two years later, now serves as a museum that houses his desk as well as his law library. The museum is even more significant because Charley Garrick, an escaped slave who made his home there after a fire destroyed all his belongings, was a well-liked man in the community who entertained the community with his violin playing. Though Garrick hadn't been educated while a slave, he ultimately attended Oberlin College, the only school of higher education to accept Black people. Contact the Ashtabula County Historical Society for tour information.

And don't forget—August is the time for the Ashtabula County Fair.

14

Lisbon

Once known as New Lisbon, this small village in Columbiana County was founded in 1803, the same year that Ohio, known then as "America's First Frontier," became a state. Iron and whiskey, which sold for twenty-five cents a gallon, were among the first products manufactured here. Mills, tanneries, salt and cement works, and even the invention of the modern drinking straw were part of the economic engine driving the village's prosperity. Lisbon also was the site of many firsts, including the county's first bank, the Columbiana Bank of New Lisbon; its first insurance business, Columbiana County Mutual Insurance; and *Der Patriot am Ohio*, a German newspaper that started printing in 1808 and was the first *newspaper* established in Columbiana County.

A stop on the Lincoln Highway, one of the first transcontinental highway routes for automobiles—or *machines*, as they sometimes called them back then—passes through Lisbon.

STAY

Available for rent on a weekly basis, the Lake House on Guilford Lake has all the comforts of home.

EAT

The beautiful Courthouse Inn and Restaurant, located in a restored 1803 building, has a lovely interior and gardens and an Old World ambience. Its gourmet dinner menu features dishes such as a spinach mushroom

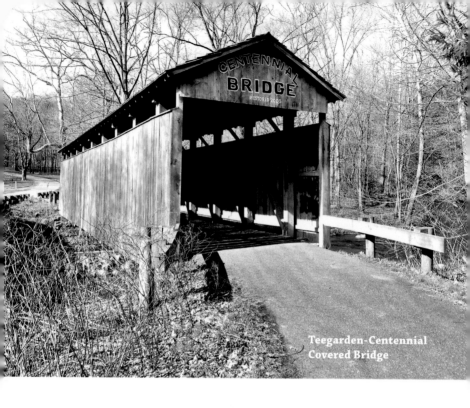

Teegarden-Centennial
Covered Bridge

risotto, consisting of traditional arborio rice toasted with shallots and then simmered with white wine and vegetable stock, tossed with sauteed cremini mushrooms and baby spinach, and finished with onion straws; stuffed mushroom Rockefeller—roasted mushrooms stuffed with creamy spinach and a parmesan-and-breadcrumb filling served with citrus arugula salad; and crispy cauliflower wings—panko-breaded cauliflower fried crispy golden brown and tossed with your choice of sauce (wildfire, buffalo ranch, Thai chili, Carolina BBQ, local honey BBQ, or inferno).

Using the same sauce as when they first opened in 1961, Mary's Pizza serves only homemade pasta dishes and fresh dough pizzas.

The Marks family opened Marks Landing in 1946 as a small diner on Guilford Lake. Over the years, it has expanded, and it now offers a full menu, including seafood, steaks, pizza, burgers, and sandwiches; indoor and patio dining; and rowboat rentals.

PLAY

Get ready for mountain music during the Dulci-More Festival, a music festival devoted to the Appalachian dulcimer and other traditional musical

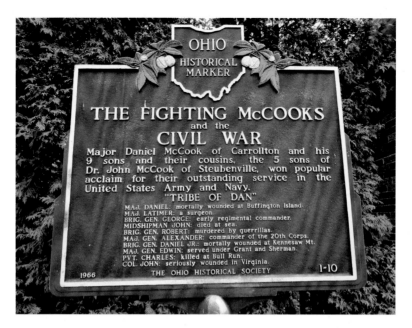

The Fighting McCooks historical marker

instruments. The festival has been held every Memorial Day weekend for over a quarter of a century at Camp McKinley, a Boy Scout camp. Lisbon also hosts both the Columbiana County Johnny Appleseed Festival and Columbiana County Fair.

Rent a pontoon boat at Marks Landing for touring Guilford Lake, constructed in 1834 as a canal feed reservoir for the Sandy and Beaver Canal.

Located on the west fork of Little Beaver Creek, Guilford Lake State Park is a pretty, quiet spot good for swimming; fishing for bass, bluegill, crappie, and channel catfish; and boating, with dock rentals. The camping area, situated on an old pine plantation, has forty-two electric sites, a play area, a fishing dock, picnic tables, and fire rings.

15

Magnolia

First inhabited by the friendly Tuscarawas Indians, some of whom still lived in the area until about 1852, the village of Magnolia was laid out by Richard Elson and John W. Smith in 1834. Two years later, in 1836, Isaac Miller founded Downingville, and a decade later the villages combined. The name Magnolia came from the mill Elson had built on the Sandy and Beaver Canal in 1834. Magnolia, with a population under one thousand, was a stop on the Underground Railroad.

EAT

Tozzi's, a family-owned restaurant for over a century, opened in 1914. In addition to dark wood and an atmospheric ambience, the restaurant boasts a menu featuring steaks, pastas (some based on Tozzi's original family recipes), seafood, and such desserts as mini cannoli and Magnolia mud pie, as well as such weekly features as Tuesday's seafood feast, Wednesday steak night, and Thursday pasta night.

Crossroads Restaurant is open for breakfast, lunch, and dinner and serves comfort foods such as beef tips over noodles, macaroni and cheese, salmon patties, battered shrimp, and liver and onions.

The Nest Café and Ice Cream Parlor operates out of the historic Isaac Taggart Inn, once a stagecoach inn that opened in 1812.

The Magnolia Market sells deli meats and cheeses, fresh produce, and wonderful pies, as well as other groceries and snacks.

Magnolia Flouring Mills

PLAY

In 1834, Richard Elson built the Magnolia Flouring Mills on the seventy-three-mile Sandy and Beaver Canal, which connects the Ohio and Erie Canal at Bolivar, Ohio, to the Ohio River in Glasgow, Pennsylvania. The canal took two decades to complete and lasted just four more before a dam in Lisbon, Ohio, burst open in 1848, wiping out a large part of the canal. Fortunately for agricultural history, the section of the Sandy and Beaver running behind the five-story red mill survived, as did the mill, which remained in the Elson family and was in continuous operation for 171 years before being acquired by the Stark County Park District in 2005. Today, it's open for tours and continues to mill prize-winning cornmeal and other products made from grains grown by local farmers. On the National Register of Historic Places in 2000, the 4.97-acre property in downtown Magnolia also includes a segment of the Sandy and Beaver Canal behind the mill, the water rights for the canal, and Dam 6.

Next to the mill is the lovely Victorian-era home that belonged to the Elson family. It's a private home and only open for tours on special occasions, such as events sponsored by the Magnolia Area Historical Society. Just across the street is a marker commemorating the site of the original Elson home, which was also a station on the Underground

Magnolia Flouring Mills

Railroad. Richard Elson's hatred of slavery runs in a similar course as that of Abraham Lincoln. Like Lincoln, he poled flatboats down the Ohio River and then the Mississippi River to New Orleans. It was there he saw slave auctions and the mistreatment of fellow human beings just because their skin color was darker. Lincoln freed the slaves; Elson helped them escape. In an aside, Elson sold his flatboat at the end of his journeys and each time walked the thousand miles back home, making that trip seven times.

The Magnolia Area Historical Society Museum is located on the second floor of the Isaac Taggart Inn.

Owners Steve and Jenifer Miller reimagined a home built in 1921 on an overgrown piece of property and created Creekside Cottage Winery, later adding a coffeehouse, the Steaming Mug, to their business. There's a limited menu of appetizers, wraps, and panini and a wine list that includes a nice selection of reds and whites, sweet, dry, and semisweet, as well as such seasonal selections as a watermelon white merlot available during the summer, cranberry chianti at Christmastime, and apple cinnamon for lovely fall days. An outdoor patio is perfect for enjoying the beauty of the property in nice weather, and there is live music on Saturdays.

Creekside is on one of over thirty wineries on the Canal Country Wine Trail, which parallels the Ohio and Erie Canal built in the early 1800s, connecting the Ohio and Mississippi Rivers, between the Great Lakes and the Gulf of Mexico.

16

Millersburg

Home to Ohio's largest Amish population and the county seat of Holmes County, Millersburg is a Heritage *Ohio* Main Street Community with a delightful historic downtown centered on an Italianate-style courthouse built in 1880 that is, along with the jail, on the National Register of Historic Places. Adam Johnson and Charles Miller plotted the town in 1815, and the town's first resident moved in four years later. But that original slow growth quickly improved, and by 1833, Millersburg boasted ten stores, seventy-three homes, four taverns, four practicing physicians, three attorneys, a printing office, a meetinghouse, and an apothecary's shop. Today it remains a bustling town.

STAY

Yoder's Amish Home opened its doors in 1847, making it among the state's oldest hostelries. Located in the Millersburg National Historic District, the hotel has a courtyard, full-service restaurant, and tavern. In keeping with its history, Yoder's Amish Home hosts the Quilt Party, a retreat space for up to forty-five quilters located in what was a jewelry shop, general store, and pharmacy. The space comes equipped with cutting tables and ironing tables, all wheelchair accessible.

EAT

It's a waste of time, so don't even try to resist the delicious hot cinnamon rolls, breads, and pies made with locally grown fruit at Miller's Bakery,

Yoder's Amish Home

established in 1967. There's more than handcrafted beer at Millersburg Brewing Company, a cool combination of historic facade and urban interior. Stay awhile, order some food, and enjoy the live entertainment.

At the family-owned fifty-two-thousand-square-foot Troyer Market, in business for more than six decades, you can choose from an assortment of house-made candies including buckeyes (an Ohio-centric candy), turtle bars, truffles, cashew crunch clusters, and crunchy butter puffs, all made with real butter and other high-quality ingredients.

PLAY

Nineteenth-century time travel starts at Hotel Millersburg with horse-and-buggy tours and tours of their schoolhouse and 1885 barn, which in the spring houses newborn animals—think lambs, colts, bunnies, and beagles. Yoder's is an Old Order Amish heirloom farm, and owners Eli and Gloria Yoder are dedicated to preservation and education about Amish culture and lifestyle. On-site, there's a petting zoo, gift shop, covered picnic area, and bakery. Here, besides the enticing aromas of the freshly baked bread lining the shelves, there are also rows and rows of such items as pickles and red beets made from recipes long used by the owner's grandmother. Who can resist buying some to take home and give as gifts?

Hotel Millersburg

The Amish Country Century Ride, an organized bike ride throughout Holmes County held every September, starts in Millersburg. Depending on your expertise, there's an easy twenty-five-mile route, a one-hundred-mile challenge, or the one-hundred-mile ride with five thousand feet of vertical gain. No matter what you choose, lunch and aid stations are available along the routes, and a post-ride Amish meal follows.

Founded by two brothers in 1905, Fenton Glass Company introduced several glass styles still popular among collectors today—carnival and hobnob. For a century, the company was the largest manufacturer of handmade colored glass and was known for its innovative colors, such as the delicate pink called rosalene and the transparent hues of colonial amber, colonial blue, and colonial green. The Millersburg Glass Museum showcases works made by Fenton Glass, which once had a plant in town.

What do you do with a twenty-eight-room Queen Anne home that's listed on the National Register of Historic Places once the millionaire industrialist who built it in 1847 is long gone? Transform it into the Victorian House Museum and highlight its Victorian roots and furnishings as well as Holmes County history.

The twenty-nine-mile Holmes County Trail, one of the first rail-trail conversions in the US and the only one built to accommodate horse and buggies, borders, in part, Cuyahoga Valley National Park, crosses bridges, winds through rural and suburban neighborhoods, and has a stop at the

Yoder's Amish Home

sixty-five-foot Brandywine Falls. The trailhead in Millersburg starts at the Hipp Station depot.

SHOP

The Village Toy Shop, designed to inspire fun, laughter, and learning, specializes in quality toys.

The Jenny Wren offers botanicals, clothing and accessories, candles, stained glass, kitchenware, DIY products like Prima Redesign, Dixie Belle chalk paints, Frenchic chalk paints and brushes.

Handmade pewterware for tables, bars, gifts, jewelry, and Celtic items like Scottish quaichs are for sale at Three Feathers Pewter.

The shelves and displays at Jackson Street Antiques show the wide variety of quality items available, from books and papers, vintage toys, vinyl records, bottles, Depression glass, figurines, and art glass to vintage clothing and American-made cookie cutters by Ann Clark.

Working with Amish seamstresses, the owners of Farmhouse Frocks create one-of-a-kind quality handmade clothing that's flattering for all. They describe their flowing farmhouse style as a marriage of many styles—urban farmhouse, boho, shabby chic, cottage, and prairie.

17

Minerva

In 1818, John Whitacre built a sawmill on 123 acres of land he had purchased. As happened with many mills, a community grew up around it, and in 1833, after the birth of Whitacre's niece Minerva Ann Taylor, the town was named after her. Prosperity came with the Sandy and Beaver Canal that passed by, later to be replaced as a means of transportation by the Pennsylvania Railroad in the 1840s.

STAY

BQ (Brewers Quarters) at Sandy Springs Brewing Company is next door to the taproom in downtown Minerva. A restored historic building, it's a perfect place to stay for those who've enjoyed dining and drinking at this award-winning brewery. It's an extremely cool space with brick walls and old barnwood.

EAT

People talk about hidden gems, but this one is the real deal. A magnificent restaurant on a hill overlooking Minerva, the Hart Mansion Restaurant is a historic destination nestled into four acres of woods amid a rural setting. The Italianate-style home dates back to 1869. Elegant with patio dining, great views and stately interiors, it is a step back in time. Be sure to try their signature dessert—chocolate peanut butter mousse pie.

Creative food like the Minervan sandwich—burnt pork ends, smoked gouda cheese, Minerva Dairy's smoked maple syrup butter on a fresh torta bun—and handcrafted ales and lagers are among the offerings at Sandy Springs Brewing Company, which is housed in what used to be a filling station before it was recreated as a brewery. The vintage barnwood used in the interior and the brewing company's name both originate from the owners' nineteenth-century family farm. They have sixteen beers on tap, along with an infusion tower that's changed regularly. Events include live music by local musicians on Saturday, trivia every Thursday with Geeks Who Drink, and an open mic night every Wednesday.

Minerva Classic 57 is a 1950s-style diner serving breakfast, lunch, and dinner. Menu choices reflect the times: meatloaf, swiss steak, burgers, their Buckeye seafood platter (a heap of scallops, jumbo shrimp, and beer-battered fish served with fries), Nashville hot chicken sliders, and fried clams. Oh, and great homemade pies.

The Normandy Inn has steaks, burgers, a salad bar, and other offerings on their large menu.

PLAY

Built in 1936 and first known as the Dreamland Theatre, the restored Roxy Theatre is the place to go for movies and community theatrical productions and other events.

SHOP

Market Street Art Spot, an artist cooperative-sales gallery, features the works of their seven resident artists and those of more than thirty other regional artists, all working in a variety of mediums.

We don't often suggest shopping for butter, but Minerva Dairy's slow-churned small-batch butter, made with 85 percent butterfat using fresh cream from pasture-raised cows on US farms, is beyond great. The fifth-generation, family-owned Minerva Dairy has been in business for more than 125 years and is the oldest family-owned creamery in the country. Their butter flavors include maple syrup, garlic herb, pumpkin spice, smoked maple wood, and sea salt.

For vintage collectibles and antiques, home decor, greeting cards, and unique gifts, check out Off the Beaten Path Gift Shop.

If you have a group of ten or more, Alpaca Spring Valley Farm offers tours of their working farm (and boy, are those alpacas cute), or you can shop at Natural Approach Farm Store, located at the farm. There you'll

Market Street

find all sorts of items made from alpaca fibers, such as sweaters, gloves, mittens, hats, blankets, and throws.

NOTABLE

Carol Costello, television commentator and former host of *CNN Newsroom*, was born in Minerva in 1961 and graduated from Minerva High School.

Willard and Isaac Pennock, two Minerva manufacturers, patented the first steel railroad car in the United States in the nineteenth century.

18

Mount Hope

For city people, the phrase *living off the grid* evokes waves of anxiety. But the simple rhythms of rural life quickly take over in Mount Hope, an adorable slip of a town located in Holmes County, home to Ohio's largest Amish population. Dating back to 1827, Mount Hope remains an Amish-centric community where horse and buggies appear to be just as popular as cars.

EAT

It's not on the beaten path, but people know how to find Mrs. Yoder's Kitchen—after all, it's right across from the Mt. Hope Auction and not far up the road from Miller's Buggy Repair. You can order their great Amish cooking off the menu or go for their salad bar and hot food buffet with its large variety of food offerings.

SHOP

For baked goods, it's hard to imagine not finding what you want at Kauffman's Country Bakery. The shop's shelves, tables, and counters are loaded with a large assortment of breads, rolls, cookies, pies, and cakes. During the holidays, they make around five hundred different varieties of fruitcakes, including their signature German-style stollen, made only with authentic ingredients imported from Germany. Among the other seasonal specialties are their breads—sauerkraut rye, Irish soda, kolach poppyseed, and braided challah—and sweets like pumpkin or mint whoopie pies. Smoothies, ice cream, and sandwiches are available at the café.

Homestead Furniture, in business for over three decades, produces Amish furniture with pizzazz that's built to last and customized to meet your home and style.

You may not want to buy, but it's intriguing to attend the Mt. Hope Auction, which holds a variety of different sales throughout the year. Their livestock, hay, and produce sales take place on a weekly basis, and they offer several periodic sales, including the Mid-Ohio Draft Horse and Carriage Sale, Machinery Sale, and the Mid-Ohio Alternative Bird and Animal sale. Each of these sales are held three times a year.

NOTABLE

Born near Mount Hope in 1843, H. D. Perky was a Denver, Colorado, attorney when, in 1892, he discovered the health benefits of whole wheat. Working with William Henry Ford, the two developed a machine that pressed wheat into tiny strips, creating what was the first prepared breakfast food. From there, Perky and his brother, John, created the Cereal Machine Company to manufacture small hand-operated machines that people could use to make wheat biscuits at home. When Perky realized that the real money was in selling the shredded wheat biscuits and not in making the machines, he established three plants in the United States as well as one in Niagara Falls, Ontario, called the Canadian Shredded Wheat Company.

19

Mount Pleasant

Quakers were one of the leading religious groups when it came to championing antislavery causes, and so it was with Mount Pleasant in southern Jefferson County. A charming village, population just under five hundred, historic Mount Pleasant is listed on both the National Register of Historic Districts and was designated a National Historic Landmark, with more than forty historic buildings, most still in use and privately owned. Founded in 1803, partially to provide a safe haven for freedom seekers escaping from slavery, Mount Pleasant is much the same as it was more than two hundred years ago. The oldest building, a log structure that used to be the Enoch Harris store, was built in 1804. Others are from the 1810s, and many date back to before the Civil War.

STAY

If you're really into historical immersion, then you definitely need to check in to the 1815 Abram Dilworth House, an Airbnb that is a three-bedroom, one-and-a-half-bath two-story brick house that has a kitchen and can host five.

EAT

It's not really in Mount Pleasant, but the Farm Restaurant and Pub in nearby Adena continues that back-in-time feel and is under three miles down the road. An interesting tidbit, the restaurant, located in

1804 log cabin

a nineteenth-century farmhouse, was at one time owned by Richard Nixon's great-aunt.

While in Adena, stop by the Black Sheep Vineyard to sample their handcrafted reds, whites, rosés, and Blitzen, a fruit wine made with Ohio blackberries. Hungry? Bring your own food or sample from one of the food trucks that may be available, and the winery also serves crackers, apples, bread, Sarris Candies, and Ohio artisan cheese from Pearl Valley Cheese in Fresno and Old Forge Dairy in Kent.

PLAY

One of the town's early structures is the two-story Quaker Meeting House, which was built in 1814 and is still standing. It was made solid and for a crowd: ninety feet long by sixty-two feet wide, with walls that are twenty-four inches thick at the base, it could seat two thousand people. Men sat on one side; women on the other. Children were upstairs in the balcony area. It is one of seven buildings, each unique, owned and operated by the Historical Society of Mount Pleasant. Tours and buildings are open by appointment. A complimentary walking tour is available on Trover.com.

The Historical Society also has other sites, such as the Benjamin Lundy House/Free Labor Store. These types of stores, typical of many Quakers and reminiscent of our fair-trade stores and goods, sold only goods made by freemen and in free states. The store, built in 1813 and the only free labor store still in existence, is listed on the National Register of Historic Places. Lundy, publisher of the *Genius of Universal Emancipation* newspaper in 1921, also organized Ohio's first antislavery society—all in Mount Pleasant. Another Historical Society property is the home of John Gill,

Mt. Pleasant Historic District

built in 1835 and now called the Elizabeth House Mansion. Persuaded by his dentist, Gill, a wealthy landowner, planted twenty-eight acres of mulberry trees and thus became one of the first successful silk mill owners in the United States. In Elizabeth House Mansion Museum, there's a quilt made from Mount Pleasant silk on display that dates back to between 1844 and 1850. Other buildings on the Historical Society's historic tour are the 1840 Historic Center and the Burris General Store, dating back to 1895 and now serving as a gift shop.

In another connection to history, after Confederate brigadier general John Hunt Morgan and his force of two thousand cavalrymen barely escaped Indiana, they rode across southern Ohio, covering more than seven hundred miles in twenty-five days. As the story goes, one of his men was wounded in nearby Dillonvale, and Morgan, also known as the King of Horse Thieves, sent his men to find a doctor. They returned with Mount Pleasant physician Ernest Findlay, who we imagined tried his best, but the patient died. His fellow cavalrymen wanted to kill Findlay because of the death, but as the story goes, Morgan saw he was wearing a Masonic pin and chivalrously told his men, "Do not harm a hair on his head. He's one of ours."

20

New Philadelphia

New Philadelphia, a port town on the Tuscarawas River, was laid out in 1804 in the same grid pattern as Philadelphia, Pennsylvania—hence its name. A former canal town, New Philadelphia is part of the Ohio and Erie Canalway National Heritage Area, a 110-mile journey along the canal's original route connecting Cleveland in the north and New Philadelphia in the south.

STAY

Stay and play at the 157-acre Woods Tall Timber Resort. You'll have a choice of cottages, camping, and primitive tent rentals for overnights, and there's a seven-acre lake with a great beach, water slides, inflatable trampolines, two diving boards, and paddle and electric boat rentals.

Schoenbrunn Inn, a boutique hotel, offers easy access to the village, the state's first settlement, and the Trumpet in the Land production—a live reenactment of the story of Schoenbrunn.

EAT

Banana bread french toast for breakfast and chicken bacon ranch flatbread or fried Lake Erie walleye sandwich for lunch are some of the many reasons that Dee's Restaurant is a family favorite. Like open-flame barbecue? Check out Hog Heaven.

J-N-G Grill has been a staple in the downtown for more than a century. Menu items include prime rib, steaks, lemon beer-battered haddock, burgers, salads, and soups such as stuffed pepper and creamy tomato basil parmesan. Check out the original bar, mirrors, and cabinetry, dating back over eighty years. While you're there, order one of their signature fishbowl cocktails and enjoy the rotating beer, wine, and mead, as well as seasonal cocktails.

Broadway Brewhouse features more than twenty beers on tap and offers happy-hour specials. It's also a great place to catch a game on one of their twenty TVs or dance to live music. Don't worry about getting in—the Broadway Brewhouse is open 365 days a year.

PLAY

Vintage amusement rides, a cotton candy stand, three different-sized swimming pools, miniature golf, the Summer Showcase (a series of Sunday-night concerts), and their annual First Town Days Festival held in July are just part of the fun at Tuscora Park, a not-for-profit organization designed to keep prices low and affordable for families. A must-see is the 1928 vintage Herschell-Spillman antique carousel, with its thirty-six hand-carved all-wood jumping horses and two chariots circling past fourteen original oil paintings while a Wurlitzer-style 153-band organ plays on. It is one of only a few all-wooden carousels still in existence in the world.

Historic Schoenbrunn Village, a historically accurate representation of the Moravian community founded by missionary David Zeisberger in 1772, represents many firsts—the settlement, church, schoolhouse, and code of laws—for the state of Ohio. At the time of the Revolutionary War, the village was the first White settlement in Ohio and west of the Ohio River. Its purpose was the conversion of the Delaware, mainly Lenape, Indians in Ohio to Christianity. At one point, four hundred Delaware lived in the village, which had more than sixty buildings, including the first school and Christian church built in the state. In the spring of 1778, Zeisberger and his followers abandoned the site. Now restored to show what a late eighteenth-century Ohio village would have looked like, Historic Schoenbrunn Village consists of seventeen log buildings, the original mission cemetery, gardens, picnic areas, a museum, and a visitor center.

The annual First Town Days Festival takes place over the Fourth of July weekend in Tuscora Park and features numerous events, including a fishing derby, a queen's contest, frog-jumping contest, turtle races, fireworks, a parade, family sack races, a tractor pull, a boccie tournament, and a kids' day.

21

Oberlin

Both Oberlin and Oberlin College were founded in 1833, and the two continue to meld well together. An amazing destination with lovely architecture and great restaurants, art galleries, museums, and shops, the town and the college were both major players in the Underground Railroad before the Civil War.

One facet of the vile Fugitive Slave Law of 1850 required that captured escaped slaves be returned to slavery; the law also made it illegal for officials and citizens of free states to try to help them. But that law didn't matter to those abolitionists living in Oberlin when eighteen-year-old John Price, a freedom seeker who had been in Oberlin for two years, was seized by a US marshal and slave seekers from Kentucky and taken to nearby Wellington as the first step in forcing him back south. Both Black and White people joined together, forming a group of several hundred and marching the eight miles to Wellington, picking up other abolitionists along the way. They found Price at the train station with his captors, who immediately hid out in a hotel, taking Price with them. Negotiations proved fruitless, and so the abolitionists stormed the hotel, found Price in the attic, and hid him in the Oberlin home of James Harris Fairchild, who shortly afterward became the third president of Oberlin College. As for Price, he made it to Canada, where slavery didn't exist.

STAY

Besides its history and luxe accommodations, guests at the 1830 Hallauer House Bed and Breakfast can enjoy such wonderful features as a four-course breakfast, an infrared dry-heat sauna, a six-person hot tub, a twenty-foot by forty-foot in-ground heated swimming pool, a music room with a baby grand piano, and the owner's large garden, named Garden of Misfit Junk.

EAT

From avant-garde food offerings (like fried avocado wedges and habanero rangoon) to classics like wings and Aunt Irene's recipe for sauerkraut balls, the Feve is an eclectic restaurant good for both traditionalists and those willing to experiment.

Overlooking historic Tappan Square, the 1833 Restaurant at the Hotel at Oberlin sources sustainable, local, and regional foods.

Get your sweet treats at Gibson's Bakery and Candy.

PLAY

The Oberlin Heritage Center, housed in a two-story brick Italianate-style building, was once the home of General Giles W. Shurtleff, who led Ohio's first African American regiment, which served during the Civil War. Built in 1866, the home offers a tour encompassing the area's Underground Railroad history. The center has several other buildings open for tours. The Little Red Schoolhouse (1836/1837) is Oberlin's oldest building and set the stage for its approach to racial relationships by defying Ohio's "Black Laws," one of which denied Black children access to public schools until 1948. From the first, the school had an interracial population. The center also offers a variety of walking tours, including Architecture History Walk, Freedom's Friends: Underground Railroad and Abolitionist History Walk, and One Step More: Oberlin Women's History Walk.

North Coast Inland Trail encompasses sixty-five miles, from Elyria to Toledo, including 3.1 miles spanning Oberlin. A twelve-foot-wide multipurpose rails-to-trails path, it's built on what was the railbed of the Toledo, Norwalk, and Cleveland Railroad.

Get high (above the treetops, that is) at Common Ground, which offers a two-and-a-half-mile Canopy Tour that encompasses seven zip lines, two spiral staircases, two aerial bridges, and one unique floating staircase.

The Frank Lloyd Wright Weltzheimer/Johnson House at Oberlin College, completed in 1949, is Ohio's first Usonian house. The term Usonian is used to describe a stylish small home. The Weltzheimer/

Johnson House is one of just a small number in the US that are open to the public.

Check out what's playing at the Apollo Theater, which first opened in 1913.

The Allen Memorial Art Museum (AMAM), founded in 1917 and run by Oberlin College, is home to fantastic collections. Its more than fourteen thousand works of art provide an encompassing overview of the history of many eras and cultures. As an example, their Ancient Art collection showcases works from Greece, Egypt, and Rome, as well as pieces from Hittite, Sumerian, Persian, Etruscan, Phoenician, and Cypriot cultures. Additionally, the collection includes a number of objects from the ancient Americas, specifically both Mexican and Peruvian. Overall, the AMAM is considered to be among the best college or university museums in the country, up there with Harvard and Yale.

Often overlooked, Oberlin's ivy-covered colonial architecture is amazing. Some buildings date back to 1813 and reflect generations of architects and styles. Take a stroll and admire.

SHOP

We love the name and the rather whimsical selection of goods at the Mad Cow Curiosity Shop. With another unusual moniker, Ratsy's Store advertises that they sell "unusual gifts & weird socks, vintage clothing, curiosities, oddities & strange stuff to keep you guessing. You may be normal when you come here, but you won't be when you leave!"

The Workshop Art Gallery offers workshops and is both an art gallery and a boutique. Ginko Gallery and Studio sells art supplies and works by artists.

Once a chain of what were called dime stores, Ben Franklin Stores first opened in the 1920s. Now the remaining ones are individually owned, including the Ben Franklin Store in Oberlin, which dates back to 1935. It's fun and funky, overflowing with a variety of goods, such as unique games and toys, sewing notions, fabric and yarn, art, office and school supplies, houseplants, and puzzles. There's a little bit of everything, like the section devoted to natural health and beauty, with brands like Tom's Naturals, Jason, and Kiss My Face, and the MindFair Books shop features both new and used trade books focusing on literature, poetry, social sciences, and arts and crafts. Adding to the fun is the occasional live music in the crowded aisles.

Oberlin College

NOTABLE

Independent filmmaker Lynn Shelton, who directed *Humpday* and *Little Fires Everywhere*, was born in Oberlin, was raised elsewhere, and then returned to attend Oberlin College.

Moses Fleetwood Walker, the first African American Major League Baseball player, later had four patents to his name. He attended the Oberlin College, where he majored in philosophy and the arts. While there, he played for their baseball team before being lured away by the University of Michigan. In 1883, he left college to play professional baseball for the Toledo Bluestockings.

22

Peninsula

Located in the middle of the Cuyahoga Valley National Park is quintessentially small-town Ohio, a pretty patchwork of family farms, woods, covered bridges, historic buildings, and walking trails.

Settled in 1818 on the banks of the Cuyahoga River, Peninsula boomed with the building of the Ohio and Erie Canal and then later with the coming of the Valley Railroad. Businesses in the 1800s included mills, boat builders, stone quarries, five hotels, and fourteen bars. If that seems like a lot of drinking establishments, remember that canal towns weren't the romantic scenes we envision but were often rowdy places where alcohol was readily available and just as readily consumed.

Much more sedate now with a population well under a thousand, Peninsula is charming. Its historic district, on the National Register of Historic Places, is a collection of such architectural styles as Greek Revival, Colonial Revival, Stick, Queen Anne, and the less well-known Western Reserve New England building type called the Upright-and-Wing—with a two-story gabled front and a one-story wing.

STAY

Located in the Cuyahoga Valley National Park, next to the Ohio and Erie Canal, the historic Stanford House has a wonderful view of the Cuyahoga River. The property dates back to 1804, when George Stanford purchased the property and moved his family here.

Kendall Lake

EAT

Fisher's Café and Pub, a third-generation family-owned restaurant first opened in 1959, continues to be a local favorite.

Order a burger basket or foot-long Coney dog at Dilly's Drive-In. It's the kind of place where a carhop brings you your food. The ambience is totally 1950s America.

PLAY

Explore the Cuyahoga Valley National Park aboard the Cuyahoga Valley Scenic Railroad. Besides scenic tours, there are special rides such as the Grape Escape (with wine tasting), Murder Mystery Train, Cocktails on Rails, and Dinner on the Train, as well as special events like *The Polar Express* Train Ride, Canvas and Wine on the Rails, Trivia on the Train, and Truffle Making on the Train.

Bike or hike the Towpath Trail. Or follow Lock 29 Peninsula Depot, where you can see views of the remains of the lock and an aqueduct as the trail winds through a section of the thirty-three-thousand-acre Cuyahoga Valley National Park. Century Cycles rents bikes and sells parts, apparel, and gear. Pedego Electric Bikes offers a variety of bikes to rent by the hour or day.

Cuyahoga Valley National Park

The Peninsula Art Academy offers classes and workshops, so why not create a visual memory of the canal or Main Street?

Szalay's Sweet Corn Farm is an agricultural destination not only because of the bounty displayed in its market but also because of their fun activities, such as the fall corn maze and the weekend outdoor eatery with stands selling roasted corn on the cob, freshly squeezed lemonade, sweet tea, grilled sandwiches, and ice cream.

Check out Gothic Revival–style Bronson Memorial Church, built in 1835 to counteract the immorality typical of canal towns with their many transient visitors and, as we mentioned before, easy access to liquor and women of wanton ways.

Ski Ohio at Boston Mills/Brandywine Ski Resort.

Learn about the area's history at the Cuyahoga Valley Historical Museum, located on the second floor of the Peninsula Library and Historical Society housed in what was the Boston Township Hall, built in 1887. The unique Honore Guilbeau Cooke mural, a focal point of the library, depicts the geographical pattern of the Peninsula part of the Cuyahoga River Valley as it appears on old maps and in aerial photographs. Cooke, who trained as a printmaker at the School of the Art Institute of Chicago, is a well-known artist whose works appear in the National Gallery of Art.

SHOP

Trail Mix Peninsula is a retail store selling jewelry, apparel, gift items, children's toys, pottery, art, wind chimes, chocolates, beverages, trail mix, and local foods to go. Sale proceeds directly support Cuyahoga Valley National Park programs.

Check out the wool blankets, yarns, roving, and fiber crafts from the Spicy Lamb Farm, located at the dead end of Akron Peninsula Road off Boston Mills Road in the Cuyahoga Valley National Park. The farm also sells their organically raised apples, pears, and plums, spicy herbs and vegetables, and flowers by appointment. They also host the annual Cuyahoga Valley Sheep Dog Trials, held since the 1880s. The competitive trials require herding dogs at the direction of their handlers to move sheep around a field, through gates, penning and shedding them with points given for each event. The farm also hosts other events open to the public, including Lyle Lad Sheep Dog Herding Clinic (in case your dogs are interested in honing their herding skills) and camp programs.

23

Sebring

Some people dream of a little plot of land and a cozy home, but the Sebring family's dreams were much larger than that. They wanted to build a pottery town and so selected two hundred acres of farmland near both a railroad line and the Mahoning River. Adding another 160 acres, they incorporated the town of Sebring in 1899 and commenced building what would become the Pottery Capital of the World, with numerous pottery and china businesses that at one time employed some thirty-three hundred workers.

Not content with just one town—and not liking the cold Ohio winters—George Sebring founded another Sebring, this one in Florida. Interestingly, only two towns exist in the US that were founded and named after the same family—Sebring, Florida, and Sebring, Ohio.

STAY

The elegant lifestyle of Frank Sebring and his family is preserved at the Sebring Mansion, an opulent and ultraluxe inn and spa. Guests are greeted with champagne in the third-floor ballroom, and it only gets better in this marvelous Italian Renaissance–style home influenced by a house Sebring visited when traveling in Italy in 1900. But Sebring was a perfectionist, and after hiring an architect, he sent him to Italy to draw up blueprints for his new home. He also hired Italian craftsmen, and they, along with all the materials for the mansion, including its stone, decorative woodwork,

Sebring Mansion

and brick, were brought to America. The thirty-thousand-square-foot building, on the National Register of Historic Places, is grandeur personified, with ornate two-story columns, twenty-five hundred square feet of balconies and porches, twelve-foot-high ceilings, elaborate dentil molding, and intricate stained glass. Added to that are a spa, indoor and outdoor pools, Wi-Fi, and special events such as wine tastings.

We can't live like the rich back then, but we can enjoy a day or two at the Sebring Mansion pretending that we do.

EAT

Who couldn't get addicted to white-gloved service for breakfast and dinner in the Conservatory with its wonderful views of the gardens?

Grab your morning cup of joe and choose from a selection of delicious edibles at Sweet Bunz Donuts and Such.

For ice cream, burgers, and specials like crab cakes, bratwurst and kraut on a bun, Italian-sausage sandwiches with grilled peppers and onions, cheese and marinara sauce served with french fries, and grilled chicken spinach salad with strawberries, walnuts, and hot bacon dressing, all at really reasonable prices, stop by JP's Snacks and Sodas.

PLAY

Explore local history at the Sebring Historical Society Strand Museum, a former opera house dating back to 1915. Built by Frank Sebring, who lived just a short walk away, the Strand also served as a movie theater. Now as a museum, it's full of wonderful objects, including pottery from the various local manufacturers as well as industrial design work and art by Viktor Schreckengost, who was from Sebring and taught at the Cleveland Institute of Art for more than a half century.

SHOP

A local favorite for almost a century, Ashton's 5 and 10 is one of the few remaining five-and-dime stores in the county.

24

Steubenville

Today, the small towns and villages of Ohio offer a pastoral beauty, emanating a sense of peacefulness and serenity. But it isn't always like that. Take Steubenville as an example. Nicknamed La Belle City, a French-English mix meaning "the Beautiful City," it sits on the mighty Ohio River, a byway that connects to the Mississippi and from there to the Gulf of Mexico and the Atlantic Ocean beyond. It was in 1786–87 that the First American Regiment built Fort Steuben to protect government surveyors as they worked at mapping the land west of the Ohio River. The fort was named after Prussian baron Friedrich Wilhelm von Steuben although he never came here to see it. In other words, it wasn't a spot chosen for its beauty but instead a strategic spot to safeguard the surroundings.

Steubenville was also a city of firsts. In 1814, Bezaleel Wells introduced the first merino sheep in the entire country in Steubenville. He also, a year later, built the country's first woolen mill—probably to go along with the sheep. And while it wasn't the first, the Steubenville Female Seminary certainly was in the vanguard when it opened in 1829. By the time the seminary closed its doors in 1898, more than five thousand women had graduated from there.

STAY

Bayberry House Bed and Breakfast Victorian Guest Houses are located in Steubenville's lovely North Fourth Street Historic District. Dating back

Jefferson County Courthouse

to 1870, the Westfall House and Garrett House have modern amenities such as wireless internet, private bathrooms (there's also one Jacuzzi suite), and cable televisions.

EAT

Try the award-winning gnocchi at Scaffidi's Restaurant and Tavern; their handmade dumpling-style pasta is prepared with ricotta cheese sautéed in the restaurant's signature pink sauce, a blend of their marinara and alfredo sauces.

Winner of sixteen awards in 2019 alone, the Ville Restaurant and Bar has a full menu of seafood, veal, pasta, beef, chicken, and pork, as well as a kids' menu and a full bar.

PLAY

Some two hundred life-size nutcrackers, carved and painted by volunteers, stand under twinkling Christmas lights at Steubenville Nutcracker Village. It's quite a display, a magical wonderland. Adding to that are the miniature Swiss-style chalets constructed by Nelson's of Steubenville,

Carnegie Library

a place for regional artisans and vendors to sell their foods, crafts, and works. At night, the illuminations from the chalet interiors add to the romance of this distinctive holiday event. The village is also the site of the Fort Steuben Gingerbread Village and Contest.

Steubenville is known as the City of Murals, so take some time to stroll through the downtown and admire these works of art, about twenty-five in all, as well as the historic buildings that now serve as businesses, restaurants, and galleries.

We told you about the fort, and while that's not there anymore, it's been recreated and open for tours. Next door is the First Federal Land Office west of the Alleghenies. Built in 1801, the log structure was the office and home of Registrar David Hodge and his family. The office was in use for four decade as the place to register land grants and deeds. Open to the public, it now showcases furnishings and artifacts of that era that would be found in a home or office. One intriguing display is the horsehair trunk that belonged to General William Henry Harrison. Also tying into the past is the Fort Steuben Herb Garden, which grows both kitchen and medicinal herbs common back then.

During the Civil War, the 98th Regiment Ohio Volunteer Infantry and the 126th Regiment Ohio Volunteer Infantry organized at Camp Steuben.

Walk through Steubenville's historic Union Cemetery, where many of the town's people who were involved in the Battle between the States rest.

SHOP

Shop like it's the early 1800s at Fort Steuben Museum Shop, where there are a variety of books, maps, documents, clothing, and charts reflective of life in a frontier town in early Ohio.

Get your nutcrackers, advent calendars, nutcracker clothing, cards, and more at Drosselmeyer's Nutcracker Shoppe.

NOTABLE

Born in Steubenville in 1917, Dino Paul Crocetti would later go on to fame under the name Dean Martin, singing such hit songs as "Memories Are Made of This," "That's Amore," "Everybody Loves Somebody," and "You're Nobody till Somebody Loves You." The handsome crooner also had success as a comedian with a long-running act with Jerry Lewis and then with the Rat Pack, a gang of heavy drinkers and carousers who spent a lot of time performing in Las Vegas. Other members of the Rat Pack included Frank Sinatra and Sammy Davis Jr.

Intriguingly, another Las Vegas–bound character was born a year after Martin, and surely they knew each other. Famed as a bookmaker and sportscaster, Jimmy "the Greek" Snyder died in Las Vegas in 1996 and now rests in Steubenville's Union Cemetery.

Moses Fleetwood Walker, the first African American Major League Baseball player, later had four patents to his name. When he was three, he moved to Steubenville, where his father, a doctor, practiced medicine. Moses played baseball for both Oberlin College and the University of Michigan before becoming playing professionally.

25

Sugarcreek

Once a railroad stop known as "the town east of Shanesville" (yes, really), this charming little village was renamed after a creek flowing nearby. Settled by Amish, Germans, and Swiss, the latter of whom brought along their cheesemaking skills, Sugarcreek became the epicenter of cheesemaking in Ohio.

These Swiss roots are on display in the Alpine facades and hand-painted murals throughout the village—and, in case you were wondering, the World's Largest Cuckoo Clock. Once featured on the cover of the Guinness Book of World Records, the clock is located smack in the middle of Sugarcreek's Swiss Village. Impressive, it's more than twenty-three feet tall and twenty-four feet wide, so you really can't miss it. On the half hour, a cuckoo bird pops out, followed by a band and dancers playing Swiss polka music. It's one of many reasons Sugarcreek is known as the Little Switzerland of Ohio.

STAY

Combining country and conveniences, the Dutch Host Inn features locally made Amish-crafted oak furniture and conveniences like refrigerators, microwaves, and coffee makers.

Lushly landscaped with added garden features like gazebos, a waterfall, and a glider swing, Carlisle Inn Sugarcreek sits on a rise with an expansive view of neatly kept farms. Country comfort and modern amenities meld: handcrafted beds, an all-season swimming pool, a fitness room, and a deluxe continental breakfast.

David Warther Carvings
and Gift Shop

EAT

Get your Amish on at the Dutch Valley Restaurant and Bakery Valley Restaurant with its all-you-can-eat buffets—a huge offering of broasted chicken, beef, mashed potatoes, macaroni and cheese, cold sandwiches, soups, salads, and house-made desserts. Want to take home some scratch-made pastries and pies? Of course you do. Thankfully, Dutch Valley Bakery is just steps away.

Try the fried pies and buckeyes at Esther's Home Bakery. Honey Bee Café sources from local farmers to serve fresh, healthy menu offerings. In season, stock up on fresh produce as well as homemade ice cream at the family-owned Harvest Barn.

PLAY

The three-story Alpine Hills Historical Museum on Main Street showcases the early days in Sugarcreek. The eighteen-stall, historically accurate reconstructed brick Age of Steam Roundhouse holds the largest private collection of steam locomotives in the world. Enjoy family-friendly entertainment at the Ohio Star Theater.

World's Largest Cuckoo Clock

Collectors Decanters and Steins is the state's largest decanter museum, featuring more than three thousand classic and collectible decanters and other unique items.

Indulge yourself in all things Swiss, including live polka music, Steinstossen (competitive rock throwing), and a yodeling contest, at the annual Ohio Swiss Festival. Founded in 1953, it's held the fourth weekend after Labor Day each year.

SHOP

At the David Warther Carvings and Gift Shop, visitors will find over seventy-five works by David Warther II, a fifth-generation carver of Swiss extract. But that's not the only reason to stop in. There's a plethora of items to examine, such as Amish brooms and furniture, clothing and jewelry, home decor items, glassware and pottery, and children's toys.

Take a look at the antiques and collectibles at Der Spinden Haus. Liven up your outdoor living area with Amish-crafted outdoor patio furniture at Swiss Country Lawn and Crafts.

26

Walnut Creek

Jonas Stutzman was the first of the Amish to settle near the rambling creek coursing through the area in 1807. Stutzman left Pennsylvania in search of fertile and inexpensive land. He found it here and was soon joined by other Amish farmers.

Now, Holmes County is the largest Amish settlement in the United States, followed by Eastern Pennsylvania and Northern Indiana. The Amish, the most conservative of the Anabaptist religious community, which also includes Mennonites and Hutterites, eschew much of what we consider the necessities of modern life, such as cars (horses, buggies, and bikes are approved transportation modes), phones in their homes, and electricity (they use propane). Their lifestyle is typically nineteenth-century rural, and it's not unusual to see horse-pulled plows tilling a field, laundry flapping in the breeze from outdoor clotheslines, and young children holding the reins of horse-drawn carts.

To drive through Amish country when Amish women are holding bake sales to raise money for church or schools is a pastry lover's dream come true. Holmes County is a fascinating trip into another world and century, and Walnut Creek is a great place to start.

STAY

If you check in, you may not want to check out of the Inn at Walnut Creek. What could be more perfect than to start the morning—or while away the day—sitting on your balcony or on a deck and gazing at expansive rural vistas of rolling hills and verdant farms.

Coblentz Chocolates

Enjoy a complimentary deluxe continental breakfast in the sun-lit second-floor wicker room at the Carlisle Inn and then take a stroll through its the garden areas dotted with fountains, secluded seating areas, and brick walkways while taking in the panoramic views of the Amish countryside.

EAT

House-made mashed potatoes and gravy, dressing, green beans or creamed corn, homemade dinner rolls, tossed salad, and a choice of meats are part of the Barn Raising Buffet at Der Dutchman. There's also the family-style table side buffet with salad bar and a large selection of options, including an Amish favorite of homemade noodles and pies fresh from the oven.

Java lovers can get their fix at the New Grounds Café and Diner, a nonprofit pizzeria, café, and coffee shop created to serve the community by providing a safe environment for people to connect as well as function as a meeting place for small groups, area churches, and ministries.

PLAY

It's family fun—think bluegrass music, comedians and actors, ventriloquists, and homemade concessions—at the twelve-thousand-square-foot, 325-seat Amish Country Theater. Learn more about the original settlers of Walnut Creek and the surrounding charming villages and towns at the German Culture Museum, a place where history is preserved.

Arts on Broadway, sponsored by the nonprofit Community Arts Council, provides a venue where local artists working in all types of mediums—including painting, sculpture, pottery, literature, music, and drawings—can display and sell their wares.

Coblentz Chocolates

SHOP

Peruse the selection of one-of-a-kind handcrafted items at Andre's Primitive Crafts and Furniture. The Victorian-style Carlisle Gifts features three floors of name-brand merchandise like Vera Bradley, Sorrento Dishware, Mona B Handbags, Crossroads Candles, and C. F. Quilts, among other offerings.

There's a lot going on at Walnut Creek Cheese. Sure, you can choose from a large selection of cheeses, baked goods from the bakery (check out their fried pies, a local favorite), and fresh farm produce purchased weekly at the Mount Hope Farmer's Produce Auction. But there's still more, like the seventy-five types of jams and jellies made from fruit grown in the area, pickled items, mustards and sauces, candies, and bulk items to buy. Enjoy the brunch and lunch menu, desserts, and ice cream at Mudd Valley Café and Creamery.

27

Zoar

Reconnecting to the early nineteenth century is as easy as a stroll along the streets of Zoar, a village in Ohio's Tuscarawas Valley settled by two hundred German separatists in 1817. For it is in Zoar, which prospered with the advent of the Ohio and Erie Canal, that townspeople built a solid and attractive community with brick homes and businesses, neat yards, and even a communal block-wide garden shaped like a seven-pointed star. Today, forty-four original structures remain and are well-preserved.

Those days can be vividly recalled by stepping into the Zoar Store, built in 1833, with its creaky wood floor and shelves and its display cases filled with local historical artifacts and Ohio artisan products, such as pottery and candles.

A totally unique feature is the seven-pointed-star-shaped Zoar Garden. Chosen by the Separatists in Germany as the symbol of their beliefs, Der Signalstern, or the signal star, represents a star or comet seen in Europe in the early 1800s.

STAY

Dating back to 1828 and once the place that made all the boots and shoes for the villagers, the Zoarite Cobbler Shop is a lovely bed and breakfast located in the historic downtown. The five rooms are filled with antiques, the grounds contain garden areas, and there's outdoor seating for warm-weather enjoyment.

1800s log cabin home

Louis Zimmerman, the treasurer of Zoar for many years, built a brick home in 1877. Now that home is the Keeping Room Bed and Breakfast (the name comes from the term used for a cozy room where the family gathered after a long day), and its amenities are very modern indeed, including free Wi-Fi, towel warmers, personal robes, queen-size canopy beds, and a full house-made breakfast.

As if that weren't enough in the way of charming places to stay, there's the Zoar School Inn Bed and Breakfast. Built in 1836, what was then a one-story building served as the village's original schoolhouse before another replaced it in 1868. A second story was added, and the home turned into a private residence. The inn features four Old World–style luxury suites.

EAT

Grab a latte or chai at the Tin Shop Coffee House, a restored historic home. Hungry? Their menu includes sandwiches, soups, salads, and pizza.

Donnie's Tavern is a chef-driven restaurant sourcing its ingredients from small local farms in Tuscarawas and Stark Counties. Their sustainable seafood comes from the Great Lakes and East Coast. The owners, who named the restaurant after their son who passed away, focus on craft cooking and offer small batch spirits and beer as well as a great cocktail menu and wine list. Contact Donnie's for a lunch in a historic Zoar building.

Enjoy a boxed lunch in the Zoar Schoolhouse from the Zoar Market or channel your inner German with a meal catered by Benson's Market and Catering.

The Canal Tavern of Zoar opened in 1829, serving travelers on the Ohio and Erie Canal. Now situated on the Ohio and Erie Scenic Byway as well as the Ohio and Erie Canal Towpath Trail, it's once again a place for travelers. As an interesting aside, the tavern is said to be haunted by a spirit known as George. A passenger on the canal, George became sick and was taken to the tavern, where he died. He liked the place so well, his ghost decided to stay.

PLAY

Although horses no longer pull barges along the canal at a maximum speed of four miles per hour, the Ohio and Erie Canal Towpath Trail follows the route they once trod. It connects to other canal towns, such as Bolivar three miles away. The super fit can hike or bike the trail's entire ninety miles between Cleveland and Zoar.

Speaking of horses, in May the Western Reserve Carriage Ride Association holds their annual carriage ride through Zoar during the village's Maifest, a fun time with lots of German food, drinks, music, make-and-take art projects for kids, a German car show, and—you guessed it—a maypole.

Other events include the April Pretzel Day, the Harvest Festival in July, Quilt Show in August, Cider and Cellars in September, Ghost Tours in October, and a big Christmas event in December.

Comprising thirty acres of shallow marsh and fifty acres of woodland, the Zoar Wetland Arboretum is a place to explore, take a walk, contemplate, and enjoy nature.

Stop by the Bimeler House and Museum, located on the southeast corner of Park and Third Streets, which was built in 1868.

SHOP

High-end antique stores abound in Zoar. At the Cobbler's House, look for nineteenth-century cupboards, wardrobes, tables, cutlery holders, and even a late-1700s immigrant chest, as well as pearlware, pewter, redware, vintage kitchen items like candy molds, muffin tins with unusual shapes, and lots more.

Zoar Museum

Antiques in the Wash House, behind the Keeping Room Bed and Breakfast, is located in the home's original washhouse.

The Weaving Haus, circa 1825 and now a consignment antique store, sells history books, World War I machine gun training charts, and military war relics and also provides such services as rope bed restoration and custom fitting for foam mattresses of unusual sizes. Items can include old sleighs, barber chairs, and looms.

Historic Zoar Village offers a wide range of activities, such as their Saturdays in Zoar: Free Speaker Series, which takes place at 11:00 a.m. on the first Saturday each month in the Zoar Schoolhouse. Topics cover the people and events that impacted local, state, and national history. Check the calendar for upcoming speaker events.

Group tours may be booked any time of the year. Groups of ten or more may tour the village's historic museums with a costumed guide for eight dollars per person. Add a tour of the Zoar Church for an extra fee.

Historic Zoar Village also puts on ghost tours in October and a Christmas celebration in December. Download a walking map of the village available on the Historic Zoar Village website.

NORTHWEST
OHIO

Barn Restaurant

28

Archbold

Designated a Tree City by the National Arbor Day Foundation, Archbold is said to have been named after James Archibald. As for the differences in the spelling, anecdotal history says the postmaster at the time made the decision, thinking that the *o* spelling was easier to deal with—and no, we still don't understand. As for Archibald, he was the vice president and chief engineer of the Michigan Southern and Northern Indiana Railroad. Credited with overseeing the development of the Air Line, a railroad route connecting Toledo, Ohio, and Indianapolis, Indiana, in 1854. Archbold, a small village on the Indiana and Ohio border, prospered because of the Air Line.

But the area's history goes even further back to 1838, when George Ditto purchased land in what was a vast track of forests. A school was built in 1852, and Frederick Stotzer opened St. Martin's Lutheran Church harness shop in 1858 and also became Archbold's first mayor.

Early settlers were French, German, and Swiss folks who brought their woodworking skills with them, a perfect fit for land with so much virgin wood.

STAY

Girlfriend weekend? Family get-together? Surrounded by eight and a half acres, Koelsch Farm, a Centennial Farm near Archbold with a pond, woods, and trail, is on the Barn Quilt Trail. Drive by to view their double aster quilt pattern. If you like what you see, download a map and tour the back roads for other patterns, like swamp angel, blazing star, garden patch, and starry night.

The large, comfy Sauder Heritage Inn offers such amenities as an indoor pool with waterfall, hot tub, game room, and fitness center. Both tent and RV campers can use the amenities at the Heritage Inn: wireless internet, a splash pad, a playground, a basketball court, shuffleboard, volleyball, horseshoes, a lake for fishing, and a walking path.

EAT

Open since 1912, the Home Restaurant has been owned and run by the same family since 1993. If you're around on the first or third Thursday of the month, stop by for barbecue ribs, beef, pork, and chicken from Brookview Farms, a family-owned farm founded over a half century ago that specializes in high-quality meat.

Barn Restaurant gets its name from the circa 1861 barn originally on the property of Moses Stutzman, two miles away from its current location, now in Sauder Village. As one might expect from a restaurant with this name, the food is hearty and homemade; they are known for such fare as their chicken, real mashed potatoes, and homemade soups, including the popular chicken and dumplings. They also feature cinnamon rolls and pies made at the Doughbox Bakery next door. If you can't decide, try the buffet.

The third-generation family-owned Homestead Ice Cream Shoppe offers a variety of ice creams, and their best sellers include sea salt caramel pretzel, buckeye, black cherry, and Cookie Monster. If the weather is right, enjoy whatever flavor you order on their large patio.

PLAY

The 235-acre Sauder Village, a living history farm and craft village, showcases how life was lived in a rural community in Northwest Ohio during the nineteenth and early twentieth centuries. The village was Erie Sauder's way to preserve and share the values that shaped our country and his determination "that we never forget" the hard work of our ancestors.

Walk through time by visiting Sauder Village Historic Buildings in Ohio's largest living history museum. The list is long and includes Erie's Farm Shop, originally located just south of Archbold, where Erie made a hand-built gasoline-powered lathe at the start of Sauder Woodworking,

Sauder Heritage Inn

now the largest manufacturer of ready-to-assemble furniture in the United States. The simple and small St. Mark's Lutheran Church, a country church with a one-hundred-year-old pump organ. In the past, St. Mark's also served as a school. Dr. McGuffin practiced medicine in the early 1900s in a nearby town, and his office exhibits the tools of his trade back then: glass syringes, splints made of rawhide, medicine bottles with cork tops, and dental tools. The water-powered gristmill continues to grind cornmeal, and there's an old schoolhouse and print shop as well.

Ride the Erie Express, a miniature replica of the original 1863 C. P. Huntington train that helped bring prosperity to the area, or take a horse and buggy through the village.

Talk about DIY. Watch craftspeople demonstrate how to make everyday necessities for life used back in the days of pioneers and early settlers, including weaving, broom making, spinning, quilting, coopering (making barrels), and tin smithing. Mark and Asher, two standardbred buggy horses; Rebekah and Delilah, a Tennessee walker mare and her foal; Jersey and Dutch Belted cows; Saanen goats; merino sheep; turkeys; chickens; ducks; and duroc hogs can all be seen at the 1928 barnyard area near the village's farm and gardens.

SHOP

Al-Meda Chocolates opened in 1924. Still family owned, the store continues to sell high-quality chocolates based on the recipes of Almeda Rupp, who was known as a great home cook and who created Al-Meda Chocolate Famous Stix—a chocolate-covered nut stick—at her son's request.

Located in Sauder Village, Sauder Store and Outlet features furniture products made by the Sauder Woodworking Company and displayed in the spacious showroom. There's plenty of other shopping here, including a village gift shop, a general store, an herb shop, Threads of Tradition (the village's quilt shop), Brush Creek Pottery, AHH Forge (the blacksmith shop), and Burlington Glass Works, where international glass artist Mark Matthews creates amazing glass forms.

Fair trade and ethically sourced with the mission of putting people and planet first, Ten Thousand Villages Archbold is one of the ultimate players in the global maker-to-market movement—a way of connecting the buyer with ten thousand villages around the world.

29

Bellevue

Bellevue, founded in 1815, was first called Amsden Corners after Thomas Amsden, who in 1823 built the town's first store. When the post office opened five years later, it was called York Cross Roads Post Office, and in the 1830s, the name changed again when James Bell, a civil engineer for the Mad River and Lake Erie Railroad called the new station Bellevue. That name stuck, and Bellevue it's been since then.

Bellevue prospered as a railroad town. In 1852, the Toledo-Norwalk Railroad connecting New York to Chicago traveled through Bellevue, as did both the Nickel Plate and the Wheeling and Lake Erie Railroads. Less than a decade later in 1891, the Pennsylvania Railroad laid tracks as well.

The city has the honor of being designated as a Tree City by the National Arbor Day Foundation.

STAY

Described as the "prettiest house in the city" by the *Bellevue Gazette* in 1908, the award-winning Victorian Tudor Inn is a luxurious bed and breakfast located in the historic downtown.

Gotta Getaway RV Park has numerous amenities for family fun, including a pool, a volleyball court, green spaces, a pavilion, a playground, laundry, and a lake.

EAT

It's not all sauerkraut balls, brats, and German beer on tap. American fare includes specialty burgers, pizza, and lots of appetizers. But there is a definite Bavarian theme going on. Of course, what else can you expect at a place named Bierkeller Pub and Restaurant? All of it is good, no matter the cuisine. Adding to the fun are live entertainment options such as dueling pianos, musicians, a comedy club night, and mystery dinner theater.

Locally owned for almost forty years, Miller's Drive-In features sandwiches, burgers, wraps, salads, and perch and shrimp dinners, as well as homemade ice cream in a choice of fifty-five flavors.

PLAY

A collection of sixteen structures dating back to the early 1800s, Historic Lyme Village is just east of Bellevue and is centered on the amazingly innovative John Wright Mansion, a Second Empire–style home built between 1880 and 1882. Back then, mansions typically had a ballroom on the third floor, and the Wright home is no exception. The second floor has eight bedrooms, and the first is an enticing entry into the world of the extraordinarily rich, with ornate woodwork in cherry, walnut, and curly maple. Wright, who owned a sawmill and brickyard, using his products to build his home, also installed two bathrooms with running water and flush toilets (no chamber pots, at least for some), and he also was one of the early innovators of the use of natural gas to light his home.

Less stately but no less interesting, other buildings include the 1836 Seymour House, the Lyme Post Office from 1824, and Groton Township Hall, now known as the John and Alvina Schaeffer Museum, which houses the Post Mark Collectors Club and National Postmark Museum. The idea for the club started in 1940, and it now boasts the largest collection in the world, with over one million postmarks. There are also three log cabins, including the one where Annie Brown lived for eighty-two years and Detterman Church, an Evangelical church built in 1846. It is one of the few remaining log churches in the state.

Take a self-guided tour of the Mad River and NKP Railroad Society Museum, where vintage trains include a Dynamometer Car X50041, an Alco RSD-12 Diesel and NKP Bay Window Caboose #423, and NKP Wooden Caboose #1047, as well as Double Outhouse, New York Central Freight House, and Troop Sleeper. Railroad paraphernalia includes Nickel Plate Road passenger uniforms and table service, a Porter sixty-five-ton "Fireless Cooker," and a B&O switchman's shanty.

The 120-acre Sorrowful Mother Shrine, one of the oldest sites of pilgrimage dedicated to the Blessed Mother in the Midwest east of the Mississippi River, was founded in 1850 by Father Francis de Sales Brunner. It's a place for peace, spirituality, and contemplation. Paths wander through a landscape of woods, flower beds, wildflowers, and forty-one grottoes and sculptures. Their annual pilgrimages begin in the spring and last until mid-fall. Also on the grounds and open to visitors are the Sorrowful Mother Shrine Chapel with its stunning al-

Sorrowful Mother Shrine

tar, paintings, and stained glass and the Pieta Outdoor Chapel, where mass is celebrated in spring, summer, and fall.

Seneca Caverns, opened to the public in 1933, called the "Earth Crack," and described as the "Caviest Cave in the USA," takes visitors on an hour-long tour through a vast underground experience. It's a descent through seven levels of cave rooms with names like the Cathedral Hall, Devil's Leap, and Fossil Room, and the bottommost level, 110 feet deep, follows the crystal-clear O Mist'ry River. Above ground, pan for gems at the Seneca Mining Company.

NOTABLE

Standard Oil tycoon Henry Flagler was the marketing genius who turned eastern Florida into a vacation destination, earning him the nickname "Father of Miami."

Stephen V. Harkness was a silent partner who, with Henry Flagler and oil titan John D. Rockefeller Sr., founded Standard Oil.

Born in Bellevue in 1884, Bradbury Robinson threw the first forward pass in American football. But that was just one of his many accomplishments, including serving as a front-line infantry officer during World War I as well as a physician.

30

Bryan

Bryan, tucked into the broad expanses of Northwest Ohio, is a quint-essential small town centered on the turrets and towers of the magnificent late nineteenth-century French baroque and Romanesque revival courthouse, listed on the National Register of Historic Places. The old-fashioned downtown bustles with businesses from the Bryan, a historic movie theater with a 1940s style marquee, to family-run stores and restaurants, some dating back to the early 1900s. Take a stroll through the Fountain City (a nickname earned because of the many area artesian wells) Historic District with its Victorian-style globe light fixtures and ninety buildings dating from the mid-1800s to the early 1900s.

Bryan, the county seat, was ranked thirtieth by Norman Crampton in his book *100 Best Small Towns in America*.

STAY

The Christmas Manor, circa 1870, on Butler is a bed and breakfast, but even those not staying there are welcome to take a peek inside at the hundreds of holiday decorations and fourteen themed trees.

EAT

A combination microbrewery, restaurant, chapel, and gardens, Father John's Brewing Company is based in a beautifully landscaped former Methodist/Episcopal church. Latte lovers will want to grab a cup of joe at Jumpin' Beanz Coffee. Frankie's is a longtime favorite for burgers,

Mexican cuisine, wraps, grinders, salads, and more. For downhome cookery, try the Four Seasons Diner.

For fancier fare, check out Kora Brew House and Wine Bar across from the courthouse in downtown Bryan. Choices include wines ninety points and higher, handcrafted coffees and beers, and a premium whiskey bar. You'll have the best time ever sitting on the patio on a warm summer evening.

PLAY

Take a Spangler Factory Dum Dum Trolley Tour and visit the candy museum at the Spangler Candy Company, founded in 1906 by Arthur Spangler and now a fourth-generation family-run business. At the company store, stock up on Spangler's famous Dum Dum Pops, Saf-T-Pops, and circus peanuts.

Music lovers can listen to the Bryan City Band, one of the oldest continuing city bands in the nation, which performs in the renovated bandstand on Wednesday nights in the summer.

For golfers, there's the Suburban Golf Course and also the Recreation Park Disc Golf Course.

The tasting room of Stoney Ridge Farm and Winery, located on the route of an old Native American trail, is set amid ten acres of vineyard that also include a large pond. Inside, the feel is restful, with a fieldstone fireplace, wood walls, and wood and tile floors. Sip a glass of wine and nibble on Amish cheeses on the beautiful patio overlooking the pond and woods beyond. Browse through the gift shop for Amish cheeses, crafts, gift baskets, and freshly baked breads.

Explore the historic downtown starting at the castle-like nineteenth-century courthouse and wander around the courthouse square. When you get hungry, grab a slice of homemade pie at Frankie's, a local favorite, and then hit the road.

31

Defiance

In 1793, the chiefs of the Miami—including those representing the Shawnee, Wyandot, Seneca, Ottawa, Delaware, Kickapoo, Pottawatomie, Chippewa, Iroquois, and Mohawk nations—gathered for a council meeting at Grand Glaize, a Native American trading center located where the Maumee and Auglaize Rivers merge. It was a strategic spot, which is why the wonderfully nicknamed General "Mad" Anthony Wayne, who was sent to subdue the Native Americans and end British influence in the area, erected a fort there a year later. Wayne had built numerous forts in the area, but he believed this one was the strongest.

As the story goes (and we love these tales whether they're true or not), Wayne said, "I defy the English, the Indians, and all the devils in hell to take it."

"Then call it Fort Defiance," suggested another general who was on the spot.

Wayne won the Battle of Fallen Timbers near what is now Maumee, Ohio—a victory that gave the US the Northwest Territories—think Wisconsin, Illinois, Ohio, Michigan, and Indiana. Shawnee war chief Blue Jacket, or Weyapiersenwah, signed a peace treaty in 1795, opening up their lands for settlers, Fort Defiance was abandoned a year later, leaving just some remains along with the name for the town. It was the place for forts, and in 1812, when Americans fought the British (again), General William Henry Harrison, who would later become the ninth president of the United States, built Fort Winchester.

As for Defiance, this location served it well in other ways, and the town boomed because it was near where the Miami & Erie Canal connected with the Wabash Canal from Indiana. There the two canals combined, flowing northward to the Maumee River and then on to Lake Erie

STAY

Consider the historic charms of the Second Story on Clinton Street and the Inn on Third, both located in the downtown.

EAT

Creamy cupcake-sized cheesecakes are the trademark of A Little Slice of Heaven, offering more fifty different flavors as well as cinnamon rolls, carrot cake, tiramisu, and all sorts of other goodies. Grab a cup of coffee and enjoy a sweet treat such as one (or more) of their caramel swirl, salted caramel, turtle, German chocolate, or white chocolate cupcakes. Located on Clinton Street in the historic downtown, A Little Slice of Heaven is just one of several great places to eat.

A step back into history, Kissner's bills itself as one of the oldest taverns in the state of Ohio. A bar and restaurant, the business opened in 1928 and continues to serve breakfast (biscuits and gravy), lunch (scalloped potatoes and ham), dinner (baby back ribs and chicken Oscar), late night nibbles, and, of course, a wide range of drinks. Check out the daily specials and who's up for live entertainment.

Take a java break at Cabin Fever Coffee, where there's not only a large selection of caffeinated items and flavor specials daily but also breakfast items and lunch offerings.

Bud's Restaurant on Second Street first opened its doors in 1939 as Bud's Hamburgers. Family owned since 1965, it's a cozy hometown diner—the kind of place where the daily specials are written on a white board and locals gather to enjoy long-standing menu items such as egg salad sandwiches and chicken pot pie.

PLAY

Besides the Maumee—which is formed in Fort Wayne, Indiana, by the St. Joseph and St. Marys Rivers—and the Auglaize, there's also the Tiffin River. These made Defiance a destination for John Chapman, who traveled primarily by river (at the time, it was really the only way to go, as roads, if they existed, were very primitive indeed) and planted a nursery outside Defiance in 1828. Of course, we know him today as Johnny Appleseed, and his legacy is celebrated not only with an annual festival but with a marker designating the site of the Old French Indian Apple Tree in Pontiac Park as well. This city park overlooks the confluence of the Maumee and Auglaize and is so named because it's very likely the birthplace of Chief Pontiac (also known as Obwandiyag), the Ottawa Indian chief who organized Pontiac's War using a coalition of Ottawa, Potawatomi, and Ojibwa nations to fight British occupation of the Great Lakes region. The park also has a boat launch.

It began with the donation of a large red barn and forty acres of land and became the Auglaize Village Museum, a project of the Defiance County Historical Society featuring a collection of restored nineteenth-century farm buildings typical of a rural settlement in Northwest Ohio during that era.

They like to party in Defiance, hosting such annual events as the Chocolate Walk (April), Lilac Festival and Street Fair (May), RibFest (July), and Fort Defiance Days (August), which includes a hot-air balloon festival and canoe and kayak competitions, as well as the Downtown Defiance Farmers' Market every Thursday afternoon during the summer.

Traces of both the Miami & Erie and Wabash & Erie Canals can be found both in town and at the 525-acre Independence Dam State Park on the Maumee River. In Defiance, what's left of Lock 37, discovered in 1997, can be seen in a pocket park on Clinton Street. In Canal Park, catch a glimpse of days gone by at the restored Miami & Eric Canal Lock.

Learn more about the canal by taking a walk (it's about three miles) along the towpath at the state park. The walk, with its historical markers and interpretive signs, runs along the remains of the Miami & Erie and Wabash & Erie Canals.

Learn more about Defiance history at the Andrew L. Tuttle Memorial Museum, located in the impressive classical Roman–style Defiance Home Saving and Loan Association building erected in 1888.

SHOP

A favorite since 1925, Meek's Pastry Shop has been serving up freshly made doughnuts, cookies, cakes, pies, pies, and more pies—pecan, pumpkin, sugar cream, cherry, and more. Looking for vintage finds in textiles, glassware, pottery, furniture, costume jewelry, military memorabilia, books, toys, prints, and more? You're sure to find it at the four-thousand-square-foot Fort Defiance Antiques. Eclectic Wallflower Boutique has a great assortment of items, including clothing, handmade soaps, essential oils, purses, wallets, gloves, and loads of fun jewelry.

No matter your decorating style—vintage, farmhouse, industrial, eclectic—Ruby Rose Market, specializing in home decor, surely has more than a few items you'll love.

32

Fort Loramie

Though some never ventured far from the village where they were born (after all, travel some three hundred years ago was less than easy), Pierre Louis de Loramie, a French Canadian who was born in Montreal, sure got around. The year 1769 found him in western Ohio, where he built a trading post at the confluence of Loramie Creek and the Great Miami River. Business was very good with French fur traders, Native Americans, early settlers, and British soldiers stopping by. Loramie stayed for thirteen years, not only working as a merchant and fur trader but also, in his dual roles as a British-Indian agent and Shawnee agitator, selling guns and ammunition to Native Americans and letting them use his trading post as a place for war parties to convene.

That all ended in the early 1790s, when Brigadier General George Rogers Clark, accompanied by Daniel Boone and more than a thousand soldiers, attacked during the Battle of Little Miami River, burning Shawnee villages and Loramie's trading post to the ground. Loramie certainly had it coming, having been part of a group who kidnapped Boone earlier when he attacked Boonesborough and brought the famed frontiersman to Ohio, where he was held captive until he was able to escape. Loramie also managed to escape and headed west, eventually founding Cape Girardeau, Missouri, where he opened another trading post and met with Meriwether Lewis of the Lewis and Clark expedition in 1803. He died nine years later in 1812.

In 1792, General "Mad" Anthony Wayne built a fort on the site of Loramie's trading post, figuring what was good for commerce would be

Gazebo in Canal Park

equally advantageous in transporting goods, weapons, and soldiers in his fight against the British and the Native Americans who had joined forces to fight the Americans. The upcoming battle, easily won by Wayne's troops, resulted in the Treaty of Green Ville in 1795, which redrew the lines of Indian Territory—and not to the tribes' advantage.

In 1843, the first canal boat came to Fort Loramie. The inexpensive fare—just one dollar—attracted a large number of German immigrants looking for land to farm and trees to fell. Land was cheap and fertile, and being industrious, they built communities up and down the river and canal. Today, many of their descendants still remain.

EAT

Brucken's Neighborhood Pub first opened its doors in the 1890s, and it remains a great place to meet friends and families. Although they're probably best known for their broasted chicken, other menu options include sandwiches and pizzas.

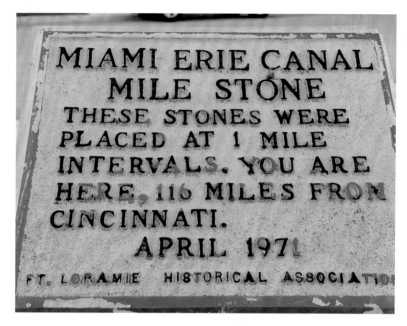

Erie Canal Mile Stone Historical Marker

SHOP

Fort Loramie Trading Post on Main Street carries Minnetonka and Hey Dudes footwear as well as hats, home decor items, concrete statuary, birdbaths, and jewelry just to name a few of their abundant assortment of goods.

Small Town Boutique carries a nice line of women's wear.

PLAY

A small island park runs the length of the downtown. It's a gathering spot with a gazebo and memorial markers for both the canal and the Buckeye Trail, a 1,444-mile hiking trail and long-distance trail looping around the state; its northern terminus is at Headlands Beach State Park on Lake Erie in northeast Ohio, and the southern terminus is at Eden Park in Cincinnati. Merging with State Route 66, the trail then follows the Miami and Erie Canal Towpath Trail and State Route 66 through Fort Loramie and on to Minster, New Bremen, and then St. Marys.

It's a lovely stroll through Fort Loramie, with its historic storefronts along tree-lined streets. Many of the buildings here date back to the canal days. One in particular is the Wilderness Trail Museum, a former boarding house and hotel for those traveling on the Miami and Erie Canal on their way to and from Toledo and Cincinnati. The two-story redbrick building had all the necessaries for an overnight stay on the canal—it was on the banks of the canal just a very few steps away and also had a bar and kitchen. The entrance takes you directly into the likeness of a nineteenth-century bar. With leaded glass windows, a working fireplace, a gun rack, and an antique cash register, the museum is a cornucopia of historic treasures from Fort Loramie's past. Also on display are uniforms and memorabilia from numerous American conflicts—the Civil War and World War I and II. The upstairs contains even more: objects from a Fort Loramie schoolhouse, antique women's clothing, and the Quinlin Bedroom, a late 1880s bedroom in an upper-class home. Additionally, the museum houses a music room and a room dedicated to fashion and retail merchandise from the early days of Fort Loramie.

From there, it's just a short walk to St. Michael Catholic Church (you can't miss it, as the two-hundred-foot-tall tower holds four original bells, the largest weighing thirty-six hundred pounds). Built in 1879, the Tuscan-Gothic-style church is also notable for its twenty-two stained-glass windows, eighteen statues, and fourteen stations of the cross imported from Germany. It's seriously large—with enough pews to seat eight hundred and a one-thousand-pipe organ with twenty-two registers.

33

Fostoria

Fostoria, a city built on rails, also benefited from a natural gas boom that brought prosperity and glass. Between the years 1887 and 1920, Fostoria had thirteen different glassmaking companies, and during the boom years 1881–92, seven or eight plants operated here. The gas was supposed to flow forever, but really in about ten years or so it was mostly gone. But the history of glass and trains is still celebrated here.

The city itself was named after Charles Foster and was formed by the combination of two villages, Rome and Risdon, in 1854. That same year, the Fremont and Indiana Railroad began laying tracks. Other railways followed, including the Chesapeake and Ohio; the Baltimore and Ohio; the New York, Chicago, and St. Louis, better known as the Nickel Plate; and the New York Central, originally known as the Atlantic and Lake Erie Road.

STAY

The sleek, stylish Hancock Hotel is within easy reach of numerous restaurants and other Fostoria-area attractions.

EAT

Sandwiches, burgers, hot dogs, and pulled pork are on the menu, but probably the biggest attraction at Whippy Dip is their many choices of ice cream.

Locally owned and housed in a building dating back to 1928 that was used as a gathering place, KemoSabes Roadhouse Grill serves a whole lot of food, from casual to more gourmet, including shrimp and chicken pasta, wings, flatbreads, barbeque, hand-cut steaks and chops, great appetizers, and drinks.

Go to Flippin' Jimmy's for made-to-order burgers and a variety of chicken chunks and sauces, like spicy parmesan, garlic butter parmesan, Korean barbecue, Asian, and more, with or without fries.

The UrbanWoody Brewery, an artisan nanobrewery using mostly Ohio grains and hops, is the place to raise a glass or two.

PLAY

The Glass Heritage Gallery focuses on ten companies that made glass in Fostoria, including Fostoria Glass Company, Nickel Plate Glass Company (named after the Nickel Plate Railroad, which ran through Fostoria), and Consolidated Lamp and Glass Company, the maker of the most colorful glass in Fostoria and maybe America at the time. At one point while they were in Fostoria, the company was said to make 60 percent of the lamps in the United States. There was also the Mosaic Glass Company, known for its tiles. Works from all of these and others are on display at the gallery.

Check out the Midwest Sculpture Initiative Walking Tour in the historic downtown.

Fostoria Rail Festival in September and their annual Santa at the Depot from Thanksgiving to Christmas honor Fostoria's heritage every year.

For a total railroad immersion, the 5.6-acre Fostoria Iron Triangle Visitor Center and Viewing Area, open 24-7, features a 360-degree viewing platform that lets viewers experience the sights and sounds of the more than one hundred trains traveling through Fostoria every day. Restrooms and vending machines are available.

The Fostoria Area Historical Society operates two museums. One, the city's oldest public building, exhibits artifacts from Fostoria's history, including an extensive collection from the John B. Rogers Producing Company, America's largest producer of amateur theatricals; a 1918 Allen Motor Car, manufactured in Fostoria; and a World War II–era Seagrave fire engine. The other, Foster Museum, named after the two-time state governor Charles Foster, displays the Foster family's belongings and other exhibits related to the city's history.

34

Grand Rapids

Once known as Gilead and founded in 1833, Grand Rapids packs a lot—six restaurants, twenty-five or so eclectic boutiques and shops, all located in historic buildings and all on the National Register of Historic Places—within their small downtown. Once a major stop on the Miami and Erie Canal, Grand Rapids has one of the few remaining functioning nineteenth-century limestone locks on the canal. The village, on the banks of the Maumee River, is a step back in time.

STAY

Sitting on the banks of the Maumee River, the historic Mill House Bed and Breakfast was once a steam-powered flour mill built in 1899. Back then it was called the Stump Mill, famed for milling Stump Best Flour. The mill's lush garden, overlooking the river as it flows by, is a wonderful place to enjoy your morning coffee or evening glass of wine.

Other overnight options include camping and cabins at the Mary Jane Thurston Park and Marina. On the National Register of Historic Places, the Grand Kerr House is a bed and breakfast dating back to 1880 with full breakfasts on weekends and continental during the week, as well as dedicated spaces for massage therapy, yoga classes, group meditation, reflexology, and other programs.

Gilead Side-Cut Canal

Isaac Ludwig Mill

EAT

LaRoe's Restaurant, located in the W. F. Kerr building erected in 1886, features wonderful murals painted on its red brick sides and back. The building was restored by David LaRoe, who was recognized by Ohio Historical Society for his work in restoring and preserving the edifice housing his restaurant, which opened in 1977. A lovely outdoor patio overlooks the park and water, and planted flowers add to the charm. Inside, there's both

a tavern and a dining room, as well as artwork by local artists. Overall, the restaurant has a cozy but stylish ambience and look.

Miss Lily's is a scratch-made kitchen with salad dressings, soups, pies with crusts made with lard, and meat they cut themselves. Check out the specials, such as beef noodles with smashed red-skinned potatoes and garlic bread or turkey avocado melt with bacon and tomato on asiago bread.

Who can resist a corner restaurant named Knucklehead's Kafé? Enjoy Wednesday's rib night and specials like a selection of different types of macaroni and cheese or Italian-style meatloaf lasagna.

Go to Wild Side Brewing for handcrafted brews and foods like smoked chicken wings, a wild game sausage board (duck sausage with apple brandy, wild boar with cranberry, rabbit with white wine and fennel), pizzas, and tacos.

The Majestic Oak Winery and Neon Ground Hog Brewery offers, besides handcrafted brews and wines made from their own vineyards, live entertainment featuring talent from local musicians.

At the Canal Experience at Providence Metropark, a restored stretch of the Miami and Erie Canal, get a feel for travel before highways or even railroads aboard the *Volunteer*, a replica of a mid-1800s mule-pulled canal boat. Costumed interpreters tell the story of Lock 44. While there, visit the Isaac Ludwig Mill, a water-powered saw- and gristmill built in 1849. At one time in the early 1900s, the mill even supplied electricity to the local area. Volunteers dressed in era-appropriate clothing demonstrate the old-fashioned way of milling, grinding out whole-wheat flour, wheat bran, yellow cornmeal, rye flour, rye bran, and buckwheat flour on the historic grindstones.

In 1928, Grand Rapids teacher Mary Jane Thurston donated fifteen acres on the Maumee River in what is now the 105-acre Mary Jane Thurston State Park and Marina, located at the west end of the village. Once the hunting and fishing grounds for many Native American tribes, the park features transient boat rentals, a public boat launch, a working canal gate, picnic tables, hiking trails, and playground equipment.

Tie up at one of the short-term courtesy docks at the Gilead Side-Cut Canal, designed by the Village of Grand Rapids for boaters to spend time in the downtown.

Held the second weekend in October, the Applebutter Fest celebrates fall's bounty and the area's heritage with historical reenactments, pioneer demonstrations including apple butter making, live music, food, and crafts.

SHOP

Download a map of the downtown on the visitgrandrapidsohio.com website and find your way to such stores as Library House Books and Art; Mary's Apple Orchard, featuring gifts and gourmet food items; and the Providence House, with its intriguing offerings of reclaimed vintage items, new arrivals, jewelry, and home decor. Also check out Angelwood Gallery, with works by regional artists using a wide range of mediums, and Just for You Riverfront Consignment, which sells new and gently used goods, including toys, clothing, gifts, and antiques.

35

Kelleys Island

Just four miles from the mainland but a world away from everyday life, the twenty-eight-hundred-square-foot Kelleys Island once was named Cunningham after a fur trapper who traded here with Native Americans before the War of 1812. Nicknamed Lake Erie's Emerald Isle, the island changed its name to Kelleys after two brothers bought up all the land in individual parcels. Now a year-round paradise for sun and fun lovers, the island has more than its share of things to do, from breweries and wineries to beaches, restaurants, biking, water sports, and more.

Boaters can take advantage of the island's marinas; for the rest of us, ferry shuttles run to and from Sandusky, Cedar Point, Put-in-Bay, and Marblehead. Several of the ferries accommodate cars.

STAY

A dazzlingly painted Queen Anne, Water's Edge Island Retreat is a short distance from the ferry and, as the name implies, overlooks Lake Erie. Rock (we're talking rocking chairs here) away—there are two large beach decks, covered verandas, and a pretty gazebo surrounded by blooms. In the morning, enjoy a breakfast that includes fresh breads and pastries and homemade apple butter made from the innkeepers' apple trees. There are also bikes available for touring the island.

For camping, there are forty-five nonelectric and eighty-four electric sites, showers, flush toilets, a dump station, two air-conditioned cabins,

Kelleys Island

two yurts, and pet-specific camping sites at the 677-acre Kelleys Island State Park on the north side of the island.

Several marinas offer daily and overnight dockage for boaters who want to spend a night or two. The pier at Kelleys Island State Park has a public boat ramp with tie-ups.

EAT

No, that isn't the Caribbean. It's Lake Erie, but it doesn't get better than eating lobster martinis, house-made crab cakes, fresh fish, meatloaf, and lobster bisque while watching the sun go down in Docker's Waterfront Bar and Restaurant's outdoor dining room, with its panoramic views of Catawba Island, Cedar Point, and Mouse Island.

Beyond gourmet coffee drinks, the menu at Taste by the Lake also features freshly made doughnuts, pastries, salads, pastas, seafood, and sandwiches.

Kelleys Island House gets creative with their seafood, sandwich, and pizza options and offers a delightful fenced-in front yard with colorful umbrellas for dining out on a nice day.

Glacial Grooves Geological Preserve

PLAY

Enjoy playing volleyball and horseshoes at the large outdoor entertainment area at Kelleys Island Wine Co. The space includes a children's play area as well as a spot for Fido to frolic.

Janet and Steve Wermuth, owners of the Crooked Tree Vineyard, give tours of their small working vineyard; just ask. Then stay to sample the fruits of their labor in their tasting room.

Known as the Walleye Capital of the World, Kelleys Island has plenty of charters for hooking a few.

No, it's not a new dance step, but the Glacial Grooves Geological Preserve is still one of the island's most popular attractions. A geological wonder, the grooves were scooped out as a gigantic glacier slowly moved across the land, moving earth, trees, stones, and whatever else stood in its way, leaving behind a four-hundred-foot-long indentation thirty-five feet wide and up to fifteen feet deep.

Caddy Shack Bar and Grill, near the water's edge, not only features subs, sandwiches, and pizza but also rents golf carts and bicycles and offers miniature golf and arcade games.

Lake Erie

SHOP

Charles Herndon, owner of the namesake Charles Herndon Galleries and Sculpture Gardens, earned an MFA in sculpture from Syracuse University and returned to the island where he spent his youth visiting his grandparents. His ten-acre sculpture garden and gallery showcase his wide range of works.

Can't decide between the praline pecan, maple walnut, Oreo cookie, or vanilla chocolate swirl? Free samples are available at the Island Fudge Shoppe, but we're afraid it will just make you want to buy them all.

Kelleys Island General Store is the place for all your tourist needs: T-shirts, beachwear, home decor, camping paraphernalia, gifts, Christmas ornaments, and golf cart rentals.

36

Marblehead

Marblehead is a delightful village of less than a thousand, poised on the edge of the Marblehead Peninsula dividing Lake Erie and Sandusky Bay. A stepping-off stop for the Lake Erie Shores and Islands, Marblehead is a viable destination in its own right, featuring beautiful views of the waters and the Marblehead Lighthouse. Built in 1820, it's the state's oldest continuously operating lighthouse, and in the summer it's open for tours.

Marblehead (the name refers to "marble headland," because the area's Columbus limestone looks like marble) was voted as "One of the 10 Most Beautiful Towns in Ohio" by theculturetrip.com and the "Best Lake Erie Beach for a Relaxing Getaway Any Time of Year" by *Travel + Leisure*.

But it wasn't always a place for peace and relaxation. Ohio's first battle in the War of 1812 took place here. Johnson Island, just a short water jaunt away, was a prison for Confederate soldiers during the Civil War, and the cemetery there, where 206 Confederate officers now rest, is said to be haunted.

STAY

An 1893 limestone three-story building, once a schoolhouse, is now the Red Fern Inn at Rocky Point Winery. As an interesting aside, the state natural area and preserve next door was a quarry that supplied the limestone used to build the school. The inn, which is on the second and third floors while the winery is located on the first, is just a short walk from both the ferry landing and the lighthouse.

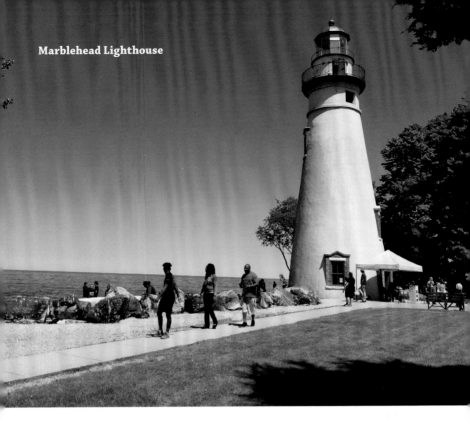
Marblehead Lighthouse

Skipper's Marina and Resort offers pet-friendly cottages, an outdoor pool, and boat dockage and is just steps away from the water.

EAT

Arrive by land or sea (make that lake) at the Hidden Beach Bar and order their specialty, a perch sandwich. There's free dockage for boats on a first come, first served basis.

You can get wood-fired pizzas, salads, sandwiches, and desserts like salted caramel pretzel-crust brownies and s'mores plus a great wine selection at the Canoe Club Wine Bar.

For live music, daily specials, and, on game days, plenty of TVs to watch your favorite team, head to Jamestown Tavern.

PLAY

Built in 1822, the Keeper's House, the home of lightkeeper and Revolutionary War veteran Benajah Wolcott, one of the first settlers on the peninsula, is the oldest surviving home in Ottawa County. For more information about this well-known Lake Erie icon and the village, the Marblehead Lighthouse Historical Society Museum displays photographs, exhibits, and artifacts. There's also a replica of the lifesaving station once located here, with more exhibits as well as an authentic vintage lifesaving boat.

Go for a swim, get some serious sun, or take a hike at East Harbor State Park. There are fifteen hundred acres of sandy beaches, a bathhouse, and eleven different hiking trails, and on weekends during the summer park naturalists present programs.

The big yellow lakeside daisies, a state endangered species and a federally threatened plant species only occurring naturally at a handful of sites, can be found blooming from early to mid-May in the nineteen-acre Lakeside Daisy State Nature Preserve located on land that was once a limestone quarry. Lakeside Daisies are considered one of the state's most spectacular wildflowers.

Bird-watch at the Ottawa National Wildlife Refuge or take a fishing charter to catch walleye or perch.

SHOP

Pamper yourself with natural handmade soaps, lotions, essential oils, candles, body oils, and more in a variety of scents at Marblehead Soap Company. Shoppers can also find canned goods, local honey, crafts and artwork by Ohio artists, gift items, and baked goods.

Ferguson Gallery features fine arts, blown glass, and other works by local and regional artists.

37

Maria Stein

Barely a wide spot in the road, Maria Stein, with population a tad over two thousand, would typically be just a drive-through sort of place, not a destination. But this farming community, dissected by Ohio State Road 119, which runs long and straight through the many German villages in Mercer County, is much more than that. It's nicknamed the Land of the Cross-Tipped Churches because of a plethora of soaring spires topping nineteenth-century Catholic churches, many built under the supervision of Francis de Sales Brunner, a Swiss priest who immigrated to the United States in 1843. Brunner landed in New Orleans, traveled up the Ohio River to Cincinnati, and then headed into the northeastern part of the state. Along the way he built churches, including Maria Stein Shrine of the Holy Relics, named after the Mariastein Abbey in Switzerland. It's an amazing place, a sprawling, architecturally astounding, and immaculately kept (but then everything around here is) brick building with white trim and architectural flourishes set on thirty acres of green lawn and woods. If you're wondering what Maria Stein means, no it's not related to beer but instead means Maria of the Rock.

EAT

This is a predominantly German American area, so it makes sense that there's a brewery in town. Moeller Brew Barn offers both core and seasonal craft beers, brick-oven pizzas, shareables, sandwiches, and even a kids' menu. What would a small town be without a hometown eatery?

Korner Kafe fits the bill. Family owned since 1961, it's a sports bar with subs, pizzas, wings, and more.

PLAY

In the nearby communities, it is all farmland and small hamlets, each marked with at least one soaring and impressive church. But Maria Stein didn't stop with just one. Besides the convent and the attached Sacred Heart Relic Chapel, placed on the National Register of Historic Places in 1976, there's also St. John the Baptist Church, built in 1889; Precious Blood Catholic Church, built in 1903; and Maria Stein Catholic Church, which is in a different location from Maria Stein Shrine of Holy Relics.

You could literally walk to each one since the farmland here is laid out in a half-mile grid pattern, but the major stopping place is Maria Stein Shrine of Holy Relics.

Self-guided tours of the shrine are free; just check in at the office. As a gal from the big city, I'm surprised at how trusting the staff members are as they wave me on my way, asking nothing but making suggestions about what to see. So off I wander, first to the stations of the cross in the garden behind the church, its walls lined with vintage photos of the convent. Also worth seeing is the Little Chapel in the Woods. Upstairs, on the second floor, someone has spent a lot of time assembling life-size dioramas of early life here—building the canal, cooking without microwaves and electric stoves, farming with horse and plow, and more—in their Heritage Museum. It's fascinating and informative, covering facets of local history.

Stop in at the lovely Adoration Chapel if you have time, but don't miss the Relic Chapel, home to the second-largest collection of Catholic sacred objects in the US. The largest is in Pittsburgh, Pennsylvania. Imagine that. Marie Stein has a population of twenty-one hundred. Here it's all gold, deep reds, stained glass, and countless physical remains and personal effects of saints and other venerated people. At the main altar are a relic of the True Cross and Saint Peregrine, the patron saint of those with cancer, as well as two removable relics to use in prayer. The base of the Sorrowful Mother Altar contains the relics of Saint Ursula and companions. Those belonging to Saint Victoria, who became a martyr around the fourth century when she spurned a pagan lover, are located in the Sacred Heart Altar.

Another nearby church is St. Rose (or St. Rosa), a High Gothic church in unincorporated St. Rose, but it's close enough to Maria Stein to sometimes be listed as part of that community.

The Marie Stein Country Fest in June of each year is a three-day family event with a plethora of activities, such as Belgian horse and wagon rides, mobile glass studios, bingo, go-kart races, a circus, vintage tractors, antique and stock tractor pulls, a diaper derby, 5K run/walk, and volleyball, cornhole, dodgeball, and three-on-three basketball tournaments.

SHOP

Oh dear, if shopping is your thing, there's not much going on here, though Maria Stein Shrine of the Holy Relics does have their Pilgrim Gift Shop selling religious gifts and keepsakes.

NOTABLE

Joseph Oppenheim, who invented the first mechanized manure spreader, established the New Idea Spreader works in Maria Stein in 1899. Hey, if it doesn't sound exciting, just imagine how happy farmers were not to have to do it by hand anymore.

38

Maumee

The history of Maumee, a pretty city on the banks of the Maumee River, goes further into the past than its historic nineteenth-century mansions on tree-lined streets. Over two centuries ago, it was a rugged wilderness outpost where a fort was built to protect American interests during the War of 1812. Fort Meigs saw itself under siege not once but twice when the British and her allies, the Native Americans, tried unsuccessfully to defeat the US.

EAT

Ever wanted to be whisked back to Edwardian England (think such TV series as *Downton Abbey* and *Belgravia*)? Then Clara J's Tea Room, located in a historic mansion, is definitely for you. Enjoy a formal tea where silver trays filled with those cute tiny crustless sandwiches, scones, sweets, and savories served with a wide selection of premium teas are filling enough for lunch.

Part of Maumee's history for over eighty-five years, Dale's Bar and Grill offers lunch and dinner and has eighteen big-screen TVs and a large patio for outdoor dining. Dale's Diner, also part of the business, serves breakfast and lunch. Menu items include sandwiches, wraps, salads, nachos, and a multitude of wing varieties. There are twenty-one tap pulls and daily specials such as avocado Caesar salad, Asian chicken salad, and Cajun peel-and-eat shrimp.

The Baker's Kitchen, a family-owned bakery in Maumee, offers a selection of fruit pies either regular or Dutch style (with a crumb or streusel topping instead of pie crust); cream pie options include black bottom, banana, coconut, chocolate, and vanilla. Also look for their petite pastries: German chocolate brownies, mousse-filled cannoli, éclairs, cappuccino brownies, cream puffs, and petits fours. They also manufacture and sell equipment for candy making and baking as well as cooking ingredients and supplies.

PLAY

Fort Meigs, a reconstruction of the US military post that played an important role in the War of 1812, is on the opposite side of the river from Maumee. Today, there's also a museum, interactive exhibits, reenactments, and events including a celebration of the victory against the enemy in 1813 held each May, a living history re-creation of battles, and camp-life and weapons demonstrations.

Maumee boasts a beautiful collection of nineteenth-century homes, some of which were built before the Civil War. They encompass a variety of architectural styles, including Queen Anne, Victorian, Greek Revival, and castle-like residences. There's also a hunting lodge with restored stables that is now a private residence. Stroll through the tree-lined neighborhoods, or take a tour like the Historic Maumee Home Tour hosted by the Maumee Senior Center, which encompasses several of the city's wonderful homes, including the Federal-style house built by steamboat-owner James Wolcott and his wife, Mary, the granddaughter of Miami chieftain Little Turtle and daughter of William Wells, a famed frontier scout.

Follow the winding ribbon of the Maumee River in Towpath Park for splendid views. Side Cut Metropark is a pretty spot for walking or picnicking. Of its six original locks—those tedious spots where the water was adjusted to let canal boats through, adding exasperating time to the journey—three remain, preserved by Works Progress Administration workers during the Great Depression. There's access here to both the river and canal for kayakers, a sledding hill, both indoor and outdoor picnic shelters, a playground, and Windows on Wildlife, a feeding station with indoor viewing areas.

Fishing spots on the river attract tens of thousands of anglers looking to hook white and smallmouth bass, crappie, bluegills, carp, catfish, walleye, gar, bullhead, red-eared and other sunfish, northern pike, and yellow perch.

SHOP

Locally owned and operated, Maumee Valley Chocolate and Candy has a lot to choose from, including retro candy, classic chocolates, nuts, and caramel and cheddar popcorn.

For the mall experience, the Shops at Fallen Timbers offers a wide selection of restaurants and stores, as well as Cinemark Theatres, a movie multiplex.

39

Milan

In 1817, Ebenezer Merry platted a small village on what was once Petquotting, which from 1805 to 1809 was a Moravian Indian mission village. Merry built a both a flour and sawmill called Merry's Mill. The village was named Beatty before becoming Milan in 1833. Because the surrounding prairie was often soggy, making it impenetrable for wagons, townspeople decided to create the Milan Mill—a connector to Lake Erie and beyond. Construction was completed in 1839, and for decades Milan was one of the busiest ports on the Great Lakes as well as a major shipbuilding center. It wasn't unusual to see numerous wagons heaped with produce and other agricultural products in line for miles, waiting to load goods onto canal boats. The peak canal year was 1847, when Milan shipped out 918,000 bushels of grain. At one point, Milan was the second-largest grain exporter in the world; the first was Odessa, Russia.

Milan, selected by the National Trust for Historic Preservation as a Distinctive Destination, is a very pretty old-fashioned village with a population under fifteen hundred, but the main focus for visitors is its native son—Thomas Alva Edison, one of America's greatest inventors. His creations include, among many others, the phonograph, the incandescent light bulb, the nickel-iron-alkaline storage battery, the fluorescent electric lamp, and motion picture cameras.

STAY

For large groups, the twenty-six-hundred-square-foot Old Tobacconist Inn, built in 1870, sleeps twenty-one comfortably. Nestled on five acres, the property hearkens back to the time when 87 percent of adult men (we don't know how many women because they had to smoke in secrecy) smoked cigars and made the home's owner, Henry R. Welschon, a tobacco grower and cigar maker, very wealthy indeed.

A Federal-style home built in 1820 is now the Angel Welcome Bed and Breakfast, situated in the downtown, just steps away from many attractions, including the home of Thomas Edison and the Milan Historical Complex and Museum. One breakfast option is to dine by candlelight in the formal dining room. Enjoy your morning coffee or evening glass of wine in the lush gardens, which feature a gazebo, art, and cast-iron accents.

The Steamboat Gothic–style Alto Inn, built in 1905, is conveniently located near the many attractions of this area. It's only five miles from Summit Motorsports Park and within twenty minutes of the ferryboat landing for Lake Erie Shores and Islands and Kalahari Resorts and Conventions, including their waterpark, the Sports Force Complex, and Cedar Point. Yet the feeling here in the grounds of this former farmhouse is one of serenity.

The magnificent Mitchell Turner House, with its wonderful white columns fronting the two-story exterior entryway, was built in 1847 by Zenas King, founder of the King Bridge Company, and is now the White Dog B&B. The Greek Revival home, which is on the National Historic Registry, is located on the Kelley Block of Milan's village square, with its impressive collection of wonderfully preserved nineteenth-century homes.

An 1845 stagecoach inn, the intriguing the 4,030-square-foot Milan Inn-tiques has an antique store on the first floor, the Coffee Station in what was the inn's old canal room, and guest quarters upstairs that can comfortably sleep six to eight adults. Located in the heart of Milan, it is a short walk from Thomas Edison's birthplace, as well as only a twenty-minute drive to Cedar Point and ten minutes from Summit Motorsports Park.

EAT

At the Milan Wine Post Pub and Bar, one of the quaint buildings in historic Milan Square, you can sample wine and beer and order from a limited menu (or you can call out for delivery). Renovated with an interior use of reclaimed barn wood, the pub has a rustic, cozy feel.

Thomas Edison Birthplace Museum

PLAY

Thomas Edison was born in a small red brick home surrounded by a white picket fence, and this house and the museum next door are now known as the Thomas Edison Birthplace and Museum, where you can see his inventions and family photos, including shots of him with such comrades as Henry Ford. Even his cane, hat, slippers, and cape are on display.

During the boom years, many mansions were built in varying architectural styles, and a majority remain in pristine shape even today, earning Milan the honor of both being known as one of the finest sites for nineteenth-century architectural history in the Midwest and of being part of the National Trust Distinctive Destinations.

Stroll through the village, taking in the Milan Township Hall, dedicated on July 4, 1876, which towers over the village square. The square is also the location of a Civil War monument.

The Milan Museum, not to be confused with the Edison Museum, is a complex of seven historic buildings and is part of the National Trust Distinctive Destinations, a network of diverse historic sites throughout the country designed to educate the public and keep the American story alive. The museum is a chance to step back in history by visiting buildings like the Lockwood Smith and Company General Store, Sisty

Blacksmith Shop, the Sayles Victorian House, once home to a sea captain, and the Hoover Innovation Gallery (where the Hoosier Potato Picker is on display). The Coulton Doll Gallery showcases 350 china, bisque, wax, papier-mâché, and composition dolls, the Robert Mowry has wonderful displays of glass, and the Galpin Galleries focuses on the history of the Milan Canal and features model ships. The Four Seasons Statue Garden, located in the courtyard between museum properties, is centered on four life-size statues representing the four seasons.

For over sixty years, the village has celebrated the harvest during their annual Milan Melon Festival over Labor Day weekend. There are a lot of typical fair happenings—runs, a classic car show, live music, and food vendors—as well as the unique: the watermelon sherbet and cantaloupe ice cream exclusively made just once a year by the Toft Dairy and Ice Cream Parlor for the fair.

40

Minster

In 1832, Francis J. Stallo and six other members of a German consortium based in Cincinnati trekked the seventy-five miles by foot to a land office in Miami County while carrying a tin box filled with $800 in silver. The silver was used to purchase 640 acres of land in what was then Mercer County. History doesn't tell us why they didn't travel by horse, but it does confirm that the mission was accomplished. Dividing the acreage into 144 shares, Stallo named the new settlement Stallostown. That changed quickly. A year later, after his death, Stallostown first became Munster. The name changed two years later to become Minster. And Minster it remains, one of many charming villages spaced closely together along the Miami and Erie Canal.

The digging of the 249-mile canal started in 1825 and would take two decades to complete, at a cost of more than $8 million or about $272 million in today's money. The German, French, and Irish immigrants who excavated rocks and soil and moved trees and other obstacles all by hand to build the canal received a whopping thirty cents a day and a jigger of whiskey.

It was a huge undertaking, but it brought prosperity to the region as it allowed farmers and merchants to transport their goods much more quickly and passengers to make their way to other locations—despite moving at a top speed of four or five miles an hour. In 1851, considered the height of canal travel for the Miami and Erie, more than four hundred

Canal mural

boats transported people and goods. As railroads were built, the cumbersome travel by canal boat became less and less popular, and by the time the Great Flood of 1913 occurred, wiping out large tracts of the canal, it was pretty much over.

STAY

Miami Erie Bed and Breakfast, on the banks of the canal towpath, is a Victorian home within walking distance of many of Minster's attractions, including the three-mile biking path and the Community Lanes Bowling Alley. Fort Loramie State Park offers 177 campground sites.

EAT

Follow the Miami and Erie Canal path to the Old Dutch Mill on Fourth Street for good grub and a lot of history. Once a general store, Canal House 65 has a side door where the barges dropped off goods.

The Wooden Shoe Inn, which opened in 1933 and is known for fried chicken and German fare, is once again serving Wooden Shoe Inn Lager. At one time the brewery was one of the largest employers in the village. Now made by Tailspin Brewing Company, the beer is a tie to the past.

At Morrie's Landing, dine on the patio when the weather warrants for the panoramic views of Lake Loramie. Once known as Mauri's Landing, it's a fun family place.

PLAY

Travel down Hanover Street to admire the double-towered St. Augustine Catholic Church, a beautiful neoclassical red brick church that dominates the surrounding neighborhood. St. Augustine's beginnings go back to 1835, when it was a sixty-foot-long, forty-foot-wide, sixteen-log-high church with seating for 330 people. If that sounds like a lot for a village that even today has a population of less than 3,000, at the time the parish covered a wide expanse of territory and consisted of two hundred families and more than 830 people. The church now standing, though it has undergone numerous renovations, dates back to 1848. As more churches were built, it became known as the Mother Church of the region.

Want to know more? Walk into the Minster Historical Society and Museum, where you can find an amazing number of artifacts and plenty of information about local history, including extensive records, local newspapers, exhibits, programs, and genealogical information. There's also a gift shop, and outside on a walkway is a lovely little garden area.

Minster Historical Society Garden

Get into canal history at Lake Loramie State Park. Initially, the 915-acre Lake Loramie was one of the original feeder lakes for the Miami and Erie Canal. Now it's a popular place for all varieties of water activities.

Boat, fish, and swim from the sandy beach, picnic, hike along the canal path, and enjoy the quiet at the 915-acre Lake Loramie. The grasses and woods abound with wildflowers, honeysuckle, flowering shrubs, and a sweet gum tree plantation. Wildlife abounds—think songbirds, Eastern bluebirds, migrating Canada geese, kingfish, and deer. Cross the footbridge, part of Blackberry Island's 4.9-mile nature trail. Flourishing in the surrounding waters of Lake Loramie are water lilies, American lotus, and cattails. On the undeveloped island, look for nesting red-headed woodpeckers, egrets, and barred owls. Take a swing at the eighteen-hole miniature golf course, swim, and take advantage of the six boat launches, ninety-one tie-ups, and docks for lease. Canoes, kayaks, and paddleboats are available for rent.

Minster's German heritage remains strong and is celebrated in the annual family-friendly Oktoberfest. Look for German-themed doings, such as the Beer Tray Relay and Heritage Beer Garden, and enjoy the foods, including typical fair items and also cabbage rolls, hot German potato salad, sausage and sauerkraut sandwiches, pumpernickel and wheat rolls, and apple strudel.

41

Montpelier

Montpelier got its start in 1845, when John K. Bryner and Jesse Tucker built a water-powered mill on a bend of the St. Joseph River and had the land just south of the mill surveyed and laid out with forty-one lots and a public square. A year later, the village boasted two stores and its own post office after the Eagle Creek Post Office was moved from the farm belonging to Conroy Mallory and became the Montpelier Post Office.

Why the name Montpelier? The story, according to historian Kevin Maynard, is that a local doctor gave a ride to Bryner and Tucker when they were working on laying out the town and, in return for the favor, they offered him the chance to name it. His choice was Montpelier, after the town in Vermont where he was born.

By 1853, Montpelier was busy enough to be described by a newspaper as "a thriving little village with three stores, two groceries, one tavern, one fine gristmill, a (wool) carding machine and various mechanics. We have but little idea of the population but suppose it to be about 200."

EAT

Drop Tine Winery and Tap House credits the success of their great brews to their use of award-winning Montpelier water—and yes, it did win an international award for water quality. Their food offerings are eclectic, with starters including a variety of pierogi, those stuffed pillows of dough, and Hungarian langos, fried bread topped with sour cream and gouda cheese. Meals include hamburgers, bratwurst with Bavarian sauerkraut, chicken paprikas, spaetzle, salads, and zapiekanka, a Polish-style bread topped with caramelized mushrooms, gouda, and their house-made ketchup.

Churn Handcrafted Ice Cream features lots of flavors and wine-infused ice creams. They also sell coffees, smoothies, pizzas, sandwiches, and wings.

Cookies on Demand serves not only that dietary necessity—cookies—but also soups and sandwiches.

PLAY

Visit the Williams County Historical Society's Museum, located on the grounds of the Williams County Fairground. The nine-thousand-square-foot building features five galleries of exhibits with artifacts ranging from the Stone Age to the Space Age. There's also a children's museum with hands-on exhibits and a dress-up room. The museum's barn houses agricultural and technological history, the depot has relics from the area's railroad days, and the Lett Log House shows how life was lived in the 1850s.

In March, the fair hosts an annual Maple Syrup Festival. It's not to be missed.

Other historic buildings in the county include the Hay Jay One Room Schoolhouse near Montpelier, unchanged since 1901—a time when slate boards and McGuffey Readers were part of the classroom.

Take a hike on the Lake La Su An Trail, a 2.5-mile loop running through the Lake La Su An Wildlife Area. The trail is rated as accessible to all levels. The wildlife area itself encompasses woods, brushland, meadows, and cropland; over thirty wooded and restored wetlands; and fourteen lakes and ponds of various sizes—from a quarter acre to eighty-two acres.

Culture mavens will enjoy the Williams County Community Theatre.

NOTABLE

Born in Montpelier in 1908, Antarctic explorer and geographer Paul Allman Siple took part in six Antarctic expeditions, including the two Byrd expeditions of 1928–30 and 1933–35, when he represented the Boy Scouts of America as an Eagle Scout. Also a Sea Scout, Siple, along with Charles F. Passel, developed the first formula and table for measuring windchill—a term Siple devised.

42

New Bremen

New Bremen, at Lock One on the canal, is a lovely little German village with a population of about three thousand.

For the first few years, it was known as Bremen, after the Bremen Company, a group of thirty-three Cincinnati investors who bought land frequently used by Native Americans as a camping site when portaging between what were then the St. Marys and the Miami Rivers. Early residents were Bavarians and Hanoverians who settled there in 1832. By 1835, the village had a post office, cabins for the families living there, and another name, New Bremen. Soon there would be a canal, turning the trip from Toledo on the shores of Lake Erie to Cincinnati on the Ohio River into a five-day journey instead of five weeks of travel through swampland and dense forests.

The peak year of the canal was 1851, with revenues of $351,897 and four hundred boats plying the waters.

EAT

It's hard to choose what to order, but rest assured you can't go wrong at the Pie Shell, where selections include pie flavors such as Butterfinger, old-fashioned cream, chocolate-covered cherry, and butterscotch, to name a few. Grab a cup of joe, sandwich, wrap, or baked good at the New Bremen Coffee Co.

Cut into a tender and juicy New York strip or an apple amaretto pork chop at 17 West, open for lunch and dinner. There's also a great wine list for every size of pocketbook and lots of by-the-glass or quartino options for red, white, and rosé lovers.

PLAY

Just steps away from the coffee shop, check out the two hundred or so bikes (there are another nine hundred in their entire collection) on display at the Bicycle Museum of America, one of the largest private collections of bikes in the world. There's a wide variety of bikes to see, ranging from nineteenth-century antiques to balloon-tire classics from the 1940s and 1950s and to the 1960s banana-seat high-rise-handle-bar bikes. One of the highlights is the Schwinn family collection, formerly on exhibit at Chicago's Navy Pier.

Take time to walk the streets near the tow path—believe me, it won't take long—and enjoy the historic architecture of this restored canal town.

For canal lovers, the old towpath is now a linear park (canal boats were pulled by mule or horse trotting alongside the waterway) where the old local wooden gates and spillway bypass have been restored to how they looked in 1910. There are displays and exhibits showcasing the canal's significance to the area.

The one-hundred-foot Crown Pavilion in New Bremen's downtown was originally built sometime around 1910 and later moved from Indian Lake to where it stands now. Perfect for festivals and events, it's the locale for Pumpkinfest, Cider Time, Bremenfest, the Firemen's Picnic, and the New Bremen Summer Concert series, free to the public.

The William Luelleman House, built in 1837 and considered a leading example of German architecture on what was the American frontier, is the oldest building in New Bremen. The twelve-room, two-and-a-half-story home, located in the downtown on North Main Street, is owned and operated by the New Bremen Historic Association. The home, listed on the National Register of Historic Places, has served as New Bremen's post office, a shop, and a Dutch Reformed church and has such architectural details as glass transom windows and a stoop instead of a porch. The historic association also owns the Pape House, built in 1865. Both are open for tours.

The seventy-one-acre Kuenning-Dicke Natural Area just north of New Bremen along the canal path at the old Dock 2 offers an oasis of outdoor beauty for primitive camping, a picnic meal, and an exploration of its prairies and woodlands. Like to fish? Throw in a line—it's catch and release—in the park's three-acre lake. A linear park, extending from Lock One south, built along the old towpath and part of the Heritage Trail system, travels all the way through New Bremen to Minster two miles south.

43

Perrysburg

Founded in 1816, Perrysburg was named after Commodore Oliver Hazard Perry, the hero of the Battle of Erie, which proved decisive in wresting control of Lake Erie from the British during the War of 1812. Perry was also noted for flying a flag reading "Don't Give Up the Ship," in honor of a dying colleague. He also famously told General William Henry Harrison, the future ninth president of the United States who was all over this area defeating both Native Americans and the British, "We have met the enemy and they are ours."

In its early days, Perrysburg was a center for shipbuilding and also a busy trading port. Located on the southern bank of the Maumee River, by 1833 Perrysburg was home to some 250 people, including two lawyers and two doctors, and the town's businesses and services included two taverns, two stores, a schoolhouse, a jail, and a courthouse. Eighteen years later, cholera killed over one hundred townspeople, as it did in many places throughout Indiana and Ohio.

Today, historic downtown Perrysburg is a delightful mélange of exquisitely restored Victorian-era commercial buildings and stately homes along Louisiana Avenue and Front Street paralleling the Maumee River. It houses shops and galleries featuring home decor, clothing, antiques, and jewelry, as well as coffee shops and an array of eateries, including an artisan brewery. There's much to choose from.

STAY

The Guesthouse, a bed and breakfast, is within walking distance of the historic downtown and all that it has to offer.

EAT

Taking the concept of beer and sausages to the artisan level, Swig in downtown Perrysburg handcrafts a variety of links, including brats, andouille, kielbasa, and hot dogs, as well as the microbrews they serve. Even the chocolate-covered bacon used for their sundaes is smoked in-house.

Rose and Thistle is all about creating the ultimate dining experience, starting with the romantic period setting, an extensive well-curated wine list, inventive cocktails, and a classic European menu based on seasonal ingredients.

For single-origin coffees, house-made syrups and baked goods, and a convivial atmosphere, perk up at Maddie and Bella Coffee Roasters.

PLAY

Take a hike or cast a line at Three Meadows Pond, one of the eleven parks equaling more than 206 acres of green space within the Perrysburg's city limits. There's also Woodlands Park for disc golf, biking trails, and Fort Imagination, a superlarge playground; Orleans Park on the Maumee is great for kayaking and canoeing and has a boat launch. For golfers, try Crosswinds Golf Course.

Hear the cannons boom during one of the many reenactments at Fort Meigs Ohio's War of 1812 Battlefield and Museum. Visit the Spafford House Museum, the 1823 Greek Revival home of Judge Aurora Spafford, which showcases historic collections telling about how both settlers and Native Americans lived back then.

For evening entertainment, there's both the Perrysburg Symphony Orchestra and Funny Bones Comedy Club and Restaurant at Levis Commons, another great shopping and restaurant venue.

During the summer, bring a blanket or lawn chair and enjoy the 7:00 p.m. Outdoor Music @ the Market Concert Series at Commodore Schoolyard, 140 E. Indiana Avenue. If it's raining, listen to the music inside the Juliet Beck Auditorium at the Commodore Building.

SHOP

For those who love home decor accents and furnishings, Sheffield Road carries distinctive brands such as MacKenzie-Childs and Paul Munro.

There's always something old that's new at Carriage House Antiques and More. That covers such merchandise as vintage and heirloom antiques, often from estate sales, including furniture, lamps, pottery, china, jewelry, gifts, crystals, paintings, and intriguing art objects.

A cornucopia of nature's treasures—freshly picked strawberries, luscious ripe tomatoes and sweet corn, handcrafted cheeses, freshly baked breads, and warm cinnamon rolls with their enticing aroma—are available in abundance at the Perrysburg Farmers' Market on historic Louisiana Avenue in the city's downtown. Open rain or shine from late spring to fall, the market, with more than fifty vendors, is the heart of the community, as neighbors and strangers come together to shop for garden art or hand-wrought jewelry, just-cut flowers and potted plants from local greenhouses, organic foods, freshly roasted coffees, and savory foods to take home for lunch or dinner.

Marsha's Homemade Buckeye Chocolates has found their niche; they make buckeyes—both chocolate and peanut butter—and that's it. This in-depth specialization may be why they're still family owned since 1984.

The Town Center at Levis Commons offers a myriad of shops, restaurants, and events.

44

Put-in-Bay

Sorry about the pun, but we can't keep ourselves from saying put in at Put-in-Bay, a charming village on South Bass Island, one of the Lake Erie Islands off the shore of Port Clinton. A summer resort with a year-round population of less than two hundred, it's just thirty minutes by water from Sandusky, home of Cedar Point, the super-popular amusement park.

Wondering about the name? There are two stories, each plausible. Put-in-Bay, or PIB as locals call it, provided shelter to schooners plying the waters in the 1700s. It was, in other words, a place to put in until storms passed. Advance to writings in an 1879 journal describing the bay as "shaped like a pudding bag with a soft bottom." Huh? It seems that sailors called it puddin' bay, a slang term that morphed into, you guessed it, Put-in-Bay.

Commodore Oliver Hazard Perry and his men hid out in the islands after learning that the British fleet, who at the time controlled Lake Erie, would be passing nearby. Thus on September 10, 1813, during the War of 1812 (we know, the years don't match, but it was part of the conflict between the US and Great Britain for domination of Indiana, Ohio, and Michigan), the Americans attacked the British fleet as they sailed by. The battle was decisive and fairly quick; starting at 11:45 a.m., it was over by 3:00 p.m. The US Navy had won and captured the entire British fleet.

Brig Niagara

STAY

With a swim-up bar, heated pool, free continental breakfast, fitness center with cardio, splash pad, and what's billed as the world's largest Jacuzzi, Put-in-Bay Resort is a great place for families. Many of PIB's attractions, including miniature golf and Adventure Bay Amusement Park, are nearby.

EAT

Once a blacksmith shop, the Forge is known for their variety of crepes— the Atlantic, filled with salmon and lemon-dill cream cheese, and the Bodee, with prosciutto, apple, arugula, and shaved parmesan in a Balsamic reduction. Other offerings include their walleye fry and duck wings. Check out their drink menu, including specialty cocktails like peach pie old-fashioned and honey lavender lemonade.

You'll have to remind yourself that you're in northern Ohio and not South Florida when dining on conch fritters, grilled grouper, and key lime pie at the Keys. Enjoy the water views and premium frozen cocktails on Fat Tuesdays.

In 1900, South Bass Island had nineteen wineries (not bad for a little 1,588.3-acre island). Of those, only Heineman's Winery survived

The Boardwalk

Prohibition—though of course there are new wineries as well. Still a family business owned and operated by the descendants of the founder, Gus Heineman, their wines are made from grapes grown on the island. Tours of the winery also include a visit to their Crystal Cave, discovered in 1896 when workers digging a well forty feet below the winery came across what is the world's largest geode. Before or after the tour, take time to relax in the pretty wine garden and have a sample or two.

A stunning Italianate home, once the Doller House and home to the wealthiest resident on the island, is now part of the Put-in-Bay Winery, located on the water. A unique venue, it shows how life among the wealthy was lived over a century ago.

PLAY

You can't miss taking a ride on the Island Tour Train, a fifty-five-minute narrated excursion of historic South Bass Island with stops at local attractions like Perry's Cave, the Butterfly House, and Perry's Victory and International Peace Memorial. The latter, which opened to the public in 1915 and honors Perry's victory, is made of seventy-eight layers of pink granite and topped with a bronze urn weighing eleven tons. Lying beneath the rotunda are the remains of three British and three American naval officers. At a height of 353 feet, the memorial is the highest open-air observatory operated by the National Park Service.

Jet Express

Historic walks and ghost and Segway tours are memorable ways to explore the island. Rent a bike, moped, or golf cart to navigate around the four-mile vacation destination. Or take the easy way and sit back for a ride with Poe's Ped-Cabs.

Visit Port Clinton or Sandusky aboard the Jet Express ferry, or travel to Middle Bass Island on Sonny-S Boat Line. J. F. Walleye's Microbrewery and Eatery, just a short walk from the dock on Middle Bass, also rents golf carts and bikes.

If you have a boat, tie up at one of three large public docks: Village of Put-in-Bay, Peach Point, and DeRivera Park. Alternatives include the family-oriented Miller Marina, with both day and overnight dockage, and the Park Place Boat Club at the Boardwalk, a bustling waterfront restaurant with live entertainment and a margarita bar.

Who can resist an annual event known as Pirate Fest? Have a pirate costume? Then bring it along.

Mark your calendar for October's events, such as the Put-in-Bay Wine Festival. Get your German on during the annual Oktoberfest for German food, drinks, polka dancing, and German music. Raise your glass, practice your polka, and imagine enjoying cabbage rolls, Wiener schnitzel, sauerbraten, and other German specialties. Grab the lederhosen and dirndl and head to your nearest Ohio Oktoberfest. Prost!

45

St. Marys

A major player on the Miami and Erie Canal, St. Marys was established in 1823, was incorporated in 1834, and officially became a city in 1904. But we can go even further back into its history than that.

Centuries ago, Native Americans traveled the St. Marys River, which flowed from Lake Erie to the Gulf of Mexico. The river at the time was so wide and deep that even the largest of flat-bottomed boats were able to navigate its waters. General "Mad" Anthony Wayne—hero of the Revolutionary War who, in winning the Battle of the Fallen Timbers, captured a vast amount of land that became Ohio—shipped supplies for his army on the St. Marys River.

Wayne wasn't the only player in the War for Independence who had a connection to the St. Marys River, though he's certainly much more heroic than Simon Girty, who first sided with the colonists during the Revolutionary War and then switched loyalties and fought with the Native Americans and British. Girty established a trading post on the St. Marys with his brother James, and the settlement was first known as Girtystown. Wayne drove out the Girty brothers, who were known for their cantankerous ways. The settlement's name changed too in 1823, when Charles Murray, William Houston, and John McCorkle purchased four hundred acres of government land and laid out sixty-eight lots of what would become the village of St. Marys.

Grand Lake St. Marys Lighthouse

What really put St. Marys on the map was the building of the Miami and Erie Canal, and that heritage is still honored in the city. The canal also gave the city and surrounding area the wonderful Grand Lake St. Marys.

It gets a little confusing here, so bear with us. St. Marys is the name of the town; Grand Lake St. Marys is the name of what was at one time the largest manufactured lake in the world. The 13,500-acre Grand Lake St. Marys was built in 1845 to feed water into the Miami and Erie Canal as it passed through west-central Ohio. Though the glory days of canals are long gone, Grand Lake St. Marys is still the world's largest hand-dug body of water, as well as the state's largest inland lake. Just to add to the confusion, there's Grand Lake St. Marys State Park as well.

The first *Belle of St. Marys* was constructed in 1990 by volunteers and donations from the community. An exacting replica, the *Belle* is permanently settled on a channel of the canal.

STAY

Tie up at Grand Lake St. Marys State Park Marina, which offers eight transient docks on a first come, first served basis at very reasonable rates. Opt to drop anchor for an overnight stay on the water. Rather sleep on

Belle of St. Marys Canal Boat

land? The West Bank Inn and Romer's Westlake Hotel Villas offer docks for their guests. The park also offers seasonal cabins and campsites.

St. Marys Canal House is exactly that, a former 1820s canal warehouse right on the Miami and Erie Canal in Memorial Park. It offers period furnishings, historic photos, and amenities like Wi-Fi in every room.

EAT

For burgers, sandwiches, subs, salads, and wings, check out JT's Brew and Grill.

For more than two decades, Xcaret Restaurant has been serving great Mexican food with menu items suitable for all palates.

PLAY

Grand Lake St. Marys, with fifty-two miles of glorious shoreline, is the state's largest inland lake and most likely one of the few inland lakes to have three lighthouses. With four boaters' beaches, six full-service marinas, seven free public launch ramps, boat rentals, and no horsepower restrictions, it's all about summer fun.

Besides hiking, fishing, dog parks, swimming, camping, and hiking trails, Grand Lake St. Marys State Park, one of the oldest state parks in Ohio, is also a destination for enthusiastic birders, and the range of feathered friends who can frequently be spotted include Canada geese, swans, egrets, loons, herons, and even eagles.

Want to go throw a line in the water? Check out fishing trips at Matt Tuttle Guide Service.

Memorial Park in uptown St. Marys and bordered by the St. Marys River is home to many community-funded projects such as the *Belle of St. Marys* Canal Boat, Memorial Covered Bridge, Veterans Walkway, Clock Tower, and Grotto. For canal history buffs, the *Belle*, a full-scale replica of the canal boat that once traveled the canal, is the major attraction. Moored to the dock on a section of the canal that's been preserved, the boat is open for tours.

The city's annual SummerFest, held the second full weekend of August, is a popular activity in the park as well. Each October the St. Marys Area Chamber of Commerce and St. Marys Kiwanis Club host the 3.5-mile "Walk with Nature" along the towpath from Memorial Park to Forty Acre Pond just north of St. Marys.

Beautifully landscaped with ponds, water fountains, bridges, and waterfall, the eighteen-hole St. Marys Miniature Golf Course is part of K. C. Geiger Park, a seventy-acre multirecreational complex with other amenities, such as three lighted tennis courts, four pickleball courts, three restroom/concession buildings, three shelter house/picnic facilities, a fishing pond, a snow hill, lighted volleyball courts, lighted basketball courts, paved roadways, concrete walkways, paved bikeways, and two playground areas.

46

Van Wert

Once the Peony Capital of the World, Van Wert was named after Revolutionary War hero Isaac Van Wart, who, along with two others, was awarded the Fidelity Medallion, America's first military decoration. They also received New York farmland and $200 a year in federal pensions (which was a lot of money back then), and each had a county in Ohio named after them.

EAT

Ice-cold beer and pan-fried chicken are just two of the reasons that the family-friendly Landeck Tavern has been a mainstay in the downtown for almost a century. The food is good and the atmosphere convivial.

Most of what is served for breakfast and lunch at Truly D'vine Bread Co. is made in-house. There are wonderful weekly specials such as homemade green pepper casserole and Grandma's homemade meatloaf with sauce and mashed potatoes. For sweets, their doughnuts are melt-in-your-mouth fresh, and they also offer fresh-baked scones; danish; pecan rolls; crisps; apple, blueberry, and cherry fritters; and croissants.

Check out the ice cream of the day at Sycamore of Van Wert, which also serves frozen custard and sandwiches. Walk in or drive in—it's up to you.

Handcrafted lattes, frappés, and other libations are available for a java jolt at Brewed Expressions.

Downtown Wall Mural

Dating back to 1932, the Peony Festival is held in June and features—besides the aromatic flowers—a grand parade, live entertainment, free concerts, self-guided garden tours, food, arts and craft vendors, fishing derby, and adult beverages on the Peony Patio.

Take in a performance at the Niswonger Performing Arts Center, a venue for concerts, ballet, Broadway-style performances, and choirs.

Back when buildings were frequently made of wood, water didn't come out of taps, and homes and businesses were gaslit, fires often could wipe out entire blocks or even more (think of the Great Chicago Fire). Antique Fire Equipment Museum—Central Mutual Insurance Company is one of the finest privately held collections in the United States.

The Wassenberg Art Center hosts the annual juried June Art Exhibit, now over sixty-five years old, attracting more than a hundred artists from Michigan, Indiana, and Ohio. The center also holds other events, like their Thursday Pint Nights, hosts classes and exhibits, and features artworks of all types in their gift shop.

We don't typically suggest heading to the library, but the Brumback Library, with its crenellated towers, looks so much like a castle that it's worth a look. Also, it holds the distinction of being the first library

Balyeat's Coffee Shop Historic District

in the US to serve an entire county. And as long as you're admiring nineteenth-century architecture, check out the Second Empire–style Van Wert County Courthouse built in 1876. A lovely pile of bricks, stone, towers (on all four sides), pilasters, columns, and quoins, it's topped with a clock tower with an eight-foot-high statue of Justice.

Now more than 165 years old, the Van Wert County Fair is held in September.

SHOP

Shop till you're ready to eat. DeShia, the Country Shoppe, offers one of the largest selections of candles selections and candle making supplies, including such brands as Woodwick, Crossroads, McCall's, and Thompson. But that's not all; there's a selection of gifts and home decor items, including framed prints, dried and silk florals, timer lanterns and lights, and plants for miniature gardens, as well as a gourmet foods section. Grab a bite to eat at their Gathering Room Café.

Look for vintage in the charmingly painted Olde Barn.

Peanut butter cup, chocolate chip, cookies and crème, salted caramel, and white chocolate macadamia are just a few of the cookies at the Flour Loves Sugar (isn't that the truth) bake shop.

You never know what you'll find, but you'll surely find something at Bob's Bargain Barn, a place for vintage goods of all kinds.

Collins Fine Foods has a deli menu and lots of intriguing food products as well as wine and beer to take home.

47

Vermillion

Call it a captain's paradise—a wonderful mix of historic and trendy—Vermilion is an adorable village situated where the Vermilion River flows into Lake Erie. Once known as the Village of Lake Captains, Vermilion is reminiscent in ways of a coastal New England village, with its sixteen-block historic downtown lined with adorable shops, sandy beaches, a lighthouse, lovely greenways and parks, recreational boating, a multitude of culinary options, and artistic and cultural flair.

STAY

Just steps away from the shores of Lake Erie is a wonderful 1885 home that once housed Captain J. C. Gilchrist, his wife, and their seven children and that is now the Captain Gilchrist Guesthouse Bed and Breakfast.

Located in Vermilion's Historic Harbour Town, the Old Vermilion Jailhouse Bed and Breakfast built in 1910 was reimagined in a luxurious European mythical castle style despite retaining its original jail bars and layout. Relax in comfort and indulge your dreams in the perfect getaway for a romantic evening, family vacation, or girls' or guys' night out, and we can even provide the backdrop for your proposal to the love of your life.

EAT

In business for more than three decades, Chez Francois serves wonderfully classic French food, a great wine list, and lovely dinners pairing wines and food courses. Their coastal eatery, Chez Riverfront Café, voted

Vermillion Lighthouse

by *Power and Motor Yacht* magazine as the second-best waterfront dining in America, serves more casual fare.

Just steps from the beach, the award-winning Old Prague Restaurant opened in 1967 and remains family owned, serving eastern European specialties such as schnitzel, paprikash, roast duck, and goulash. As befitting this beach town, the menu also lists Lake Erie perch, salmon, and frog legs. Pivos (beers) include Czech selections, and there are American and European wines.

Step under the red and white awning and into the 1950s at Big Ed's Main Street Soda Grill, where dining fare includes burgers, chili dogs, chili cheese fries, and old-fashioned soda fountain drinks like floats, shakes, and malts.

What is summer at the beach without ice cream? Indeed, what is any time of the year without sampling the newest flavor or your own standby? Check out the creatively named Granny Joe's Ice Creamatorium and Romp's Dairy Dock.

PLAY

The wide expanse of sandy beach, observation platform, concession stand, and red and white Vermilion Lighthouse make for a perfect day at Main Street Beach. Beach chair and umbrella rentals are available.

Lake Erie

Architectural styles such as beautifully maintained Victorian, Italianate, Arts and Crafts, and Queen Anne abound in Vermilion's Harbour Town Historic District, home to many wealthy ship captains from days of yore. Take a stroll and admire their beauty.

Travel the Vermilion River like its 1927 in a twenty-six-foot Model 826 three-cockpit or like it's 1926 in

Nokomis Park

a twenty-six-foot Chris-Craft three-cockpit runabout. These antique wooden speedboat rides are available at Moe's Marine Service.

Look for bald eagles and great blue and green-backed herons who make their habitat in the Vermilion River Reservation, or cast a line in the river for steelhead and bass. In the reserve's ponds, you can find more bass, crappie, and catfish. Rent a kayak and paddle the river, part of the twenty-seven-mile Vermilion-Lorain Water Trail that flows through the village, enters Lake Erie, and then finally ends at the Bur Oak Picnic Area of the Black River Reservation in Elyria.

For boaters, Vermilion's marinas have over three thousand boat slips including transient docks, and there are numerous boat ramps for easy river access. West River Paddling Co. rents canoes, kayaks, and paddleboards. Fish Lake Erie aboard Lucky Duck and Trolling Eye Charters.

Held each June, the Festival of the Fish is a three-day fish-frying event. The intriguingly named Dick Goddard Woollybear Festival is a one-day event held every year around the first of October, attracting large crowds of about 150,000. There's a wide range of choices for music

The Wine Vault

aficionados. In the summer enjoy such outdoor events as Third Thursday Music, Flowers & a Sunset and Summer Concerts in the Park.

Christmas at the Brownhelm Heritage Museum is a marvelous annual celebration of the holiday season, but the museum, once a German Evangelical and Reformed Church built in 1870, is worth the trip anytime to see exhibits of local history. The same holds true with the Historic Brownhelm School and Museum housed in the former redbrick Brownhelm School, which opened in 1889 and closed in 1989.

What were second-floor classrooms now are filled with displays of historical artifacts from the school's past and the area's history of places no longer in existence, such as Swifts Mansion and the Light of Hope Orphanage.

SHOP

Shopping options abound as Vermilion has adorable, colorful boutique stores and galleries. There are gift, home decor, furnishing, art, fashion, and antique stores like Ancient Celtic Shop, Swan Creek Candle, Lee's Landing, Silly Goose, Burning River Boutique, and Szabo Apparel.

Foodies should check out Brummer's Homemade Chocolates and the Olive Scene for a myriad of fresh olive oils and balsamic vinegars. Stock up on seasonal local and regional produce as well as a variety of wines, cheeses, meats, and jarred goods at the Vermilion Farm Market.

48

Wapakoneta

Early on, before White settlers took their place, Wapakoneta was one of the Shawnee tribe's principal towns, and by 1808 over five hundred Shawnee, Seneca, and Ohio Seneca-Cayuga lived here. Using cultivation skills taught to them by the Quakers, this large group of Native Americans established the first sawmill and gristmill in Northwest Ohio. But, of course, all this wasn't good enough, and in 1831 they were forced from their lands. In 1880, the population of Wapakoneta was twenty-eight hundred, and supposedly the manufacturing of butter churns was a big business, with more produced here than in any other single location at that time in the US.

STAY

Like a camp for both adults and children, Venture Out! Resorts' Arrowhead Lakes Resort offers a plethora of fun nature experiences—land and water sports, hiking, biking, fishing, golfing, entertainment, children's activities, and festivities.

EAT

Hamburgers, fried bologna sandwiches, hand-breaded tenderloins, weekly specials, and patio dining are just part of the allure of the Alpha Café. The café is known for its back bar, a resplendent hand-carved white oak twenty-four-foot long bar built by Brunswick Balke Collender Company in 1893. Opposite the bar is a matching eight-foot-tall elaborately carved wainscoted wall with arched mirrors.

Auglaize County Courthouse

The history of the Alpha and its owner are steeped in rich tradition, stories, and personal narratives. When the bar was moved from across the street, many of the men from town helped move the large pieces of the back bar. On occasion a patron will stop in and begin telling personal narratives of how he was one of those volunteers. Bill and the mover will sit and brag about how they moved the back bar on a Sunday and, with all the help of movers, plumbers, and electricians, "Never missed a day of business."

J. Marie's Wood-Fired Kitchen and Drinks serves pizzas, salmon burgers, spinach dip, and ham and cheese sandwiches, all made in their wood-fired oven. Other foods include vegetarian lasagna, steak and potatoes, chicken alfredo, burgers, and salads. The drink menu includes handcrafted cocktails, local craft beers, and an extensive world-class wine selection.

PLAY

Neil Armstrong Air and Space Museum is dedicated to Bellevue's own hero, Neil Armstrong, who was the first man to walk on the moon. An interactive museum exhibit here includes the Gemini VIII spacecraft, Armstrong's Gemini and Apollo spacesuits, an Apollo 11 moon rock, and even the plane that Armstrong learned to fly when he was fifteen.

1937 mural

Fort Amanda Memorial Park is the site of Fort Amanda, built in 1812 as a base of supplies for General William Henry Harrison as he and his men fought the British for control of the Northwest Territories. Seventy-five soldiers, their names no longer recorded, rest on the banks of the Auglaize River, under markers reading "Unknown Soldier." A 1915 monument marks the site of several firsts here—the first shipyard, post office, national cemetery, and religious meetinghouse. There are trails going through the woods, over bridges spanning ravines, and along the river.

Definitely a one-of-a-kind attraction, the one-acre Temple of Tolerance is a plea for peace and a destination showcasing what can be done with a lot of imagination. A terraced rock garden and maze with art installations, garden art, and such unique objects as the door to the jail cell that once held two of members of John Dillinger's gang, and an eight-foot-high plastic tube containing 71,388 bullet casings representing every member of the military from Ohio killed in a war. Jim Bowsher created the Temple of Tolerance over more than a quarter century, adding to his creation constantly. It's free and open to the public daily.

NOTABLE

Head civil chief of the Shawnee Indians, Black Hoof, also known as Catecahassa, was described as a statesman as well as a fierce warrior who fought in the Battle of Fallen Timbers and attended the signing of the Greenville Treaty in 1795.

49

Waterville

A large outcropping of natural limestone known as Roche de Boeuf (French for Buffalo Rock or Rock of Beef) on the east bank of the Maumee River had long been the gathering place for council meetings among Native Americans. But the lives of the Indians who lived in villages throughout the region ultimately changed, and not for the better, when General "Mad" Anthony Wayne and his troops arrived on the Maumee's west bank and built Fort Deposit, the starting point for the Battle of Fallen Timbers. But for Wayne, winning the battle was just the start. For three days after, his men destroyed Native American communities and cornfields up and down the river until the signing of a treaty that paved the way for the western expansion of settlers on lands that once belonged to the Native Americans.

In 1795, the year the treaty was signed, Isaac Richardson opened a tavern, always a money maker back in that era. Thirty-three years later, John Pray built the Columbian House, a two-story building that functioned as a tavern, trading post, and inn and then later became a stop on the stagecoach line.

The Miami and Erie Canal opened in 1843, and at its peak eight years later, four hundred boats traveled along at least a part of the canal. For Waterville, that meant prosperity, the establishment of the Pekin Mill in 1846, and the coming of hotels, diners, and stores to accommodate passengers on the uncomfortable canal boats. Interestingly, when winter came and the canal froze over, it was used for ice-skating, and according

Columbian House

to the Waterville Historic Society, it wasn't unusual for some to skate to Grand Rapids and back, a distance of about ten miles one way, in an evening. That must have made for a long, cold evening when you consider that today's Olympic speed skater, using the finest most technologically advanced blades, can go about thirty-one miles per hour or so. In 1848, the first all-iron ice-skating blade was invented, but we're not sure when that made its way to Waterville. Ice skates weren't the boot-like contraptions we wear now; instead, the blades were attached to a wood platform and held in place on a boot or shoe with straps.

EAT

Dale's Diner, a popular eatery with another location in nearby Maumee, offers a great selection of handhelds, specials, beverage options, salads, and wings. The restaurant itself has been in business for almost nine decades.

For seafood, check out such menu offerings as Buffalo shrimp, crab cakes, crawfish bites, lake perch, and lobster macaroni and cheese at Chowders 'N Moor.

Waffle or sugar cones? Sundaes or banana boats? Turtle topping? Flavors like peanut butter, chocolate peanut butter, or blue raspberry are just some of the choices at Sweet Retreat. Sandwiches, hot dogs, tacos, and pretzels are also on the menu.

PLAY

The Roche de Boeuf Festival held in downtown Waterville in September is an annual celebration that includes a parade focused on local history, food vendors, crafts, and the Rue des Artistes where over thirty local artists sell such wares as mosaic glasswork, beaded serving utensils, leaf castings, photographs, metalwork, jewelry, paintings, drawings, and more.

Though it's an uncommon name today, the Side Cut Metropark was once just that, a side cut extension for the Miami and Erie Canal, connecting its main line to Maumee—a water version of an off-ramp on today's interstate. Three canal locks remain from those days, and kayakers can easily access the canal and river from the park. Side Cut is also home to the largest spring run of walleye on the Great Lakes when they swim upriver to spawn. For those who don't fish or kayak, the park has picnic tables, a playground, great views of the water, and wildlife feeding stations with indoor viewing areas.

It's a somewhat steep climb following the 1.6-mile Wabash Cannonball Trail Connector to Fallen Timbers Monument, one that passes through copses of buckeyes, that iconic Ohio tree. But the view from fifty feet above the Maumee River makes it worth the trip. A National Historic Landmark, the nine-acre Fallen Timbers Monument honors both the early American troops and the Native Americans who originally lived here. A ten-foot bronze statue of General Wayne is mounted on a fifteen-foot-high granite pedestal, and on either side is an early pioneer. Two stones nearby list the number of casualties on both sides.

SHOP

Garden Smiles by Carruth Studios is a gift shop and gallery as well as the only place carrying the entire collection of George Carruth's quirky and extremely original sculptures, more than 250 in all. Beyond that, Garden Smiles is the place to discover his new creations.

We dare you—no, make that a double dare—to find another shop specializing in colonial and War of 1812 clothing, patterns, books, music, movies, camping gear, sewing supplies, and such necessary accessories for the colonial gentleman and gentlewoman as a complete fire-starting kit, sixteenth-century German or French playing cards, rifle flints, and those small grease-burning lamps called Betty lamps. That's just the beginning of a long list of items at Smoke and Fire Company. Want to cook like it's 1812 all over again? There's a selection of cones of sugar and bricks of tea. And for those looking for tomahawks, your search is over. Smoke and Fire Company sells a versatile forged throwing tomahawk that can also be used for camp work.

50

Whitehouse

Once a railroad town, the village of Whitehouse, tucked away in the northwest corner of the state, is just fifteen minutes from Toledo, but life here is at a much gentler pace. So take the slow lane and enjoy its small-town charm.

EAT

In business for over a quarter of a century, the Whitehouse Inn in the downtown is charming inside and out. Outside there are gardens and window boxes overflowing with colorful blooms, as well as a pretty patio. Inside, the walls are lined with presidential photos and all sorts of historical artifacts. Known for their prime rib and some of the best margaritas around, they have a full bar and popular menu options such as steaks, seafood, burgers, and flatbreads.

Planting a vineyard behind an old barn more than a century old, Wheeler Farms now makes their own wine, served in their Wine Room, which is also the setting for their farm-to-table dinners featuring produce from local farms.

Local Thyme Restaurant and Bar, open for brunch, lunch, and dinner, takes the concept of bar food up several levels with house-smoked chicken, ten or so burger varieties, and flatbreads.

Specializing in more than forty types of sundaes, hard-serve and soft-serve ice cream, Dole whip, soft-serve yogurt, and lactose-free soft-serve

Whitehouse Inn

Wabash caboose

ice cream, Generals Ice Cream also offers shakes, floats, and slushes as well as pulled pork sandwiches.

PLAY

For over twenty years, Wheeler Farms has turned rural into entertainment with pumpkin patches, buggy rides, and an intensely detailed corn maze that changes its form every year. Stroll into the Wheeler's Butterfly House, the only one in the area, and immediately floating butterflies flitter by. They come in all colors, sizes, and patterns—pink with black and pale green with red spots. There's an identification chart nearby to try to match them all. But there's also a bench near the masses of colorful blooms, and instead you can just relax and be immersed in the whole experience. Wine Room, stables, and interaction with friendly animals are what Wheeler Farms are all about. Take a tour at the farm, where the owners originally planted a small vineyard behind the century-old barn and made their own blends. They also planted a one-acre organic vegetable garden and raise cows with care and dignity and dispatch them in the same way. Come back in the winter and enjoy their Christmas tree farm.

Celebrate the bounty at Whitehouse's annual Cherry Fest each May.

If you're in town on Saturdays in May, stop by the Flower Market. The Whitehall Farmers' Market is also on Saturdays from mid-July through September.

Jump on the Wabash Cannonball Trail, which spans sixty-three miles and traverses four Northwest Ohio counties: Fulton, Henry, Lucas, and Williams. Designed for nonmotorized access for hikers, bikers, equestrians, and cross-country skiers, the trail follows the old tracks (dating back to 1855) of the Wabash Railroad Line.

Take the Tree Tour by first logging on to the village's website (https:// whitehouseoh.gov/having-fun/tree-tour/), which provides photos and identifying characteristics of local trees tucked along the streets and in parks, and then start walking and see how many you can locate. There's a lovely variety of tulip trees, Crimson King Norway maples, and seven-son flowers.

Take a stroll through the downtown, stopping at the 1910 historic depot and the 1927 red Wabash Cannonball Railroad Caboose to take photos before heading across the street for coffee and pastries at Share Our Grounds, a 501(c)(3) training and education center for adults with developmental disabilities to help them learn the work and life skills necessary to run every aspect of the café.

Once the Nona France Stone Quarry, the eighty-plus-acre Blue Creek Recreation Area/Nona France Park now features a 20,873-square-foot barn with a gambrel roof and plank frame dating back to the late 1920s. With walking paths, a small quarry for fishing and nonmotorized boating, and abundant flora and fauna and places to picnic, this is a beautiful spot to spend time.

CENTRAL
OHIO

Alexandria Museum

51

Alexandria

Sometimes the tiniest hamlets, the type you could drive through in a minute or less, instead hold surprises making it imperative to stop. And so it is with Alexandria in Licking County. It's just a few streets but already has the inviting look of a place that's going to happen.

The village, population around six hundred but growing (there are now at least one hundred more citizens than during the Civil War), was platted in 1830 by Alexander DeVilbis, who moved there with his family in 1815 and built a mill two years later. He must have decided that DeVilbistown or whatever was too much of a mouthful and so settled on Alexandria.

There's a lot of history in the village and township, including Indian mounds; the Buffalo Trail, once a roadway for American Indians; and historic buildings.

STAY

The Tudor-style WillowBrooke Bed 'n Breakfast was featured on the cover of the twenty-first edition of *Bed & Breakfasts and Country Inns*. Overnight guests can choose from the two-bedroom cottage or luxury rooms. A full breakfast is included.

EAT

Judging by the number of cars in front of Ragamuffins Coffee Shop on weekday mornings, this is the place to be for baked goods such as bagels, scones, croissants, and muffins, as well as breakfast and lunch sandwiches and handcrafted coffee drinks. There's a cozy fireplace with comfy chairs and, for warm weather, a deck out back overlooking a copse.

PLAY

Located in a pre-1860s home in the heart of the village, the Alexandria Museum preserves and displays the history of Alexandria and the surrounding region. Exhibits include a large clock collection from Dr. Fred Nichols, wood carvings and cameras, items belonging to Willoughby Dayton Miller (more about him below), vintage clothing, and more.

Two hundred ten acres of woods, meadows, cliffs with panoramic views, and a stream corridor make Lobdell Reserve a great place to explore on foot, mountain bike, or even horseback. There are eight trails for every level of ability and a championship-caliber disc golfing course.

SHOP

Owned by award-winning artist Meredith Martin, who studied pre-Columbian art in Mexico and New Mexico, Sunbear Studios and Gallery displays her works as well as those of other artists who create in a variety of mediums—painting, jewelry making, woodworking, and stained glass, among others.

NOTABLE

Check out the Ohio Historic Marker paying homage to the wonderfully named Willoughby Dayton Miller, who, born in Alexandria, is considered the father of modern dentistry. Educated in a one-room schoolhouse near the village, in 1890 Miller published the rather dry-sounding tome *The Micro-organisms of the Human Mouth*. Hypothesizing that cavities were the result of bacterial activity, he caused an immense increase in the interest of oral hygiene.

52

Bellefontaine

French for beautiful spring, the name refers not to the season but to the springs found in the area. Known also as Blue Jacket's Town after the Shawnee war chief Blue Jacket (whose Shawnee name was Weyapiersenwah) built a settlement here in 1777. Nine years later, Blue Jacket's Town was decimated by the Kentucky militia during Logan's Raid in the Northwest Indian War.

With the building of tracks for the wonderfully named Mad River and Lake Erie Railroad, Bellefontaine became a railroad town, and in the 1890s, the Big Four Railroad built a main terminal here with the largest roundhouse between New York and St. Louis.

EAT

Get your morning blast at Sweet Aromas, which serves gourmet coffee, fresh fruit smoothies, teas, and other hot and cold beverages, as well as a wide variety of fresh-baked pastries.

The Food Network and *Guy's Grocery Games* have been to town to order pies at Six Hundred Downtown. Set in the city's historic district, the pizzeria has won a myriad of awards for its creative pizzas, including the Montana, topped with locally made kettle-cooked potato chips as well as buttermilk ranch, mozzarella, extra cheese, black pepper, potatoes, grilled chicken, and bacon. There are also sandwiches, salads, and appetizers plus local beers and wines.

Bellefontaine Courthouse

Hope you brought along a cooler so you can stock up on scratch-made doughnuts, confections, cupcakes, and other yummies at City Sweets and Creamery. If not, you'll just have to eat as much as you can here, but be sure to save room for their hand-dipped ice cream.

Fresh eggs from Sugar Creek Farms in Buckland, Ohio, sure go a long way to explain the deliciousness of the pies, waffles, and other dishes at the Homecoming Family Restaurant.

Featuring a variety of roasts and beans depending on the season and availability, Native Coffee Co. has your favorite caffeine fixes plus tea, frozen drinks, and smoothies.

Once home to the 1950s Johnson's Restaurant, Brewfontaine has frequently been voted the number one beer joint in Ohio. They're also known for foods such as their mustache-shaped hand-rolled pretzels made in partnership with Rise Bakehouse, served with Saucy Sows sweet pepper mustard locally made in Jackson Center, Ohio (you can also order beer cheese to go with them), and their fried bologna sandwiches, a half pound of their pork and beef blend of bologna pan-fried in garlic butter and topped with lettuce, tomato, onion, a choice of sauce, and a slice of cheese.

PLAY

Learn more about Bellefontaine and the surrounding region at the Logan County History Center, including their Transportation Museum—besides railroads, the area is also home to Honda Motorcycles. Also not to be missed is the 1906–1908 William Orr Residence, part of the center's complex. Built at a time when the average earnings were $2 a day, the

Holland Theatre

stately home with its columns, peaks, gables, and unique double rounded porches cost $40,000.

If you need an excuse to quaff an artisan brew or ale, then explain that the Roundhouse Brewery, the first in Bellefontaine, is also a paean to the city's rich railroad past. So there, enjoy your drink and soak up some history.

Street fame is rampant in Bellefontaine. The twenty-foot McKinley Street is said to be the shortest in the US, and the city is also known for Court Street next to the Logan County Courthouse, the first paved with concrete in the country. It was 1891 when George Bartholomew, founder of the Buckeye Portland Cement Company in Bellefontaine, convinced the city council to let him pave a street using his newly developed cement. It worked, as we all know, and the rest is history.

The Bellefontaine Courthouse in Bellefontaine, built in 1931, with its Flemish-style gable and rose-colored brick, is the only Dutch-style atmospheric theater in the United States and most likely the only one still in existence in the world. Open for events, it's definitely a trip back in time to when theaters were more than just cineplexes—they were works of architectural delight.

Work off the ice cream, beer, and goodies at the twenty-nine-acre Fred Carter Park. A wilderness area great for hiking, birding, and wildflowers, it also has a three-acre lake for swimming.

The Logan County Fair is held each July on the Logan County Fairgrounds in Bellefontaine.

SHOP

Nest 1896 gets its name from its location in the downtown, a beautifully restored building dating back well over a century to, you guessed it, 1896. Nest also comes from the great vintage finds filling three stories, including home decor, boutique clothing, jewelry, upscale crafts, creative artisan works, and just about everything you can image in this well-curated seventy-five-hundred-square-foot space.

If you're looking for a place to shout your Ohio pride as well as locally made items, check out Four Acre Clothing Co.

You're sure to find something you love at Olde Mint Antiques, with three floors of vintage treasures.

We love the name Just U'NeeQ as well as their treasure trove of handmade finds, farmhouse decor, furniture, and the latest in home trends.

PeachTree has a fantastic selection of apparel for women and children, as well as jewelry, handbags and other accessories, kids' activities, and gifts for men. Look for their Yellow Brick Road in the kids' boutique area.

NOTABLE

Norman Vincent Peale, a minister and the author of books about the benefits of positive thinking, graduated from Bellefontaine High School.

53

Canal Fulton

A vital stop on Tuscarawas River and the Ohio and Erie Canal, the village of Canal Fulton still retains its historic charm.

The canals and waterways opened up the ability to transport goods and people to the villages, towns, and cities along its way. In Stark County, the Tuscarawas River begins in its northern section and then meanders—as rivers do—southwest to join the Muskingum River. That in turn flows into the Ohio and then into the Mississippi, meaning the reach is wide, as that river spills into the Gulf of Mexico at the port of New Orleans. Thus the canal connected ports like Canal Fulton, just a small rural area, to the world. The boom days for many canals ran from 1827 to 1850, ending because of the arrival of the railroad. And so it was with Canal Fulton. But at its height, some three hundred boats passed through the village each month.

Downtown Canal Fulton, with more than ninety buildings, is listed on the National Register of Historic Places.

EAT

Quiche, soups, salads, panini, and decadent desserts are part of the high tea options at the Dragonfly Tea Room. Also on site is the Dragonfly Winery, serving a full menu and offering tastings either inside or out on the patio overlooking the scenic Tuscarawas River. Above the English-inspired tearoom is a bed and breakfast.

St. Helena Heritage Park–Canal

Sisters Century House Restaurant, located in the downtown historic district, is right on the canal. Enjoy breakfast and lunch while watching the *St. Helena III*, a replica of a real canal boat.

For ice cream, shakes, house-made drumsticks, burgers and other sandwiches, and fries, visit Cherry Street Creamery. Or choose from over seventy-five flavors at Oser's.

We think the name Peace, Love and Little Donuts of Canal Fulton says it all.

Enjoy drinks and food at the Canal Boat Lounge, situated on the water.

PLAY

For outdoor laser tag, F-22 Raptor go-karts, miniature golf, teacups, bumper boats, Professor Marvel's Ferris Wheel, and other family fun for all ages, plan on stopping at Sluggers and Putters Amusement Park. If you're hungry, then take a break and visit Auntie Em's Food Court and Ice Cream.

At St. Helena Heritage Park–Canal, purchase tickets for a ride aboard the *St. Helena III*, a reproduction of a freighter that traveled along the Ohio and Erie Canal more than one hundred years ago. The boat ride, pulled by two huge Percherons, lasts for about an hour. There's also a video about the canal's history. Other places to visit in the park include the Heritage House, Towpath Trail, and Olde Canal Days Museum.

Lock 4

Pack a picnic basket and head to Lock 4, among the best examples of a lift lock on the Ohio and Erie Canal.

Follow the Ohio and Erie Canalway Hike/Bike Path.

The Canal Fulton Canoe Livery, located on the banks of the Tuscarawas River, rents boats and bikes and offers different excursions, such as the paddle and pedal, a six-mile river trip and a return by bike on the towpath.

A popular fest for almost a half century, the Peddler's Festival is time travel back to the years between 1776 and 1825. Enjoy dining on food cooked over an open fire, learn to make colonial crafts, meet vendors dressed in period garb, and get lost in that post–Revolutionary War feel. The fest is held three weekends in September.

A traditional colonial saltbox-style house built in 1847 and furnished in nineteenth-century antiques, the Oberlin House Museum showcases the life of a family during the town's canal days. A costumed interpreter tells the story of the home and the families that lived there.

SHOP

Like fudge? Then check out the multitude of flavors—peanut butter overload, cherry cordial, German chocolate cake, and orange dream, among many others—at Deliciously Different Candies.

Looking for the toys of your childhood? Toys That Time Forgot, specializing in vintage toys, is the place for you.

Keillor's Teddy Bear Shoppe sells, well, you guessed it, the fuzzy, furry bears we all love. Brands include upscale bear makers like Charlie Bears, Gund, Clemens (a German bear brand), and Chantilly Lane, maker of musical bears.

A hot blown-glass studio and a mixed-media art gallery exhibiting original works by some fifty Ohio artists, the Canal Fulton Glassworks is housed in the oldest building in town, built in 1814 and located on the Tuscarawas River. On display are more than twenty-five hundred individual handmade works of art.

54

Canal Winchester

When construction of the Ohio and Erie Canal was slated to cut through Reuben Dove's wheat field in the 1820s, he wanted to sue. Instead, canal workers convinced him to plat the town, as it was equidistant between Columbus and Lancaster. Dove listened, and in 1828, Canal Winchester was founded.

Three years later, the first canal barge passed by, and Canal Winchester was on the road—or should we say water—to prosperity. Stagecoaches also brought travelers to town, as did the railroad.

An intriguing tale (which we're choosing to believe) recounts how two mischievous local boys decided to pull a Halloween prank in 1841 and attached two horses to the Waterloo post office and hauled it across the street to Winchester. That was it for Waterloo, which now had no post office, and good news for Canal Winchester, which suddenly did have one.

EAT

The restored Shade on the Canal, formerly the Shade, a longtime community favorite, once again is open, serving such appetizers as Buffalo shrimp, wild fries (fries, boneless wings, spicy cheese, bacon, cheddar, tomato, and green onion drizzled with a choice of Shade wing sauce), salads, soups, and globally inspired sandwiches like German fried bologna, parmesan chicken sandwich and Jamaican jerk chicken sliders.

A neighborhood spot open for breakfast, lunch, and dinner, the Harvest Moon Craft Kitchen runs a scratch kitchen where the majority

O. P. Chaney Elevator and Caboose, Historical Society Complex

of the food is made in-house or locally sourced from region food producers.

There are lots of options for those who love their meat slow smoked until it's falling off the bone at Barrel and Boar BBQ Gastropub.

We know you didn't ask for it, but we think you'll love it once you get past the idea that your brew is orange and white. That's Dreamsicle Searchlight Shandy, one of the many creative artisan offerings at Loose Rail Brewing. Try a few, listen to music, and enjoy the outdoor patio if the weather is right.

Live acoustic music and special food nights (Monday's burgers are half price and Wednesday's pizzas are the same) are on offer at the Ugly Mug Bar and Grill.

Stop by for comfort food at the Old Town Tavern.

PLAY

Displaying a number of military exhibits, Motts Military Museum showcases military memorabilia from America's wars, including the Revolutionary War, Civil War, World Wars I and II, Korean War, Vietnam War, and Desert Storm. There are also exhibitions dedicated to NASA and prisoners of war. Tours are available. You can buy patriotic items and military books in the museum's gift store.

Canal Winchester Area Historical Society's main complex consists of the one-room Prentiss School, two cabooses, a monument honoring Civil War private Alfred Cannon, the Hocking Valley "Queen of the Line" railroad depot, and the O. P. Chaney grain elevator, the latter two individually listed on the National Register of Historic Places.

You don't often come across a museum devoted to all things relating to barbering from the 1700s to the present. Indeed, we can't think of any

Fall Festival

other than National Barber Museum, and since they claim to be the only one, we believe them. So go ahead and enjoy the unique collection of barber poles, chairs, signs, razors, mugs, and tools. But there's more. Since barbers often substituted for surgeons, there's bloodletting equipment as well. Call for a tour.

Take a walk across the last remaining covered bridge in Franklin County. Built in 1874, the 134-foot Bergstresser/Dietz Bridge spans Little Walnut Creek, a tributary of the Scioto River, and is located in Kelley Preserve, one of Canal Winchester's Metroparks. The preserve, with forty-five acres of hiking trails, is one of the largest in the city, as is the trail. The vast seventeen-hundred-acre Slate Run Metropark is five miles from downtown and has trails, picnic areas, and woodlands.

Recreating life on an Ohio farm in the 1880s, the Slate Run Living Historical Farm, situated inside Slate Run Metropark, is centered on a Gothic Revival farmhouse. Here, both staff and volunteers wear period clothing as they go about the daily chores using tools, farm machinery, and household goods typical of that time period. And yes, if you want to pick up a hoe or help out in other ways, you certainly can. The live animals, including pigs, merino sheep, and Percheron draft horses, represent the same type of livestock common back then.

Within the 1,705-acre park's confines, sandhill cranes have found a nesting spot in the 156-acre wetlands. The 1.5-mile Bobolink Trail, labeled as easy and ADA accessible, leads to a viewing area overlooking the wetlands—a great place to look for birds and other animals.

Sample the more than seventeen proprietary wines at the family-owned Slate Run Vineyard.

They like to party in Canal Winchester, so check out the many festivals and events throughout the year, such as the three-day Labor Day Festival, the two-day Canal Winchester Blues and Ribfest, the Taste of Canal Winchester in June, and Art in the Park, a summer-long series of free concerts with a roaming clown and refreshment stands. Christmas in the Village is a magical transformation where the historic downtown becomes a winter wonderland with a tree-lighting ceremony, a parade, carriage rides, and, of course, Santa Claus.

SHOP

Sticks and Stones Studio sells gifts, home decor and furnishings, jewelry, and artworks, many made by local craftspeople and artisans. They also carry Annie Sloan chalk paint and offer painting classes teaching how to make one-of-a-kind items that are uniquely your own.

Georgie Emerson Vintage sells made, worn, handcrafted, and gathered items created by local and regional artists such as April Smith, who repurposes old windows and frames into quotable works of art, and Linda and Larry Chapman, who recreate old jewelry, silverware, and wood into art. They own One 4 You Originals in nearby Lancaster, Ohio.

It's old, new, or a little of both at CornerSmiths, a store filled with a variety of fun items including furniture, jewelry, scarves, lavender items, forgotten household items, scented lotions, candles, unique microfiber cloths (yes, I know, but they're really sweet), intriguing household cleaning items, and so much more.

Had to leave Fido at home? Make up with natural dog treats from Nom Nom Nom.

55

Circleville

As European settlers pushed the Delaware Indians, also known as Lenape, farther west, the Wyandot Nation gave them permission to settle in Ohio. One such settlement was called Maguck, a village on the Scioto River consisting of about ten families. In January 1751, they were visited by Christopher Gist, the first known European explorer to arrive in the area, who stayed with them for four days. In an intriguing aside, Gist was a British surveyor and frontiersman who accompanied a young colonel by the name of George Washington on wilderness missions. In 1854 at the start of the French and Indian War, he twice saved the future first president: once when he prevented an assault on Washington by a Native American and the second time when he pulled Washington out of the glacial waters of the Allegheny after he fell off a makeshift raft. I think we're all in agreement that we owe Gist a big thank-you.

There would be more Europeans coming, of course, and they wouldn't stay for just four days. After the Revolutionary War, the US government, short on money but with a lot of land, started handing out acreage, and in 1810 the town of Circleville was established. They chose the name Circleville after the ancient circular earthworks built by the Adena culture more than two thousand years ago.

STAY

Intriguingly, the fantastic Castle Inn Bed and Breakfast is on Court Street—I mean, what could be a better street name for this 1895 house that, with its crenulated turrets, gables, and porticos, indeed looks like a castle. In keeping with staying in a castle—OK, we mean a house—the owners host weekend murder mysteries, where guests dress in character and try to figure out the whodunit.

A cozy getaway, the Winery Romantic Cabin, tucked away in the extensive vineyards at the Manchester Hill Winery, also comes with a wine tasting for two.

A. W. Marion State Park has sixty tent and trailer camping spots open year-round with latrines and drinking water available.

EAT

They're famous for their pumpkin doughnuts, but don't stop at those. Instead keep on ordering from the wide selection of scratch baked goods at Lindsey's Bakery, family owned for more than fifty years. And yes, it's still home to the world's largest pumpkin pie.

Want to watch a game and still get great food? Unlike a lot of restaurants with multiple TVs turned to sporting events, the chef (not cook) at Watt St. Tavern prepares a curated menu designed to satisfy everyone's taste buds. Order one of their craft brews on draft and some food off the menu or one of the daily specials and enjoy local entertainment in the backroom and patio area.

Calling themselves the "Home of the Bourbon Chicken," the Thirsty Parrot Bar and Grill is also the place to grab a burger (either beef or turkey), wings, fresh-cut fries, a taco salad, and cheese curds.

Q Mixers and Boar's Head are some of the items featured at Richie's New York Corner Deli.

It's delicious and hearty cooking—think country-fried steak with mashed potatoes and gravy, broasted chicken, or a buffet and salad bar—at Goodwin's Family Restaurant, in business for over forty years and open for breakfast, lunch, and dinner. Don't forget dessert—homemade pies and gigantic cream puffs.

PLAY

October is the time for the popular Circleville Pumpkin Show; now heading to its 115th year, it's a three-day extravaganza of all things orange and round.

When Ted Lewis, whose trademark was a battered top hat and clarinet, died, the Smithsonian as well as Harvard and Yale Universities wanted his archives, music, and memorabilia. But his widow, Ada Becker Lewis, donated it to his hometown, a place Lewis thought of as "the Capital of the World." Over his long sixty-five-year career, millions of fans bought Lewis's records, including his signature song, "Me and My Shadow." He spanned entertainment mediums from vaudeville to television. Admission to the museum is free.

Explore Hargus Lake in A. W. Marion State Park. Take the 3.9-mile intermediate-level trail circling the lake, where you can fish and canoe.

SHOP

Open for over 180 years, Wittich's Candy Shop is the nation's oldest family-owned and family-operated candy shop. Stock up on old-fashioned candies, buckeyes, hand-dipped chocolates, and candy-making supplies and then take a break at the old-fashioned soda fountain and order a sundae, soda, or shake.

We're taking it you don't need a prom dress, but you can still stop at Maggie and Me's for casual clothing perfect for vacationers to restock their wardrobe with.

Looking for a favorite comic book from your past, or are you a collector willing to scoop up a copy of *Iron Man* #55 CGC 7.5 for $800 minus 10 percent? Stop by Journey into Comics and take a look.

With an amazing number of craft and hobby supplies, Creative Chaos also offers classes and runs retreats for crafters.

The family-owned, award-winning Manchester Hill Winery handcrafts wines and hard ciders, all made from locally sourced fruits that are fermented, created, bottled, corked, and labeled on-site along with some of their estate vineyard grapes.

NOTABLE

Storm chaser Tony Laubach, a meteorologist featured on the Discovery Channel, attended Circleville High School.

56

Granville

A New England village tucked away in the hills of eastern Central Ohio? That's what settlers from Granville, Massachusetts, and Granby, Connecticut, wanted when they set roots here in 1805. It's a dream that persisted, and even today Granville—population under six thousand but seemingly so much larger when Dennison University students are in attendance—is a lovely stretch of tree-lined streets and gracious nineteenth-century buildings filled with eclectic shops, galleries, restaurants, and boutiques.

STAY

In 1812, Orrin Granger, who hailed from the other Granville, opened an inn, which over time would also serve as a stagecoach stop on the line connecting Columbus and Newark. Besides rooms for guests to stay, there was a dining room, ballroom, and stagecoach court, and the village's post office was also located there. The inn's attractive salmon color accented by white exterior staircases, railings, and columns served a purpose. For travelers who couldn't read, the color served as signage telling them they'd arrived at the right place.

Three presidents are among the famous guests who stayed here, including William Henry Harrison, who overimbibed one night and rode his horse up the stairs of the stagecoach court. Harrison fell asleep in his room, and the horse was led downstairs and into the stables.

The food is exquisite, the rooms luxurious, and the basement where coach drivers once slept on straw and made their meals over the large

Buxton Inn

open-hearth fireplace, which remains, is now a cozy bar with thick stone walls and wood beams seemingly little changed since then—except, that is, there are no straw beds on the floor for taking naps.

Guests at the inn can also choose to stay next door at Founders Hall. Built in 1840, it was originally a boardinghouse for those attending Granville Female College. Balconies at the back of the hall overlook tiered gardens and a lovely fountain.

Just across the street from the Buxton Inn is the amazing Granville Inn, a grand Tudor surrounded by a large swath of emerald-green lawns, leafy green trees, and garden beds. Built in 1924, the inside of the inn is just as old English—a mélange of high-end antique furniture, Asian carpentry, sandstone fireplaces, and burnished wood glowing under numerous chandeliers. There's dining in the bar, in the grand dining room, and outside when weather permits.

EAT

Wake up with your favorite brew and pastry at River Road Coffeehouse.

Even a burger isn't just a burger at Snapshots Lounge, known for their New American cuisine. Instead, it can come with such toppings as blueberry preserves, caramelized onions, spinach, and whipped goat cheese, with a side of macaroni and cheese. Specials are indeed culinarian

Robbins Hunter Museum

specialties like the seared scallops with skillet corn, Old Bay and truffle aioli, or the filet with sautéed asparagus and roasted potatoes sauced with hollandaise.

Vietnamese-style street foods like banh mi sandwiches, pork dumplings, Japanese fried chicken, and tempura shrimp are what's sizzling at Mai Chau Kitchen. Quaff a few at the Three Tigers Brewing Company next door and order from the Mai Chau Kitchen's menu.

Get your cold sweet fix at Whit's Frozen Custard.

PLAY

With some eight hundred vines and ten varieties, Three Oaks Vineyard offers a lot of ways to enjoy their wines—in their pavilion, under the covered porch, on the outdoor patio, and inside. All of it's good, set on fifteen acres of hardwoods and meadows filled with wildflowers in season, it offers a meandering brook, a ravine and spring-fed pond, and an apple orchard.

The 16,500-acre Dawes Arboretum is a delightful patchwork of beautiful landscapes such as a Japanese garden, rolling meadows, thick woods, a small lake with an island, three ponds, a cypress swamp, over one hundred types of holly, indoor beehives, and the type of old-growth forests now mostly gone. In the spring, learn how to tap the arboretum's maple trees and make syrup.

The sixteen rooms of the American Greek Revival–style Avery-Downer House, built in 1842, are filled with the collections of Robbins Hunter Jr., who lived in the house from 1956 to 1979 and filled it with eighteenth- and nineteenth-century antiques and decorative arts for future generations to enjoy.

Pre-Columbian cultures left their mark on this region well before European settlers showed up. The Alligator Effigy Mound, listed on the National Register of Historic Places, was originally thought to have been built by the Hopewell people of 100 BCE to 500 CE, who also built the vast Newark Earthworks just a few miles away. Now the mound, which sits on a bluff overlooking the Raccoon Creek Valley, is believed to be somewhat newer, built by the Fort Ancient culture between 800 and 1200 CE. And no, despite its name, it's not an alligator but most likely an underwater panther, a supernatural creature believed by many Native Americans to live in lakes and rivers.

The Bryn Du Mansion is so beautifully restored, it's hard to image that it was built in 1865 and operated as a cattle ranch and sandstone quarry. Once called McCune's Villa, it is now owned by the Village of Granville and has a myriad of events—Sunday's Polo on the Green Lawn; the summertime Concerts on the Green; the Daffodil Show in mid-April; Taste of Granville, usually on the last Saturday in April; and the Rendville Art Show, featuring over two hundred pieces of original folk art and typically held the weekend before Thanksgiving.

In the village's downtown, there's the monthly Granville Art Walk, HotLicks Bluesfest, and Christmas Candlelight Walking Tour.

SHOP

For foodies in the downtown, stop by Wetzel's Candy Kitchen, Whit's Frozen Custard, and Granville Gourmet Whoopie Pies, where shoppers face hard choices among three sizes—mini, individual, and party pies—in a myriad of homemade flavors.

If you brought along a cooler, then you'll enjoy visiting Lynd Fruit Farm, one of the state's largest apple orchards, with over eighty thousand trees. You can pick your own, find your way through the corn maze, take a hayride pulled by classic antique John Deere tractors, and visit the show orchard to learn the history of apples. Also for sale are other fruits and vegetables, Christmas decorations, flowers, gifts, and Lynd Fruit Farm jarred goods, such as salsas, jams, and jellies, at their Market on Morse.

NOTABLE

Woody Hayes was a graduate of and football coach for Denison University before leaving to coach at Ohio State University. During his career, he compiled a career college football record of 238 wins, 72 losses, and 10 ties.

57

Heath

Take a guided tour of the Newark Earthworks, the world's largest set of geometric earthen enclosures in the world. It was inhabited by the Hopewell Indians until early into this millennium, and of the three segments that originally covered four miles, some were destroyed by the arrival in the nineteenth century of European settlers who used the land for farming. Luckily, the efforts of preservationists and historians saved much of the enclosures. Both a National Historic Landmark and Ohio's official prehistoric monument, the earthworks are also regarded by American Indians as a sacred site. In Heath, the Great Circle Earthworks segment was thought to have served as an immense ceremonial center and has eight-foot-high wall surrounding a five-foot-deep moat is nearly twelve hundred feet in diameter.

EAT

The Coffee Shack Coffee Roasters offers a seemingly limitless menu of coffee drinks made from fairly traded, organic green coffee beans roasted on-site, smoothies, specialty drinks, and food offerings like breakfast sandwiches and toasts (avocado, bacon, and egg; peanut butter and banana), sandwiches, and salads.

Shade on Thirtieth Street is a family-friendly sports bar with loads of comfort foods, such as chopped brisket sandwich and fries, wings, wraps, salads, and burgers, as well as a full bar and a happy hour.

Dizurts Custom Cakes and More specializes in custom cakes, doughnuts, cinnamon rolls, cupcakes, cake pops, and desserts.

PLAY

At the Great Circle Museum, visitors can learn more about the Hopewell culture and the earthworks by touring a one-thousand-square-foot exhibit showcasing Ohio's numerous ancient cultures and explaining the reason American Indians regarded the Newark Earthworks as sacred. There are also self-guided tours, an interactive video showing the site's significance, and another display with details of how the earthworks were designed to align with the rising and setting of the moon.

Sand Hollow Winery has a limited menu but lots of handcrafted, small-batch wines made using 100 percent Old World–style juices from Italy, Chile, and America. Blended to suit every taste, there are dry full-body reds, delicate whites, and sweet and fruit wines.

SHOP

When it comes to gifts, antiques, vintage, crafts, home decor, and whatever else, what can't you find at Finders Keepers Village, with its theme houses, storefronts, barns, back porches, and two hundred stores within a store? Probably not much.

58

Johnstown

A charming place with tree-lined streets, tubs of flowers, and a historic downtown, the first Euro-Americans to settle in Johnstown were George and Diadema Green, who arrived from Virginia in 1806. But in the race to build the first log cabin, they were beaten out by another pioneer, named George W. Evans. Think about that: of a handful of early settlers, two were named George. Johnstown remained a sleepy place until it became the agricultural hub for Liberty, Jersey, and Monroe Townships in the 1880s.

EAT

With an intriguing name and menu, Ghostwriter Public House partners with local purveyors such as Jeni's Splendid Ice Cream, Lucky Cat Bakery, Black Radish Creamery, and North Country Charcuterie to create such fascinating menu items (though note, in keeping with the season, items change) as tempura cheese curds, "Japanese Style" crispy fried chicken, and gnudi—ricotta dumplings with brown butter, red pesto, speck, and basil. For desserts, those old campfire favorites become a s'mores torte, Mom's recipe for banana bread has gone up more than a few notches with the addition of cocoa nibs and a side of Jeni's honey vanilla bean ice cream, salty caramel sauce, and brown butter powder.

Whit's Frozen Custard, once housed in a gas station back in the 1970s, now has locations in eight states and continues to grow. They offer vegan, no-sugar-added, and gluten-free versions besides regular and such specials as O'Henry (hot fudge, hot caramel, and Spanish peanuts) and

Buckeye Madness (Reese's cups, peanut butter, and chocolate), as well as cones, banana splits, shakes, malts, and the old-fashioned but always-delicious black cow.

Get your fired-meat fix at Route 62 Barbecue.

PLAY

Johnstown Town Hall and Opera House, dedicated in 1885 and on the National Register of Historic Places, is one of only five opera houses remaining in Ohio.

Autumn Rush Vineyard serves wines and hard cider made on-site and also has an eclectic menu of wine slushies and wine and cider cocktails. Family and pet friendly (though they encourage both dogs and kids to be well-behaved), it has a large lawn with picnic tables (you can also bring lawn chairs if you like) to enjoy libations. Meats and cheeses are served in the tasting room, and food trucks are scheduled regularly. Check the schedule, and if no food truck will be on-site, you can pack your own. Take a stroll through the vineyards and by the pond. The property is accessible.

SHOP

Timber Tunes Gifts and Antiques for Home and Garden features a variety of products, including wooden spoons, spatulas, rolling pins, bowls, cutting boards, and candlesticks all made on-site at the farm; ornaments; home decor; goods from Sugar Loaf Pottery in nearby Granville; works by local artists; cookies from Hometown Cakes and Cookies, a Johnstown bakery; and consignment items in the large barn out back.

Find vintage goods, furniture, home decor, gifts, unique finds, crafts, painted furniture, fabrics, books, and arts at Antiques on Main. Peruse antique furniture and home decor from local vendors at Heart of Home.

My Soaps sells handmade lotions, salves, and soaps like their peaches and cream, Himalayan salt soap bar, and patchouli. Malone's Shoppe 740 sells furniture and home decor, as well as vintage finds and lines like Martha's Bath and Body products.

59

Loudonville

A river definitely runs through Loudonville, first settled when Stephen Butler built a cabin in 1810 on the east bank of the Black Fork River. Part of Ohio's Amish region, Loudonville is named after James London Priest, another early settler who purchased one thousand acres and laid out the town in 1814. But it's the Mohican River, a designated State Scenic River, that defines the town, earning it the title of Canoe Capital of Ohio.

STAY

The amazing Landoll's Mohican Castle surely is one of America's most unique lodging and dining venues, just as they advertise. The castle sits high at twelve hundred feet on twenty acres of land. Gordon Ramsey stayed here while filming an episode of his *Hotel Hell* series, and the menu showcased then is served at their Copper Mug Bar and Grille.

On the National Register of Historic Places, the 1856 Blackfork Marken Inn Bed and Breakfast is a magnificent Victorian-era home in Loudonville's downtown, making it within walking distance of much the town has to offer.

Mohican State Park features 118 campsites with electric hookups; another 33 full-hookup sites with electric, sewer, and water; 35 nonelectric sites; and 12 walk-in tent sites. There are also camper cabins, a guest lodge, and two-bedroom cottages, several of which are pet friendly. Amenities include a swimming pool.

Located on the Mohican River, Wally World River Resort offers a wide range of amenities—access to the river for kayaking and tubing, themed activity weekends, miniature golf, a swimming pool, a dog park, beach volleyball, an arcade, a game room, and horseshoes. Accommodations at this family-oriented campground include RV and tent campsites and garden cottages.

EAT

Ugly Bunny Winery—gotta love the name and the wines ranging from sweet to dry and bourbon barrel–aged. There's live music; just bring your own food (they have their own vendors as well), order a glass or two, and enjoy.

Located on the Black Fork of the Mohican River, the River Room Lounge has good views and good grub—burgers, pizza, subs, and such appetizers as wings, sauerkraut balls, and jalapeño pretzels. Check out their specials on Facebook and their website (see "Destination Information"). Behind the falls is a cave, and at some point, over two hundred years ago, Johnny Appleseed carved his name and the date in the rock ledge. Those have been worn away with time, but we're sure there's still an apple tree or two around.

PLAY

The Loudonville Canoe Livery, the oldest canoe-leasing business in the state to remain in the same location, offers a selection of canoes, kayaks, and tubes. Day trips range from forty-five minutes to six hours, and you can also take a lazy river overnight trip with primitive camping, a forty-mile two-day trip, or a sixty-mile three-day trip.

Pack a picnic, take a walk, explore a historic village, and enjoy an immersion into early Ohio pioneer history at Wolf Creek Mill Museum and Historic Park. In 1998 while they were camping, Mike Smith and his family discovered the abandoned mill dating back to 1831 and painstakingly restored it. Adding to its history, Smith now has on the premises an 1880 sawmill and seven other historic log cabins that were donated and moved on-site.

Once the hunting grounds as well as the site of villages belonging to the Delaware nation, the centerpiece of the eleven-hundred-acre Mohican State Park is the Clear Fork River Gorge. Thirteen miles of hiking trails follow or rise above the gorge, offering dramatic views of the stunning surroundings. Lyons Falls, located within the park, also follows the Mohican River, and it's spanned by the Mohican Covered Bridge.

Landoll's Mohican Castle

If you love local museums that retell an area's history through artifacts and displays, then the Cleo Redd Fisher Museum, open to visitors for free, is for you.

Cool down by wading and tubing or try fly-fishing on the Clear Fork River.

The stretch of the Mohican River running between Loudonville and Greer, near the Wally Road Scenic Byway, is considered Ohio's largest outdoor recreational complex. Here paddlers cross between Knox and Holmes County, and the wonders of several scenic routes—Gateway to Amish Country, Wally Road, and Amish Country Scenic Byways—are easily accessible.

Formerly the Loudon Opera House, built back in 1909 when many small towns had such places, the Ohio Theatre, on the National Register of Historic Places, hosts a variety of shows, movies, and performances and also offers classes.

SHOP

Beyond farmhouse decor, furniture, handmade soaps and lotions, jewelry, fabric, yarn, weaving items, and Scottish tartan wool blankets, the Alabaster Mouse also offers a unique assortment of pottery, garden art,

Landoll's Mohican Castle

and other classes and retreats, such as their Eco Printing and Shibori Dyeing Retreat and Rolling Waves Quilt Retreat.

Creative Outlet Indian Crafts and Jewelry, is the largest retailer of Native American goods in southern Central Ohio, with items like Minnetonka Moccasins, rocks and crystals, artwork, jewelry, dream catchers, and the like.

Blackfork Marken Inn Bed and Breakfast also has a gift shop, so even if you're not staying there, stop on by.

NOTABLE

Antarctic explorer Danny Foster was born in Loudonville, as was Robert Bacher, a nuclear physicist and one of the leaders of the Manhattan Project.

Born and raised in Loudonville, Charles Kettering developed the all-electric starting, ignition, and lighting system for automobiles (before that, you had to hand-crank car engines), founded what is now Delco, headed research at General Motors from 1920 to 1947, and holds 186 patents. But if his name is familiar, it's because using a large chunk of his fortune, he helped fund, along with Alfred Pritchard Sloan, the Sloan-Kettering Cancer Research Institute in New York in 1945.

In 1912, Hugo H. Young was operating a motorcycle sales business in Mansfield, Ohio, when he had an idea for a new type of motorcycle sidecar attached by a flexible connection allowing it to always follow the direction of the motorcycle, whether when rounding curves or going straight. Taking his idea, Young founded the Flxible Company in Loudonville. By 1919, Flxible was the world's largest exclusive manufacturer of motorcycle sidecars. The business grew, producing not only sidecars but also hearses and ambulances, as well as intercity and city-transit coaches such as a Studebaker twelve-passenger sedan.

60

Lucas

Founded in 1830, Lucas, a charming village, was once a stopping place for John Chapman, also known as Johnny Appleseed (1774–1845)—and yes, there was a Johnny Appleseed—who had several nurseries in the area. Appleseed not only spread apple seeds but also was a missionary for the Swedenborgian Church. The folkloric stories about his travels and lifestyle were passed down through the generations, and while some if not most may have changed somewhat over the last two centuries, what we know is this: The son of a minuteman during the Revolutionary War, Chapman constantly wandered. He was friends with Native Americans, often bringing them medicinal plants, and some in turn considered him touched by the Great Spirit.

"I have traveled more than 4,000 miles about this country, and I have never met with one single insolent Native American," he is quoted as saying. During the War of 1812, when he heard that the British were inciting an Indian attack, he ran thirty miles from Mansfield to Mount Vernon, Ohio, to warn the settlers living there.

STAY

There's primitive camping at Malabar Farm State Park, or you can stay at the park's Maple Syrup Cabin, a rustic place sleeping four with views of a small pond and a chance of spotting wildlife.

Set amid forty-six scenic acres and just a mile from Malabar Farm, AngelWoods Hideaway Bed and Breakfast has stabling for horses, an

in-ground pool, a lovely deck, and a large hot tub. They also have over-night and weekend packages for scrapbooking and crafting.

EAT

The French, European, and American food served at the Malabar Farm Restaurant just down the road from Malabar Farm is a whole lot more upscale than travelers probably ate starting in 1820, when David Schrack and his sons built this two-story red brick building that served as a stagecoach stop for the Marietta-Cleveland line. Back then, dinner was definitely seasonal, and free-run animals meant scrawny chickens and cows or game like raccoon (said to be one of Abraham Lincoln's favorites), goose, duck, and beaver, often cooked in the same large pot. That's a lot of history, which is evident in the ambience of this attractive building with a three-sided large deck, elegant interior, large windows, and white trim accenting brightly patterned old-fashioned wallpaper. The Schracks were attracted to the location because of the bubbling Niman Spring. When author Louis Bromfield, owner of Malabar Farm, bought the inn in the late 1930s, it needed lots of work. Once completed, it was good for extra guests, and the cool spring waters, which were filtered through sandstone troughs, kept the organic produce for sale at his roadside farm stand cool.

Malabar Farm State Park

Rainbow Gardens is the place for hot dogs, sloppy joes, burgers, subs, and sandwiches.

Wood-fired pizzas, pasta, sandwiches, and salads are on the menu at Open Door Café, open for breakfast, lunch, and dinner. It's also a great stop for coffee.

PLAY

The nine-hundred-acre Malabar State Farm, the country estate of Pulitzer Prize winner Louis Bromfield, was not only a working farm where he practiced sustainable farming and conversation but the hangout of Hollywood stars such as Dorothy Lamour, Errol Flynn, William Powell, Clark Gable, and Shirley Temple, and that golden couple Humphrey Bogart and Lauren Bacall were married here. Bromfield, who was not only a prolific novelist but also a screenwriter, was good friends with the Hollywood elite.

Once known as Poverty's Knob, Mt. Jeez is certainly rich when it comes to views. Rising 1,310 feet above sea level, it is one of the highest spots in the state and is worth the side trip for its panoramic scenes. From the top you can see Malabar Farm and, on a clear day, three counties.

Malabar, which means "beautiful valley" in a Native American dialect, is indeed lovely. Bromfield knew the area well, having graduated from

Mansfield High School and returning here after fleeing France with his family at the outbreak of World War II. It's furnished as it was when the Bromfields lived here, and there are both tours of the home and a tractor-drawn tour of the working farm with an Ohio State Park naturalist. There's also a Visitor's Education Center with exhibits and a gift shop and bookstore, as well as hiking and bridle trails, including the 0.83-mile moderately challenging Butternut Trail, which leads through a mature beech and maple forest to a small cave area.

When snows fall, get out the snow skis and shoes for both Pleasant Valley Bridle Trail at Malabar Farm and the Clear Fork Valley Scenic Trail.

Scenes from the 1993 movie *The Shawshank Redemption* were filmed at Malabar Farm as well as other places in the area. The Shawshank Trail Driving Tour includes a stop at Malabar Farm's Pugh Cabin, which is on the Doris Duke Woods Trail and was the opening setting in the movie.

Lucas is also a stop on the Johnny Appleseed Historic Byway, a thirty-mile route along State Routes 39 and 603 celebrating the life of John Chapman. The byway highlights some fifty sites and former locations, including Appleseed's land holdings, his apple nurseries, and Native American villages, as well as the site where the Delaware Indians stayed after being forced to leave Greentown.

When the sap flows, check out the events page of Malabar Farm and attend their Maple Syrup Festival.

61

Mount Vernon

Founded in 1805, Mount Vernon is named after George Washington's plantation. Known for having some of Ohio's most beautiful historic districts, Mount Vernon is the county seat of Knox County and is located in the rolling hills and valleys of Central Ohio. Mount Vernon is also home to Mount Vernon Nazarene University, a Christian liberal arts college. John Chapman, known throughout history as Johnny Appleseed, owned acreage in Mount Vernon, though he didn't record the deeds and thus lost it. But still, at his death, he was able to leave an estate to his sister consisting of twelve hundred acres of expensive nurseries

STAY

On the Square in historic downtown Mount Vernon is a luxe boutique bed and breakfast with a Victorian-era atmosphere and elegance but with twenty-first-century amenities such as complimentary high-speed Wi-Fi, a business center, and a fitness center.

No matter whether your stay is short or long, the Mount Vernon Inn has accommodations to suit your needs. Offering homes, suites, guest rooms, apartments, and corporate and extended stay, the inn also has a lovely perennial garden for enjoyment, a full-course breakfast, and a complimentary drink in the evening.

EAT

Settle in for a caffeine boost, boot up your computer, and check your emails at Happy Bean, a coffee shop.

Knox County Courthouse

The menu at the Half Baked Café is a delicious list of mini cream puffs with a large assortment of fillings—pomegranate, mango, cherry, and chocolate, just to name a few—cobblers, pies, cupcakes, and muffins.

At one time a small ice cream parlor and sweets shop opening in 1910, the Alcove has upped its game over the last century or so. Garnering numerous awards, its menu is an intriguing mix of classics—steaks, prime rib, lamb, and pork chops—and more esoteric offerings, such as stout mustard barbecue chicken, roasted cauliflower with romesco sauce, and baked cheese fondue.

Established in 1939, Mazza's is a classic upscale Italian restaurant with very reasonable prices. Menu items are based, in part, on family recipes brought over from Italy when they immigrated to America in the early part of the twentieth century.

PLAY

Learn about the downtown and its architecture, history, shops, and artisans and sample foods and libations by taking one of several tours offered by Walk Eat Mount Vernon, such as their Yesteryear Tour or Sensation Tour, or, for parties of ten or more, arrange a customized private tour.

Entering Harmony Salt Spa's Himalayan Salt Cave is like entering another world. Relax in one of the zero-gravity lounge chairs and let the enriched microclimate help you relax, heal, and regain your physical and emotional balance. Or you could opt for other healing therapies, including the far infrared sauna treatment, Swedish massages, and yoga classes.

Woodward Opera House

Stop by Y-Not Cycling and pedal through the downtown, Ariel-Foundation Park, or, if you're up for more of a challenge, the fourteen-mile Kokosing Gap Trail, a paved trail built on what were the tracks of the Pennsylvania Railroad line with endpoints in Mount Vernon and Danville, Ohio.

Even if you don't bike it, take a stroll through the 250-acre Ariel-Foundation Park, a stunning recreation of what was once a glassmaking factory. It's all a marvel of steel sculptures, lakes, observation tower, and walking trails. There's also a River of Glass—crushed glass and chunks of glass designed to look as if it's flowing down one of the park's hillsides in honor of those who worked at the former glassworks. Also, stop to admire the Tree of Life Labyrinth and architectural ruins as well as the museum before taking the connectors to the Kokosing Gap Trail and the Heart of Ohio Trail.

The wonderfully restored Woodward Opera House, the country's oldest authentic theater from the nineteenth century, once held minstrel and vaudeville show. Today entertainment remains key, with comedy and musical performers.

The Knox County Fair takes place the last week in July and has all the wonderful things we love about fairs, including rides, live entertainment, tractor pulls, games, animal exhibits, and, best of all as far as we're concerned, fair food. The premier event of the year in Downtown Mount Vernon is the Dan Emmett Music and Arts Festival. There's always something going on, including numerous stages with live acts, entertainment inside the Woodward Opera House, a kids' zone, and arts, crafts, and trade shows every day of the festival.

Take a stroll through this very pretty town with numerous historic districts, including the Downtown District, which surrounds the public square, and three residential districts all on the National Register of Historic Places. These are the East Gambier Street Historic District, the East High Street Historic District, and the North Main-North Gay Streets Historic District. Architectural styles represented in these districts include Victorian, colonial revival, art deco, Greek revival, federal, Queen Anne, and Richardsonian-Romanesque. The earliest building is from 1829.

Rent canoes or kayaks and paddle on the Kokosing River, the first designated water trail in the state of Ohio by the Ohio Department of Natural Resources.

SHOP

Butcher Family is a 133-acre farm producing high-quality maple syrup and making such products as maple creams, maple candies, maple syrups, and maple-flavored coffees. Check their website (www.butchermaple.com/) for dates of their tours during maple sugar time.

Paragraphs Bookstore is a place to enjoy perusing books, talking about books to fellow literary fans, and enjoying the conviviality of an independent bookstore.

The Makery on Main is the place for yarns, thread, needlework patterns and kits, classes, advice on your latest projects, and even a lounge.

NOTABLE

Daniel Decatur Emmett, who was born and died in Mount Vernon, was a comedian who performed in circuses, was inducted into the Songwriters Hall of Fame, and is credited with writing the song "Dixie."

Actor and comedian Paul Lynde was born in Mount Vernon in 1928 and played bass drum at Mount Vernon High School. He was a regular on *Hollywood Squares* and appeared frequently on the popular TV series *Bewitched*.

NFL player Robert Kelly was born in Mount Vernon in 1974.

62

Orrville

Settled in the early 1800s by pioneers of Irish, Pennsylvania Dutch, and German descent, Orrville got its first home 1828, built by the son of James Taggart Jr., who was awarded 160 acres for his service as a soldier during the Revolutionary War. That home at 421 E. Fike Street was a stop on the Underground Railroad. Still standing, it is a private residence. When word got around in 1851 that the Pittsburgh and Fort Wayne Railroad would be laying tracks through Orville, Judge Smith Orr persuaded the railroad to build a water tower on land in what would become incorporated as Orrville in 1862. That was a huge deal, as steam-engine-pulled trains needed to replenish their water supply every one hundred miles or so. After securing the deal, Orr and several prominent citizens sold forty-two lots for fifty dollars each to help develop the town.

STAY

The family-friendly Cobblestone Hotel and Suite is convenient to many of Orrville's attractions and offers such amenities as a pool and free Wi-Fi.

EAT

Check out the daily specials at Jerry's Café, open since 1979. The large menu means you'll definitely find something you like while watching sports on the ten big-screen TVs. And don't forget that Thursday evenings are Burger Night.

Grab breakfast or brunch at Mrs. J's.

Get caffeinated with fair-trade, micro-roasted, single-origin, and organic beans at Sure House Coffee Roasting Co.

Family owned since 1969, Dravenstott's Restaurant is a reasonably priced family restaurant that's open for breakfast, lunch, and dinner.

PLAY

J. M. Smucker Company Store is the big deal here. Whether you're a jam lover or not, this place is definitely for family fun and even for those traveling without kids. The company, headquartered in Orrville, has been in business for over 120 years. The store has an amazing display of products, row after row of gleaming jars containing ice cream toppings, syrups, fruit spreads, peanut butter, and items such as coffee, baking products, and pancake mix. Represented here are all the Smucker brands—and there a lot of them, including Smucker's, Jif, Café Bustelo, Adams, Meow Mix, and Natural Balance. Take a break from it all and enjoy burgers, salads, pizzas, and sandwiches, including a grilled peanut butter with the jam, jelly, or preserve of your choice. But be sure to save room for a treat from their ice cream bar.

A boardwalk runs through Johnson Woods State Nature Preserve, one of the largest and best old-growth forests in the state. Many trees—such as red and white oaks and hickory, some four hundred years old—reach forty to fifty feet before the first limbs appear. The preserve also teams with birds such as pileated woodpeckers, hooded warblers, ovenbirds, scarlet tanagers, and Acadian flycatchers.

In 1913, Jacob B. Stauffer, in memory of his late wife, Martha, donated the clock that is now on display in the Orrville City Hall. Now that the clock has been restored, its features include a computer control system and Westminster chime/strike as well as a carillon that plays a variety of songs.

Orrville Historical Museum owns and operates the house at 365 West Market Street, built in 1844 by Christian Horst.

SHOP

Journey in Time holds twenty-thousand-square-feet of primitives, antiques, farmhouse and other home decor, jewelry, pottery, glassware, gift items, furniture, candles, and just about everything else you might be hunting for.

J. M. Smucker Company Store and Café

Family owned since 1958, Shisler's Cheese House sells a variety of cheeses, chocolates, sausages, Bahlsen cookies, and Amish Wedding products.

In business for almost forty years, Michael's Bakery is the place for doughnuts, cakes, and other delectables.

NOTABLE

Born in Orrville in 1961, Mike Birkbeck played Major League Baseball for the Milwaukee Brewers and the New York Mets.

Perhaps you don't recognize him by his real name, Robert Montgomery Knight, but we bet if we say Bobby Knight or the General, you'll recognize this former head basketball coach at Indiana University. He grew up in Orrville and played at Orrville High, then at Ohio State.

63

Utica

Named after Utica, New York, the little village of Utica was platted in 1815 and sits on the northern bank of the North Fork of the Licking River.

EAT

Walleye, ham with raisin sauce, fried chicken, hot beef sandwiches, clam strips, beef and noodles, pies, and banana splits are all part of the home cooking at Watts Restaurant, a former fish shop bought by the Watts family in 1912.

Open for breakfast, lunch, and dinner, the Rivers Edge Grill has a menu full of temptations, starting with blueberry hotcakes in the morning and moving to dinner dishes like charbroiled ribs, chops, steaks, and prime rib. Finish it off with such desserts as a velvet sundae or housemade cream pie.

PLAY

We do all scream for ice cream, so head to Velvet Ice Cream, a mandatory stop for just about everyone. Named by Frommer's as one of America's 10 Best Ice Cream Factory Tours, Velvet's Ye Olde Mill welcomes 150,000 visitors each year for tours, tastings, and events. Founded in 1914, the family-owned fourth-generation company turns out some five million gallons of premium ice cream every year, and their headquarters is a vast

Velvet Ice Cream

sprawling compound centered on a three-story old mill. Here you can take a tour, dine, order your favorite flavor, and indulge both inside and out. There's also, of course, a gift shop, and the decor is heavy on vintage ice cream advertisements and makers—creating a museum-like atmosphere that takes away some of the sin of indulging in that double scoop of your flavor choice with both caramel and hot fudge sauce.

Tours of the ice cream factory are conducted regularly and, if the weather is good, usually involve a walk down to the banks of the North Fork of the Licking River. The proximity to the river made it a good stop on the Underground Railroad, and escaping slaves, led by conductors (the term used for those helping freedom seekers find their next stop on the labyrinth of unmarked paths crisscrossing Ohio), came ashore and found shelter at the mill. There are also walking paths for those who'd rather just wander on their own and a very modern glassed-in viewing room with large expanses of windows overlooking the making of yummy vats of ice cream. Sorry, no jumping in allowed.

The grounds themselves are lovely with picnic areas, a playground, benches, a catch-and-release fishpond, live music and entertainment every Thursday and Sunday throughout the summer, a fountain, and statuary (including, of course, a few cows).

Celebrated for half a century or so, the Utica Sertoma Ice Cream Festival is held every Memorial Day weekend.

Water wheel, Velvet Ice Cream

SHOP

The family-owned fifth-generation Legend Hills Orchard offers a bounty of fresh produce in season, including veggies, strawberries, apples, peaches, and plums. Open year-round, the shelves of their market are lined with jams, jellies, preserves, apple butter, Amish cheese, chocolates, Amish Wedding jarred goods, trail bologna, maple syrup, beef jerky, fried pies, candles, home decor, and even Amish furniture. Open in season, Branstool Orchard has trees laden with peaches, apples, and pears.

SOUTHEAST
OHIO

Ohio Pawpaw Festival

64

Albany

Deep in the hills of Southeast Ohio, Albany was home to a large number of abolitionists and was a pioneer of education for African Americans in the 1800s, with three academies.

STAY

The campground at Lake Snowden at Hocking Hills College has ninety-five campsites with electricity and thirty primitive sites that are available on a daily, weekly, monthly, or seasonal basis. According to your interest, choose the camping area that is closest to that activity. Those with horses should opt for Locust Grove, which is near the horse trails. Hilltop Camp amenities include hot showers and flushing toilets, compared to the vault toilets at the other areas, and there are some lakefront lots at Big Oak, which also has a shelter and play area. Off the beaten path, Hickory Hill is near the camp shelter house. There's a grass and sand beach for swimming and an inflatable water park with slides, obstacle course, ramps, and rafts.

EAT

Located in former school building, the Albany Café serves up creamed chicken over mashed potatoes or biscuits with a side; stuffed pork chops with mashed potatoes, gravy, and slaw; or baked chicken breast with noodles and slaw, with Oreo cake and pineapple sunshine cake for dessert—and it's all so much better than any of the school meals we ever ate. Instead, we're talking about good ol' home cooking dishes to order.

Ohio Pawpaw Festival

It's country cooking at Ray's Harvest House as well. Think pulled pork sandwiches with fries, smoked briskets, wings, ribs, meatloaf, house-made chips, and lots of pie.

PLAY

Ohio Pawpaw Festival is an annual celebration of all things pawpaw, an almost forgotten fruit except down in the rolling hills of Southeast Ohio. Located on Lake Snowden in Albany, it's all about this sweet custard-like fruit—competitions for the best pawpaw, best pawpaw-related work of art, pawpaw cook-off, the ever-popular pawpaw-eating contest, hands-on activities for kids, and live music.

NOTABLE

Olivia Davidson Washington, a student at Albany Enterprise Academy, was the second wife of Booker T. Washington, a noted African American leader and author of *Up from Slavery*.

One of twelve African Americans awarded the Congressional Medal of Honor for bravery in the Civil War, Milton M. Holland studied at Albany Manual Labor University and Albany Enterprise Academy.

65

Athens

When the first permanent Euro-American settlers arrived on the banks of the Hocking River in 1797, they decided to name their new settlement after Athens, Greece. But the history of this region of hills and woods—home to Ohio University, one of the largest research colleges in the United States, chartered in 1804—had previously been home to two major mound-building Native American groups: the Adena, a pre-Columbian culture that flourished in this region from around 1000 BCE to 200 CE, and the Ohio Hopewell tradition, circa 300 BCE to 700 CE. Later the Shawnee, an Algonquian tribe, lived on these lands.

STAY

Who can resist a name like Bodhi Tree Guesthouse and Studio? Not far from uptown Athens and Ohio University, this is a nurturing sort of place with lovely vistas of the rolling hills that make this part of Ohio a beautiful destination. Accommodations includes luxe rooms; yoga instruction; a spa for massages, including a Thai massage; a flotation tank that offers a relaxing float in Epsom salts; and integrative health and wellness coaching.

Close to uptown Athens with its plethora of restaurants and shops, as well as the Hockinghocking (and no, that's not a spelling error) Adena Bike Path connecting Athens to nearby Nelsonville, the Athens Footpath Bed and Breakfast is a three-bedroom apartment set above a local store.

Dairy Barn Arts Center

On the border of Strouds Run State Park and therefore with access to all the outdoor activities available there, Lake Hill Cabins are woodland retreats just a short distance from Athens.

There's a family camping area for tents and trailers at Strouds Run States Park and two camper cabins.

If you're for sleek, modern, and luxe, Athens Central Hotel is a boutique hotel with twenty-two rooms and just a minute stroll to uptown Athens.

EAT

Zoe Fine Dining is all about American regional cuisine, its menu offerings creative fusions of local, international, and southern ingredients, like their shrimp and shagbark coarse-milled grits with bacon, tomato, collard greens, and Snowville Creamery cheddar or their local short ribs braised in a chipotle, tomato, and tamarind sauce with queso fresco, rice, and shagbark black beans with chorizo. A nice wine list complements the meal, and, of course, there's dessert, like their milk chocolate praline cheesecake.

Pleasant Hill Vineyards, surrounded by a pretty garden, has outdoor and indoor seating and offers tastings and an appetizer menu.

Miller's Chicken, open for breakfast, lunch, and dinner, serves fried chicken and seafood, sandwiches, macaroni and cheese, soups, and sides like mashed potatoes and green beans.

Hot dogs like their cheesy bacon jalapeño footlongs, fried macaroni-and-cheese bites, cheesy bacon tots (we're seeing a trend here), and burgers are for lunch and dinner at Larry's Dawg House, followed by such sweets as banana splits, artic swirls, milkshakes, and old-fashioned malts.

Dutch Creek Winery specializes in small-batch, handcrafted honey wine (or what we usually call mead), cider, and fruit wines. The owners keep bees and grow their own apples, pears, and peaches to make their products.

Locally sourced, sustainable artisan beer and foods are not to be missed at Little Fish Brewing.

Wayne National Forest

PLAY

Feel the rush in uptown Athens, north of Ohio University's College Green. It's where students congregate, filling the streets, restaurants, shops, and galleries and just hanging about. There's a great vibe here no matter your age.

O'Betty's Hot Dog Museum is all things wiener—hot dog–shaped cars, toys, cooking utensils, cookers, cookbooks, kids' books, games, buildings. Oh, and they have real hot dogs—lots of them with names like Hootchy-Kootchy along with a multitude of toppings like fresh sauerkraut, diced jalapeño peppers, Cleveland Stadium mustard, and fresh crunchy sweet relish. Order what sounds best along with a variety of hand-cut fries, such as a Cajun, very cheesy, and fresh garlic. Jazz it all up with sauces—Casa Nueva's hot habanero salsa and wasabi mayonnaise, to name just two.

Once a mental hospital open from 1874 until 1993, Ridges is part of the Ohio University and home to the Kennedy Museum of Art, which has exhibits on American artwork, including Southwest Native American textiles. The former cow barn, a Georgian revival–style building built in 1914, now houses the Dairy Barn Southeastern Ohio Cultural Arts Center. Their mission is to offer exhibitions, events, and educational programs that nurture and promote area artists and artisans, develop art appreciation among all ages, provide the community access to fine arts and crafts from outside the region, and draw attention and visitors to Southeast Ohio year-round. Besides classes and exhibits, they also host several major events, including the Quilt National and an annual auction.

Also part of the thirty-two-acre property is the Ora Anderson Trail at the Dairy Barn Arts Center, named in tribute to one of the members of a group that saved the barn from being torn down.

Boasting 153 acres with seven miles of shoreline, Dow Lake is part of Strouds Run State Park and is annually stocked with such fish as rainbow trout. The state park's amenities include campgrounds, a swimming beach, boat docks as well as boat and kayak rentals, picnic areas, and hiking paths including the Rockhouse Trail, where you'll find the Turtlehead Cave. It's also open for hunting during the season. Consisting mainly of narrow valleys, ridges, and steep hillsides (the highest point is about 1,022 feet above sea level), the park has springs and springhouses (from when it was private land).

The sixteen-mile Moonville Rail Trail runs between Vinton and Athens, passing through several tunnels, including the Moonville Tunnel, said to be haunted because of its many rail accidents.

SHOP

Look for vintage clothing, collectibles, and antiques at Athens Underground. Furniture, home decor, and art are among the many antique offerings at Random House. Looking for just the perfect present or piece for your home?

Check it out at the Little Professor Book Center for books and periodicals. Can't find what you're looking for? They do special orders for hard-to-find tomes.

Fashion, both local and international, can be found at such boutiques as the Figleaf, Kismet, International House, and Artifacts Gallery.

At Beads and Things, sort through an international collection of goods, including a variety of beads made from such materials as glass, seeds, and metal, along with gemstones. Choose what you like, and if you want, sit down and work with one of the staff to design and make the perfect piece of your own. Other items include tankas, prayer flags, sculptures, incense, sarongs, bags, polished rocks, and gemstone specimens.

66

Beaver

With a population of about 450, Beaver might be the type of place to just pass through—that is, unless you're a big fan of America's western frontier and vintage cowboy series, particularly husband-and-wife team Roy Rogers and Dale Evans. Then Beaver, founded in 1839 and most likely named for Beaver Creek, which flows nearby, is a must-stop. It's here that the Mike Montgomery family created Dogwood Pass Old West Town and Roy Rogers Memories Museum, a replica of an Old West mining town with thirty-nine buildings. The overall effect is complete with costumed reenactors populating the town, dirt roads, and plenty of Wild West action.

PLAY

It all started with a saloon that Mike Montgomery, a former horse trainer, built on two acres of the family farm in 2010. From there it grew, and it now has all the typical stores and civic buildings particular to that period and place. That includes, besides the saloon, a jail, bakery, school, general store, bunkhouse, bathhouse, bank, freight office, gun shop, livery stable, undertaker, and, of course, that most modern necessity of any tourist destination—a souvenir shop.

Roy Rogers was known as the King of the Cowboys, and his Roy Rogers Memories Museum is filled with the movie and TV star's memorabilia. As for Dogwood Pass, the action really gets going on the weekends.

Dogwood Pass Old West Town

That's when it's typical for guests to see gunfights, bank robberies, and shoot-outs between good guys and bad. Special events include turning Dogwood Pass into a haunted town in October and a big Christmas extravaganza in December. Check their website for other upcoming events (see "Destination Information").

67

Belpre

French fur trappers who landed here before the first American settlement was founded called this scenic valley Belle Prairie or Beautiful
Meadow. Now known as Belpre and located in Ohio's Appalachian
Country, it's a small village across the river from Parkersburg, West
Virginia. The second settlement in the Northwest Territory (Marietta was
the first), Belpre also had several firsts—the first female public-school
teacher in the state and the first library in the Territory.

EAT

Because it's open twenty-four hours, you can always get your doughnut fix
at McHappy's Bake Shoppe, with their long list of freshly made doughnuts
and baked goods—jumbo cinnamon rolls; doughnuts filled with such
cream flavors as maple, coconut, Bavarian, and chocolate; muffins; cookies; and fritters.

Check out the Unicorn Wine Guild. They offer fifty-two wine varieties,
coffees, teas, and a small menu of appetizers, entrées, sweets, soups, and
sandwiches.

PLAY

Take a gander at Belpre's heritage homes. The Charles Rice Ames Home,
a Greek revival–style house built in 1843, is one of the four buildings on
the National Register of Historic Places. Another is the Captain Jonathan
Stone House, the oldest home in the city, built just ten years after Belpre

Charles Rice Ames Home

was founded in 1789 and considered a rare surviving example of Ohio's earliest residential architecture. There's also the 7,140-foot Parkersburg Bridge spanning the Ohio River and connecting Belpre to Parkersburg, West Virginia. At the time it was completed in 1871 by the Ohio and Baltimore Railroad, it was considered the longest bridge in the world.

Most likely built around the time that Captain S. J. Spencer moved to Belpre in 1858, his Federal-style home with its gray slate Mansard roof, elaborate staircases, and ornate fireplaces, had floor-to-ceiling windows overlooking the river and his riverboat docked in front of his home.

The twelve-mile Belpre Multi-use Trail takes hikers and bikers on scenic routes along the Ohio River and through Belpre. Points of interest include the Belpre Historic Society, the Civil War Cemetery, a scenic lookout over Blennerhassett Island State Park from Civitan Park, and an Underground Railroad stop.

One of the exhibits at the Belpre Historic Society is on the Southeast Ohio Underground Railroad. Other displays include a model of the ferry boat *Nina Paden*, which made the crossing between Belpre and Parkersburg, West Virginia, before the bridge was built in 1915, and an archaeological collection spanning twelve thousand years.

68

Cambridge

Located on the National Road, one of America's first east–west roads, and snuggled at the edge of the Appalachian foothills in Southeast Ohio, Cambridge was one of many towns and cities that boomed in the late nineteenth century during the natural gas boom spawning numerous glassmaking businesses. Its charming historic downtown is lined with nineteenth-century buildings housing boutiques, cafés, and galleries and offers lots of outdoor activities, including peaceful parks. There's much to see here.

STAY

The Colonel Taylor Inn, located in a lovely historic neighborhood, is just a short walk from Cambridge's picturesque downtown and Northside Park, where the historic Armstrong Covered Bridge was built in 1849. A beautiful 1878 bed and breakfast, the home is listed on the National Register of Historic Places and Save America's Treasures. Besides breakfast, the Queen Anne–style inn also offers dinners and, by advance reservation, live music.

You can choose to stay in a cabin or room at the Salt Fork State Park Lodge, located on the shores of 2,952-acre Salt Lick Lake in Ohio's largest state park. There's also camping at the 17,229-acre state park.

EAT

The Georgetown Tavern on the Hill is a great place to sit outside and enjoy the expansive view of the five acres of grapevines and the city of

Guernsey County Courthouse

Cambridge in the distance. In winter or summer, enjoy one of their brick-oven pizzas and a glass or two of wine, craft brew, or one of their specialty slushies made using their concord or peach wines. There are also sangria and pineapple margarita slushies.

Everything is made from scratch at Kennedy's Bakery, in business since 1925 in downtown Cambridge and family owned for generations.

Handcrafted coffees and teas are the thing at Ladders Coffee Bar.

PLAY

There are few survivors of the natural gas boom when it comes to glass-making, but in Cambridge there's the still-functioning Mosser Glass Factory. Take a tour and see glassmaking in action and then take time to peruse the gift shop.

Cambridge Glass was a big player in the town's economy, and though it's no longer in business, having closed in 1954, the National Museum of Cambridge Glass is a fascinating collection of more than ten thousand pieces of glassware made by the Cambridge Glass Company. The museum also hosts demonstrations of how glass was created from gathering to shaping, etching, and engraving. Visitors can also do their own rubbings from original etching plates in the Education Center and watch a 1940s movie made by the Cambridge Glass Company.

Every year the National Cambridge Collectors, a nonprofit organization established a half century ago that runs the museum, hosts the Annual Glass Show and Sale at the Pritchard Laughlin Civic Center, as well as an auction in October.

From May through October, the Cambridge Main Street Farmers' Market offers the best in local produce. In October, there's the Living Word Outdoor Drama, a nondenominational outdoor theater showing the life of Jesus Christ.

Besides hiking trails, fishing, swimming, birding, boating, a marina, and more, visitors to Salt Creek State Park can explore Hosak Cave and the fifty-foot Hosak Cave Falls. Take the Stone House Trail Loop to the Kennedy Stone House, listed on the National Register of Historic Places and restored to how it looked in the 1840s, when it was first built.

From November through December, downtown Cambridge transforms into nineteenth-century England during their annual Dickens Victorian Village. The village has some ninety-two tableaux with 180 lifelike Victorian-era figures that depict scenes from *A Christmas Carol*. The 1881 county courthouse, spectacular in its own right, is festooned with tens of thousands of lights synchronized to holiday music and thirty-six animated light displays. There are costume guides and trolley cars, and the 1800s-era buildings of the downtown are decorated as well.

Follow the Hopalong Cassidy Trail (maps and a display are at the Cambridge/Guernsey County Tourist Information Center) highlighting the life of William Boyd, the local boy who became a TV- and movie-star cowboy. The stops include a six-foot bronze statue at the Guernsey County Senior Center.

SHOP

As far as we're concerned, Nothing but Chocolate is a great name for delicious candies.

For handmade items, home decor, vintage goods, and Klienkinecht Candles, stop by Ellie's Cottage Candles.

Over fifty years in business, Cambridge Wooden Toy Company offers hardwood, handmade toys including "Snoopy's Flying Circus" airplane, rocking horses, push-and-pull toys, dollhouses, and games, as well as rolling pins and oven-rack pullers for the kitchen.

69

Chillicothe

Chillicothe was the capital of the Northwest Territory in 1800 and then three years later became the first capital of the state of Ohio. Chillicothe was the name of a village where only Shawnee chieftains could live. At one time there were five Ohio villages with that name; now there is only one. But the Chillicothe we're talking about here was never one of those five. Yes, it's confusing, but so is the city's history as Ohio's state capital.

Back and forth, founded in 1796, its designation as state capital happened when Ohio became a state in 1802. But then in 1810, Zanesville won the honor. Their time lasted until 1812, and then it was Chillicothe's turn once more. Four years later, in 1816, the capital moved again, for good we assume, to Columbus. Whew.

Nestled in the foothills of the Appalachian Region of America, in 1831 Chillicothe was linked to the rest of the state by the Ohio and Erie Canal, and then two decades ago, the Marietta and Cincinnati Railroad brought even more connections and thus prosperity to the city. Intriguingly, while railroads supplanted canals in most towns, not so in Chillicothe because they traveled in different directions. It wasn't until a flood in 1907 that their canal days finally ended.

STAY

A beautiful Greek Revival built in 1843, the Atwood House Bed and Breakfast is located in the historic downtown near restaurants, shops, and galleries.

Second Street

Built by Governor Tiffin in 1826 and located just a block from the historic downtown, the Guest House Bed and Breakfast is a two-story Victorian with a lovely English garden to enjoy.

EAT

Step back into the 1950s at Carl's Townhouse, a classic hamburger joint.

Specializing in smoked meats and offering both classic and traditional barbecue dishes, the Old Canal Smoke House located in the historic downtown is worth the trip.

Though it's said to be haunted, that shouldn't stop you from enjoying the ambience, food, and live music at Cross Keys Tavern. Besides, maybe the ghosts are just hanging around for one of their famous perch dinners with a side of house-made potato salad.

A gastropub with everything from mahi-mahi to bourbon burgers and a great drinks menu, check out the Pour House at Machinery Hall.

Highland's Ice Creamery, located in the downtown, serves hand-dipped Johnson's Ice Cream in shakes, cones, and sundaes.

Lake Ellensmere Covered Bridge

PLAY

The oldest continuously operating theater in America, the Majestic opened in 1853 featuring vaudeville shows and operas with such old-time greats as Milton Berle, Laurel and Hardy, and Sophie Tucker. Nowadays, the Majestic Theatre hosts an annual concert by country music star John Berry, movie nights, workshops for aspiring musicians, and the productions by the Chillicothe's Civic Theater.

The spectacular three-hundred-acre Adena Mansion is that kind of place—eighteen rooms; fine antiques dating to the time when owner Thomas Worthington, his wife, and their ten children lived there; wonderful landscaping; barn; smokehouse; and springhouse. In other words, it's how the very wealthy lived back then. Worthington was twice elected as a US Senator and twice elected as governor of Ohio.

The Hopewell Culture National Historical Park showcases the vast Hopewell tradition, which thrived for five hundred years starting millennia ago. They left behind an extensive complex of earthworks, embankments forming geometric enclosures, burial mounds, and relics. The area was a sacred place where the Hopewellian people came together for feasts, rites of passage, and funerals. Admission is free.

Junction Earthworks/Arc of Appalachia is a new archaeological park and nature preserve with nature trails, a seventy-acre prairie, and two-thousand-year-old Native American earthworks. It's open 365 days a year, and admission is free.

The story of Tecumseh, the great Shawnee leader who tried to unite all tribes to fight the invading settlers, is a regular feature at Sugarloaf Mountain Amphitheater, a beautiful outdoor venue.

Lucy Hayes, wife of President Rutherford B. Hayes, was nicknamed Lemonade Lucy because that's what she served instead of alcohol. We're not sure what her guests thought in that hard-drinking era but her birthplace, the Lucy Hayes Heritage Center, presents life as it was in the early 1800s.

SHOP

Antiques and vintage items can be found at Old Canal Antiques and Primitives, American Vintage Warehouse, Porch Swing Days, A Touch of Charm Mercantile, and Buried Treasures, to name just a few.

Grandpa Joe's Candy Store is a step back in time when it comes to confections. Rows and rows of glass jars are filled with a myriad of sweets, including nostalgic candy among the 250 candy bars and over 100 bulk candies for sale here. Also a blast from the past, there are 225 flavors of old-fashioned glass-bottled soda, such as birch and ginger beers, sarsaparilla, and something called bacon soda.

NOTABLE

Joseph Hanks was born in Chillicothe in 1843 and served under Ulysses Grant in the Battle of Vicksburg, where under heavy fire he carried his childhood friend Antone Eppenhauer to safety and then returned to the battle. It took Eppenhauer three decades to find Hanks, and when he did, he notified federal officials about what had happened. Hanks was awarded the Civil War Medal of Honor in 1917.

70

Coshocton

Situated where the Walhonding River and the Tuscarawas River meet to form the Muskingum River near land once the site of a Lenape village, Coshocton was a canal city originally named Tuscarawas by American colonists. It is known for its famed Roscoe Village, a restored canal town that is a definite step back into the mid-1800s.

The 6,004-acre Muskingum River Navigation Historic District, listed on the National Register of Historic Places and encompassing Coshocton, Morgan, Muskingum, and Washington Counties, is the most intact system of large hand-operated locks in the United States and consists of twelve buildings, thirty-two structures, and ten hand-operated locks. Completed in 1841, it was the first location to be designated a Navigation Historic District in the United States by the National Park Service.

ROSCOE VILLAGE

When James Calder went bankrupt in 1816, he managed to retain a parcel of land on the Muskingum River. Taking a gamble that local farmers would rather buy from him than pay the exorbitant price of twenty-five cents to ride the ferry to Coshocton, he built a general store and named his settlement Caldersburg. Fourteen years later, the name changed to Roscoe in honor of the English poet and early abolitionist William Roscoe. Other changes were coming too.

In 1844, the *Montezuma* docked at Roscoe. It was the first canal boat to do so along the recently opened Erie and Ohio Canal, a laboriously

Shops at Roscoe Village

hand-dug 350-mile waterway connecting Portsmouth on the Ohio River to Cleveland on Lake Erie. Prosperity followed for Roscoe. Times were very good indeed until the 1860s, when the days of canal travel were ending, replaced by a newer mode of transportation: steam engine trains. The Flood of 1913 wiped out the majority of the canal and locks, as well as what was left of Roscoe's prosperity. Once-stately commercial buildings and lovely Victorian and Queen Anne homes fell into disrepair.

And so when nationally famous artist Dean Cornwell painted a romantic mural for Roscoe's Sesquicentennial Celebration, the scenes from the past he created stood as a stark contrast to the present. They were also an inspiration to manufacturer Edward Montgomery, who drove past Roscoe every day on his commute to his glove company in Coshocton. He and his wife, Frances, bought several properties along the intriguingly named Whitewoman Street.

Edward Montgomery envisioned creating "a living history museum." Their first project was restoring the old toll house, the home of Jacob Welsh, who started collecting tolls. The Montgomerys paid $1,200 for the place and spent another $41,000 to bring it back to its former glory. The red brick house with its white wood trim again collects tolls of a sort, selling tickets for activities, and also houses a gift shop. The Toy Cellar is located in its cellar.

Now on the National Register of Historic Places, Roscoe Village is a delightful step back in time, its historic buildings restored and housing restaurants and shops and offering a plethora of things to do.

Historic water wheel,
Roscoe Village

STAY

The Apple Butter Inn, circa 1840, is a six-bedroom bed and breakfast perched on a hill overlooking Roscoe Village and the canal. With spacious porches on both the first and second floors, hardwood floors, fireplaces, and antique furniture (but modern conveniences), it provides the perfect ambience for exploring the historic village. Nestled in the Appalachian foothills and surrounded by woods, Roscoe Hillside Cabins are within walking distance of the village.

PLAY

Travel like it's 1840 on the *Monticello III* for a horse-drawn canal boat ride. Get hands-on at the Visitor Center by learning such essential nineteenth-century skills as tin punching, candle dipping, toy top painting, rope making, and weaving. Go on a guided Living History Tour in which costumed interpreters showcase life over 150 years ago. Frances Montgomery was an avid gardener, and the village boasts nine gardens, including her first creation, the Toll House Garden. Schedule you visit for many of the village's numerous events, such as A Roscoe Christmas Lantern Tour and the annual Apple Butter Stirrin' in October.

EAT

Once the Roscoe Hotel (circa 1856), McKenna's Market at Medbery has a café, deli, and olive bar and sells an assortment of foods and beverages—craft beer, wine, imported cheeses and meats, old-fashioned candies, and unique soda pops. Uncorked, a restaurant and bar as well as coffee shop and wine bar, is located in the two-story William Roscoe building, once a general store that opened in the early 1840s. Enjoy outdoor dining when weather permits, and be sure to visit the adjacent wine shop with its selection of over two hundred distinctive wines.

Built around 1838 and used as a warehouse for canal cargo, a general merchandise store, and even the Roscoe Post Office, this three-story brick building is now home to Warehouse Steak n' Stein, famed for their onion rings, steaks, and chops, as well as intriguing items like crawtail macaroni and cheese, Reuben pizza, and Rajun Cajun crawtail alfredo.

SHOP

Vintage candies—Bonomo Turkish Taffy, Moon Pies, and Charleston Chews to name a few—are a perfect fit for Roscoe Village Sweets and Treats, located in the John Dredge Building (circa 1846), but they also have a large selection of other yummy confections, including over a dozen varieties of fudge and Marsha Buckeyes, handmade in Columbus. John Bankhurst built his pharmacy and drugstore in 1870, and it was restored by the Montgomerys 101 years later and is now the Roscoe General Store. Here you can shop for a myriad of goods, like candles, home decor, antiques, and collectibles. Peruse their Christmas room and stock up on Roscoe Village shirts, caps, and souvenirs.

NOTABLE

Whitewoman Street, Roscoe's main thoroughfare, gets its name from Mary Harris, who was ten years old when she and 111 other townspeople were kidnapped from Deerfield, Massachusetts, and taken on a three-hundred-mile march to Canada. Harris, among the 86 to 89 who survived the trip, was adopted into the Kahnawake Mohawk nation. She married a member of the Mohawk Nation and settled with her family near Roscoe in 1748, never taking advantage of the opportunity to return to her White roots. She was so respected by the Mohawks that they named both the village and trail leading to where she lived Walhonding (Whitewoman) Town and Walhonding Trail, the latter becoming Roscoe's Whitewoman Street.

Chief Netawatwees, also known as Netahutquemaled, Netodwehement, Netautwhalemund, and in English Newcomer, was a principal chief of the Delaware (Lenape) who first settled Coshocton and was an ally of Continental forces during the American Revolutionary War.

71

Gallipolis

Founded in 1790, making it the second-oldest settlement in the Northwest Territory, Gallipolis was at first the home of about five hundred French immigrants, including professionals, aristocrats, and artisans, who thought they were buying prime property and instead ended up in a vast wilderness on the Ohio River. They quickly found out their fancy furnishings brought from back home didn't quite work in this raw pioneer environment. For the most part, these weren't the types of people used to embracing or ready to embrace the hard labor needed to tame a wilderness, and half hightailed it out of there.

The other half worked hard, taking advantage of transportation opportunities on the river.

PLAY

One early frontiersman was Henry Cushing, who built a two-story inn he called Our House Tavern. That way, he could meet travelers at the docks and invite them "to come to our house," where they would dine on fine French china in a home filled with magnificent furniture. It was not by any means a typical river tavern.

Marquis de Lafayette, who convinced France to support our revolution, stopped by on May 22, 1825, for a two-and-a-half-hour visit.

Now a museum open by appointment, the place displays the coat Lafayette wore when visiting and one of the violins played during his stay. The tavern is filled with lovely and expensive French furniture from that time.

Our House Tavern

Bob Evans—yes, that Bob Evans—didn't like the sausages he was serving at his twelve-seat restaurant near Gallipolis and so started making his own from the hogs he raised on his farm. They were so well received he started manufacturing his own, branching out into other food products and opening more restaurants. Currently there are about five hundred Bob Evans restaurants in eighteen states, and in 2017, a private equity firm bought the business for $565 million. Not bad for a hog farmer from tiny Gallipolis. Evans and his wife had six children, and the Homestead, the name they gave their farm where they made their sausages and had their restaurant, was once a stagecoach stop and inn and now is on the National Register of Historic Places. Now open to visitors, the Bob Evans Farm is a complex including the Homestead Museum, the original restaurant, and Craft Barn.

For more than half a century, the French Art Colony Museum, located in a historic mansion built in 1855 on the banks of the Ohio River, has been the destination for art classes, art exhibitions, and community outreach. It's also the home of the Riverby Theatre Guild, which offers an annual schedule of community and children's theater.

Gallipolis from Mound Hill

Dating back to 1880, Mound Hill Cemetery, also known as Fortification Hill, overlooks Gallipolis and across the Ohio River into West Virginia. Buried among intriguing cemetery art and historic connections to the town's history are thirty Revolutionary War soldiers as well as at least two of the original founding French.

The 8.5-mile Gallia County Hike and Bike Trail traverses an old railroad right-of-way connecting Gallipolis at the Ohio River to Bidwell, an unincorporated community that's also in Gallia County.

SHOP

The grass-based sustainable producer of grade A Jersey milk, the family-owned Laurel Valley Creamery crafts naturally aged raw milk and several pasteurized cheeses, including Jersey drover, a raw-milk natural-rind cheese, an Appalachian take on the Swiss gruyère, and such fresh offerings as cheese curds, pimento, mozzarella, and Aphrocheesiac, a soft cheese seasoned with Mediterranean herbs and spices. Call for an appointment (https://www.laurelvalleycreamery.com/).

72

Ironton

The name about says it all. Located on the Ohio River, Ironton is the county seat of Lawrence, one of the six counties constituting the Hanging Rock Iron Region of southern Ohio. Poised on the northern banks of the Ohio River, it's connected to Russell, Kentucky, by the Oakley C. Collins Memorial Bridge, which, when lit up at night, is a spectacular sight.

This is iron-ore region, and the towns have names like Coal Grove and Franklin Furnace. For those who don't know (and we sure didn't), at one point forty-six iron furnaces used for smelting ore dotted this rugged hilly area. In production from 1818 until 1916, the ore mined and produced here was used to build the steel hulls of both the *Merrimack* and *Monitor*, the iron-clad boats used during the Civil War. At its peak, in 1875, Southeast Ohio was the leader in the amount of iron produced in the US.

STAY

There are two family campgrounds and one group campground at Lake Vesuvius Recreation Area in Wayne National Forest. Spectacularly beautiful, the 143-acre lake has a beach and swim area, picnic facilities, stunning rock outcroppings, hiking, fishing, a scenic overlook, an archery trail, and the 46.6-mile Lake Vesuvius Horse Trail System, consisting of nine trails, four trailheads, and a horse campground. The recreation area is named after the Vesuvius Iron Furnace (which in turn was named after Mount Vesuvius), which produced ten tons of iron every day. It closed—or "blew out" as it's called in iron-ore language—in 1905, and most of the furnace is gone except for the rock chimney and a wall now on the National Register of Historic Places. Also gone is the company town, where workers were paid in company scrip, of Vesuvius.

EAT

Peddler's Home Cooking offers family-style comfort food like chicken and dumplings, baked chops and steak, macaroni, and breakfast all day.

Chow down on old-time Italian favorites from a long list of menu offerings such as baked ziti, ravioli, lasagna, chicken or shrimp fettuccine alfredo, and seafood specialties such as shrimp, mussels, and clams with a choice of pastas—capellini, linguini, spaghetti, penne, farfalle, rigatoni, fettuccine, whole wheat spaghetti, whole wheat penne, and gluten-free penne—at Melini Cucina.

For hickory barbecue, stop by the Armory Smokehouse for ribs, chops, chicken, grilled shrimp, and a whole bunch of great side dishes.

PLAY

Check out the Nannie Kelly Wright room at the Lawrence County Museum, a rich load of area history. Nannie, the daughter of a riverboat captain, married the owner of the Center Furnace in Lawrence County, and when he died in 1902, she took over running the furnace and also the other company her husband left her, Kelly Nail and Iron Company in Ironton. When iron fortunes declined, she lived a hard life and was said to even work the furnace herself, dressed in men's clothing. She managed to regain her fortune and at the turn of the century was thought to be the second-richest woman in the world (Queen Victoria was the first). In 1906, she sold the furnace to Portland Cement, receiving a check for $100,000, which, when she cashed it, was the largest check ever cashed in a local bank at the time. She lost her fortune again during the stock market crash of 1929 but lived well thanks to her jewelry collection.

The museum also tells the history of Reverend Rankin, a conductor on the Underground Railroad. Ohio—bordered by Kentucky and West Virginia, two slave states located on the Ohio River—was a natural escape route for freedom seekers. More than fifty men, women, and children in Lawrence County are documented as having been conductors on the Underground Railroad. Conductors, including Black, White, and biracial people, their backgrounds varying from rich to poor, were typically Methodists, Presbyterians, and Quakers. One such Presbyterian was Reverend John Rankin, whose home stood high on a three-hundred-foot-high hill overlooking the Ohio River. From there Rankin, who established the Ohio Anti-slavery Society in 1835, signaled by lantern that it was safe for fugitives on the Kentucky side to cross the river. Once they crossed, the freedom seekers were led north following the iron furnaces.

73

Logan

The only city in Hocking County, Logan is the epicenter of all that is grand and beautiful in Hocking Hills, located on the Hocking River in the foothills of the Appalachian Mountains. Hocking Hills provides a plethora of outdoor drama with spectacular waterfalls, woodlands, cliffs, gorges, hiking trails, kayaking, zip-lining, and nine state parks and forests. Oh, and did we mention caves? Yes, they've got several of those as well. And Logan's historic downtown offers shops, restaurants, art galleries, and even a pencil sharpener museum—yes, you read that correctly. More to come on that later.

STAY

Hocking Hills Canoe and Livery offers rentals for kayaking and canoeing, including moonlight and torchlight paddles. Spend the night at either their tent camps or camping cabins. Bring your own bedding, and the restrooms and showers are close by.

Built around 1853, White Pillars Inn is a bed and breakfast on the National Register of Historic Places.

The pet-friendly Inn and Spa at Cedar Falls, located on seventy-five wooded acres, offers a unique range of sleeping options: 1840s log cabins with fireplaces, a luxe lodge, bed and breakfast rooms, romantic cottages, and twenty-foot-diameter yurts with heat, air-conditioning, kitchens, and a view of the sky above. They have a wonderful restaurant as well,

Ash Cave at Hocking Hills State Park

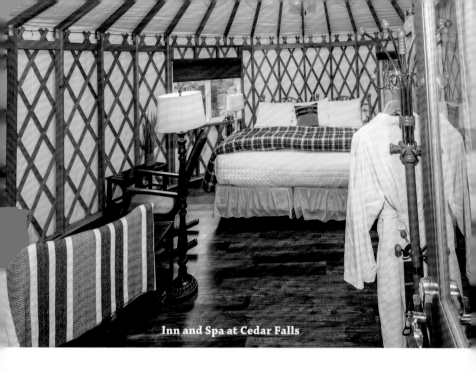
Inn and Spa at Cedar Falls

serving breakfast, lunch, and dinner. Surrounded on three sides by the Hocking Hills State Park, there's a spa as well as breakfast, lunch, and dinner at their Kindred Spirits restaurant with its three-seasons enclosed patio dining area located in the largest of the original 1840s cabins.

The Hocking Hills Inn and Coffee Emporium is multifunctional, with four suites in a historic home, beautiful gardens, and their Coffee Emporium with its menu of artisan coffee drinks, breakfast, lunch, and smoothies. There's also a gift shop selling coffee by the bag, mugs, beanies, hoodies, and other accessories.

EAT

The annual Hocking Hills Comfort Food Cruise is a way to experience twelve local restaurants, each with a signature dish to try.

For wine and craft beer lovers, there's a long list of places to try, including Brewery 33 Hocking Hills, Hocking Hills Winery, Shade Winery in nearby Shade, and Rockside Winery and Vineyards, known for their French hybrid grapes, in Lancaster. Hocking County's only moonshine distillery, Hocking Hills Moonshine, offers tours, a history of Prohibition, and samples.

With a name like Pearl's Diner and the tagline "Cooking like Granma's," you know you're going to get some great biscuits and gravy, home fries, creamy chicken noodle soup, great pies, and all sorts of home cooking.

Amish-style food—fried chicken, mashed potatoes and gravy, house-made noodles and roast beef—is on the menu at the Olde Dutch Restaurant.

Ever had a split cream doughnut? We hadn't either, but oh my, are they delicious. But then anything coming out of the oven at Penny's Pastries, in business for over a century, is sinfully delicious, including their glazed doughnuts, iced sugar cookies, and apple fritters.

Millstone BBQ is the place to go for slow-cooked barbecue-style meats, beer, mixed drinks, wine, and weekly specials such as Monday wing night and prime rib on Friday, as well as lots of sports on their flat-screen HDTVs.

Ice cream lovers can order their favorite flavors, toppings, cones, and sundaes at the family-owned Treehouse Treats and Treasures.

PLAY

You probably didn't even know such a place existed, but it certainly is worth a stop. The Paul A. Johnson Pencil Sharpener Museum, located in its original one-room shed now on the grounds of the Hocking Hills Visitor Center, is a twenty-year-plus collection of 3,479 pencil sharpeners with no two alike. Really.

Another improbable museum is also a working factory—the Columbia Washboard Museum, the only remaining washboard company still in business. And yes, people still buy washboards. See how they're made using machinery that dates back to when they first opened, and learn how to make music playing a washboard. And yes, we guarantee you're go home with a washboard. We did.

Logan is outdoor central, and we can barely even begin to list all the state parks and forests, caves, waterfalls, rock formations, and hiking trails in Hocking County. But we'll give it a try. Take your pick of caves to explore—Ash, Old Man's, and Whispering. For falls, consider Cedar, Big Spring Hollow, Ash, Upper, Lower, Whispering, Minor, Top of Broken Rock, and a few more.

There's always a celebration. June is the Washboard Music Festival and Duck Creek Log Jam, a combination of music festival and classic camping trip. Airstream trailers, music, and authentic moonshine are all part of the Urban Air Wake Up Downtown, and in September it's both the Hocking Hills Artists and Craftsmen Annual Fall Show and the Hocking County Fair.

Day or night, the John Glenn Astronomy Park, the gigantic twenty-eight-inch telescope in the roll-off-roof observatory can view the sun, stars, moon, and sky.

SHOP

Take an hour or so to create your own personalized scented soy candle at Hocking Hills Candle Works, located inside Christmas Treasures, a fun shop for holiday aficionados, with over eighteen thousand Christmas decorations, decor pieces, gifts, and collectibles in stock.

With more than one hundred dealers, you can find pretty much anything you want at Logan Antique Mall, open seven days a week.

At Midwest Glassware Outlet, you'll find crystal, china, bakeware, beverageware, vases, barware, jugs, specialty jars and lids, votives, cake domes, trifle bowls, dinnerware, and such name brands as Anchor, Lancaster Glass, Dansk, Fostoria, and L. E. Smith.

Wren Valley Truffles can be purchased at a variety of Hocking Hills locations, including Hocking Hills Winery, Hocking Hills Moonshine, and Hocking Hills Inn and Coffee Emporium.

NOTABLE

Retired four-star general of the United States Army Curtis Scaparrotti was the Supreme Allied Commander Europe and Commander United States European Command.

Katie Smith, an Olympic gold medalist and a Women's National Basketball Association player, was born in Logan and was named the Gatorade National Player of the Year at Logan High School in her senior year.

74

Malta

A tiny village with some 670 people, Malta is conveniently located close to several gorgeous parks and recreation areas, including, just fifteen minutes away, Burr Oak State Park and Blue Rock State Park. The Wilds and Dillon State Park are thirty minutes from the village.

STAY

Perfect for getting away from it all, the Sandstone Retreat is set on twenty acres and has three bedrooms, two full baths, and a loft. The luxury vacation cabin can accommodate eight and has such amenities as a hot tub, game room, fire ring, pond, fireplace, wood stove, air-conditioning, and laundry facilities.

PLAY

The Morgan County Historic Society, with its wonderful collection of interesting sites, has opened to the public the Rock Hollow School, a one-room school built in 1877, and the rather disturbing Morgan County Dungeon. The latter was discovered in the basement of the old jail in 1964 and had been used for incarcerating prisoners convicted of rioting, larceny, and adultery in Morgan County between the years 1833 and 1839. Located on Main Street, the dungeon's stone-encased entrance leads down to an eleven-foot-high, twelve-foot-long, and five-foot-wide underground room adjacent to the Rock Hollow School.

Wildcat Hollow Trail

McConnelsville Dam

The 1,444-mile Buckeye Trail meanders in all directions throughout the state, connecting Lake Erie to the Ohio River. Near Malta, the Buckeye Trail links to two loops of the Wildcat Hollow Trail. The short loop of 6.1 miles is known for its beautiful spring wildflowers and is suitable for all skill levels. The moderate-level long loop, offering river views, is 16.5 miles with an elevation gain of 1,669 feet. Both loops wind through pine forests, meadows, and rock formations, along streams and country roads, and are accessible year-round. Dogs are welcome but must be kept on a leash.

NOTABLE

Born in Malta in 1838, Colonel Rufus R. Dawes was an officer in the Iron Brigade during the Civil War, fighting for the Union and most well-known for his service during the Battle of Gettysburg. He went on to serve as a US congressman. His son, Charles G. Dawes, not only won the Nobel Peace Prize but also worked as a composer and served as vice president of the United States under President Calvin Coolidge. It was quite some family. Sarah Jane Dawes Shedd, the sister of Rufus, was also born in Malta in 1836, and after she graduated from college and married a minister, the couple worked together as missionaries for Assyrian Christians at Urmia, a city in what was then Persia but is now Iran.

75

Marietta

Marietta, located where the Muskingum River flows into the Ohio River, is the first permanent settlement in the relatively new (the pioneers showed up in 1788) United States. At the time, this large swath of land was known as the Territory of the River Ohio. But the Hopewell lived here long before that, building the Marietta Earthworks, a complex more than fifteen hundred years old that still defines parts of this city.

A riverboat city, Marietta (named in honor of Queen Marie Antoinette) exudes a European-style charm with its historic homes, commercial buildings, and cobbled streets. Marietta College, founded in 1835, was a stop on the Underground Railroad.

STAY

Located in downtown Marietta, making it an easy saunter to shops, restaurants, bars, museums, and coffee shops, the Parkview House is a spacious, historic home more than a century old. The neighborhood has a large city park, and there is a riverside bike and walking trail close by.

A grand dame of a hotel, its brick facade shaped like the bow of a steamboat, the Lafayette Hotel opened its doors in 1918 near the spot where the Marquis de Lafayette, French hero of the American Revolution, disembarked in 1825. Lovely Victorian-era antiques and memorabilia from the days when steamboats, transporting goods and people, made their way up and down the Ohio River, such as paintings, brass pilot

Muskingum River

instruments, vintage photos of local scenes, and a pilot wheel, all add to the feel of having stepped back into time. Check out the Gun Room, one of the hotel's restaurants; this one has a unique decor—a famed collection of long rifles, each made by hand and dating from 1795 to 1880, all numbered and accompanied by a description. Its most famous gun is likely the percussion rifle made by the well-known gun-marking family, J. J. Henry and Sons, who traveled with Benedict Arnold in his failed attempt to conquer Quebec.

EAT

Built in 1879 as a private residence and listed on the Ohio Historic Register, the Buckley House is a now a marvelous restaurant. The Victorian-style house, its upstairs veranda, and downstairs porch are flanked with tall white columns. Dine inside, outside on the porch, or in the lovely gardens.

Marietta Brewing Company, in the historic downtown, crafts such beers as their flagship Cooper's Copper Ale, a medium-bodied amber ale; Happy Trail Ale, a wheat-based IPA generously hopped with Mosaic and Simcoe hops; and the intriguingly named Estella's Raspberry Wheat, an American wheat ale with a heaping of raspberries. Burgers, wings, pizzas, and sandwiches are on the menu.

The century-plus Harmar Tavern near the Harmar Bridge is famous for their bologna sandwiches, but you can also get stuffed pepper soup, spaghetti and meatballs, pizza, wings, and sandwiches, as well as such weekly specials as prime ribs on Thursday or barbecue ribs on Friday and

Saturday. The building itself dates back to around the 1840s, and so you shouldn't be surprised to learn there's a least one ghost on the premises —a harmless one named Mollie who sits in the corner and seems to mind her own business. Oh, and don't worry about the place being closed. They're open 365 days a year.

PLAY

The Hopewell who lived here between 100 BCE and 500 CE built what are known as the prehistoric Marietta Earthworks. Some parts of the earthworks now lie below Marietta, but some are now parks. The first (not counting a sketch of the mounds in Circleville) to be documented in America, they were ninety-five acres of mounds, embankments, and passageways, and portions remain, including the thirty-foot Conus Mound in Mound Cemetery. Stand atop the Quadranou Mound, where ancient astronomer-priests analyzed the movements of the sun, moon, and stars.

Marietta Adventure Company rents bikes, kayaks, cycling and paddling accessories, and climbing and outdoor gear and provides information about local trails and waterways. There's plenty of recreational opportunities. Just for starters, within the city limits alone, there are over thirty miles of single-track mountain biking trails plus close proximity to four other regional trail systems.

Ohio River Museum

Nearby, you will find the Marietta unit of Wayne National Forest, Mountwood Park, North Bend Park, and the North Bend Rail Trail. A visit to the region is a must for mountain bikers, history lovers, and active families.

An older George Washington recalled his young days as a surveyor and the beauty of the Ohio River Valley to his general, Rufus Putnam. Leading a forty-eight-man party, Putnam and his men built a walled fortification with four blockhouses he called Campus Mauritius, meaning field of wars, to repel Native American attacks. His home was within the fortification, and now, over 220 years later, it is a museum, with furnishings from the Putnam family and objects from the city's early days, like antique musical instruments, surgical tools, Putnam's sword, and muskets used by early settlers.

The *W. P. Snyder Jr.*, the last steam-powered stern-wheeled towboat to operate in this country, is now an outdoor attraction at the Ohio River Museum. A big boat at 175 feet and 342 tons, it's docked on the Muskingum River behind the museum.

Hikers can enjoy the six marked hiking trails at the five-hundred-acre Broughton Nature and Wildlife Education Area or, farther afield, the three hundred miles of trails for hiking, mountain biking, and horseback riding at the Wayne National Forest.

First opened in 1919 as Hippodrome Theatre, the wonderfully restored Peoples Bank Theatre shows movies, entertainment, and music. The entertainment at the Adelphia Music Hall features regional and national musicians, comedians, and actors. On a warm summer's evening, spread a blanket on the grass of a nearby park and dance and jive to the soothing sounds of jazz, bluegrass, and rock.

Considered one of the best-executed examples of Gothic Revival architecture in the state, the Castle was once the home of Ohio senator Theodore Davis and is furnished with items of historical significance to Marietta and the surrounding region. On the National Register of Historic Places, the home, open to tours, includes such wonderful architectural details as a scagliola fireplace, an octangular tower, a trefoil attic window, and floor-to-ceiling shutters on the parlor's bay window.

The weekend after Labor Day, the city celebrates its river heritage with the Ohio River Sternwheel Festival, with fireworks, music, food, and the arrival of between thirty and thirty-five authentic sternwheel boats traveling the river.

Stroll down to the landing under the Washington Street Bridge at Front Street and board the *Valley Gem Sternwheeler* for a river cruise.

SHOP

Putnam Chocolates offers a wide assortment of hand-chopped chocolates.

Check out the handcrafted assortment of works at Riverside Artists Gallery.

A specialty cut-flower farm, Wildroot also offers farm workshops and seasonal flower picking.

Take a class and stock up on cookware, linens, coffee, and spices at the Cook's Shop.

Connecting to local and regional artists and crafters, Wit and Whimzy features a curated stage of distinctive products, including artisan jewelry, apparel, paper goods, tableware for kids, retro-style key chains and coin pouches, socks, and totes.

76

McConnelsville

A historic village on the Muskingum River, McConnelsville was named after Revolutionary War officer General Robert McConnell, who bought land here in 1817 at a cost of $1.75 an acre. Like many who followed him, he was attracted by the vast forests and rich bottomland, as well as the riches offered by the Muskingum River, including fishing and furs from trapping animals. The mighty Muskingum River winds its way through 112 miles of Ohio's gorgeous hill country, starting where it's formed by the confluence of the Walhonding and Tuscarawas Rivers in Coshocton. From there, its path travels south through Zanesville, where it is joined by the Licking River, and on to the Ohio River. Its path takes it through quaint villages and into early Ohio history.

STAY

The fully furnished, eight-hundred-square-foot Morgan County Cabin in the Woods is just a mile outside of McConnelsville and has a wrap-around front porch and, for those who like to cast a line, a stocked pond for fishing.

EAT

Cast-iron seared rib eyes, extra-crispy chicken fritters, honey-glazed pit ham, barbecued ribs, freshly baked bread, mashed potatoes, gravy, and green beans are just some of the menu items at Boondocks BBQ and Grill.

Located in a one-hundred-year-old brick building in McConnelsville's historic downtown, the Old Bridge Brewing Company has the convivial atmosphere of a local hangout and the urban vibe of a trendy taproom.

Get your coffee at Repo Kafe Roasters; check out the baked goods and sandwiches, including cream horns, Bundt cakes, feta pie, sausage gravy and biscuits, and pressed ciabatta sandwich at Seraphinea's Crumb and Coffee.

Little Dog Deli offers a selection of pizza, sandwiches, salads, fried chicken, wraps, and sweets.

PLAY

Built in 1890 and in continuous operation since its grand opening two years later, the wonderfully restored Twin City Opera House is located on the village square. There are weekend movies and live events, including regular performances on the third Saturday by the Ohio Valley Opry. Tours of the Twin City Opera House are available by appointment.

Intriguingly, there are tunnels under the theater (though they're not open to the public) leading to other locations in the village and to the riverbank. Speculation is that they were used by freedom seekers before the Civil War. It makes sense, given that the Muskingum feeds into the Ohio, a river frequently traveled as slaves made their way from Kentucky and other southern states.

Shake hands with President Lincoln and meet Civil War era soldiers, cavalry, and civilians, including women wearing hoopskirts. Watch the sky light up at night as cannons fire over the Muskingum River, see skir-

mishes and a battle reenactment, and take a lamplight tour of both Union and Confederate camps. It's all part of Malta-McConnelsville Civil War Encampment Days, the largest annual Civil War reenactment in the state, held each August.

Held in October, the annual Morgan County Heritage Day is a celebration of the area's Appalachian heritage—a day of local food, live music, and lots of pioneer activities.

Mail Pouch Barn

For children, that includes Make Your Own Quilt Book. For adults, there are beer and wine tastings. The entire family can enjoy museum tours, the quilt show, a scavenger hunt, and a historical photo exhibit.

The Morgan County Historical Society Museum is home to genealogy collections, photographs, prints, and printed records, as well as an extensive collection of memorabilia and artifacts showcasing the history of the county and its people. Also, they have several historic structures that are open to the public in both McConnelsville and Malta.

Twin City Opera House

One is the Federal-style Button House, the residence of Mrs. Evelyn True Button, a teacher, author, world traveler, and advocate for women's rights. Built in 1836, the home has been restored and preserved as if Button still lived there, including furnishings and decor dating between 1830 and 1890. The daughter of a physician and a graduate of Ohio Wesleyan University, Button traveled to the Philippines to train teachers in 1898. She died in the house where she was born in 1975 and willed it to the Morgan County Historical Society.

The Carriage House and Blacksmith Shop are in back of the Button home. Showcasing relics from the times of horse-drawn transportation, the Carriage House features a horse-drawn hearse and vintage fire wagon. Call for information about live demonstrations at the Blacksmith Shop, once located in nearby Malta and now adjacent to the Carriage House.

77

Nelsonville

An Appalachian town located on the Hocking River, Nelsonville at one time depended on the coal and salt mining industries and, because of an abundance of clay, had numerous brickyards.

Now the beauty of the surrounding area is also reflected in the charming historic downtown, centered on a historic fountain dating back to 1904.

STAY

Be at one with the forest by opting for a perch high up in one of the treehouses at Among the Trees. Or go for Victorian-era glory at the Hyde House Bed and Breakfast, built in 1882, with its wraparound front porch; dining, sitting, and parlor rooms; and four bedrooms.

EAT

Located on Nelsonville's lovely Public Square and featuring local Appalachian cuisine and live music, Rhapsody Restaurant features a pub and fine-dining menu as well as a Sunday brunch with extensive offerings.

When George Stuart's showboat sank in 1869 and he and his minstrel troop were no longer able to travel along the Ohio canals, he took to land, building the Stuart Opera House a decade later. Coinciding with the coal boom, the opera house prospered until moving pictures and the value of coal went bust. Stuart's closed its doors in 1924. It remained closed until the 1970s, caught fire, and then was restored and has now achieved its former glory.

Hop aboard the Hocking Valley Scenic Railway, a vintage train consisting of such cars as a 1918 B&O heavyweight combination baggage and passenger car, three Rock Island commuter cars built in the 1920s, and a heavyweight day-coach railcar that originally served the Baltimore and Ohio Railroad through the 1950s. Using the same tracks as coal trains traveled in the late 1800s and early 1900s while moving coal to Central Ohio, Hocking Valley Scenic Railway offers daily trips through Hocking Valley and special event trips such as the Nelsonville Halloween, New Year's Eve Train and Fireworks, Elegant Dinner, Easter Bunny Train and Egg Hunt, and more.

Robbins Crossing, a completely restored 1850s-era Ohio village, is both a historic destination for those who like to take a step back in time as costumed interpreters show how life was lived back then and also a living lab for Hocking College students learning interpretive services. The village consists of several nineteenth-century buildings, including a general store and blacksmith shop as well as several old homes. You can arrive by car, by bike on the Hockhocking Adena Bike Path, or by train when the Hocking Valley Scenic Railway pulls to a stop there.

SHOP

Locally owned, the Nelsonville Quilt Company has everything a quilter could need, including twenty-four hundred bolts of material. For those who want to get away from it all and quilt in peace, Needles-n-Pines Retreat is dedicated to making it the perfect place for quilters to work.

The Nelsonville Emporium features the works of more than a hundred local craftspeople and artists with such goods as pottery, garden art, paintings, soaps, glassware, artisan chocolates, and wines, as well as a wide selection of tools, glazes, and clays for potters.

Major League Baseball outfielder Estel Crayton Crabtree, who lived in Nelsonville and is buried there, played for the Cincinnati Reds and the St. Louis Cardinals.

Actress Sarah Jessica Parker is probably best known as Carrie Bradshaw in the long-running TV series *Sex and the City*.

Dave Wyatt, Negro Leagues infielder and manager, was born in Nelsonville in 1871.

78

Portsmouth

The place where the Scioto River flows into the Ohio River, overlooking Kentucky, was once land occupied by the Ohio Hopewell, who constructed what is now known as the Portsmouth Earthworks, a sprawling prehistoric mound complex built millennia ago. Those mounds still remain, and Portsmouth, located at the confluence of the Scioto and Ohio Rivers, is a river port.

As an interesting aside, in 1897, the Enos Reed Pharmacy was the first store to offer Coca-Cola.

STAY

The Shawnee once lived on land that now makes up the sixty-thousand-acre Shawnee State Park, founding an important village called Lower Town, where the Ohio and Scioto Rivers joined together. As an aside, the meaning of the word Shawnee is "those who have the silver," as they traded that valuable metal. The landscape here is all rolling hills, forests, waterways, and valleys sculpted by wind and erosion. This beautiful park is part of the Appalachian foothills, which are called "Ohio's Little Smokies," and it offers an eighteen-hole golf course, camping sites, cabins, and a lodge with spectacular views.

EAT

Ohio's oldest brewery, the Portsmouth Brewing Company, opened back in 1843, built on the stone foundation of the former Ohio and Erie Canal.

Turkey Creek Lake

Handcrafted brews and a full menu are served in this wonderful brick (made locally when Portsmouth was big in brick manufacturing) building. It's definitely a trip to the past.

Patsy's Inn Restaurant has been a family favorite for good comfort cooking since opening in 1948.

Get cakes, cupcakes, cookies, and more at Scent from Heaven Bakery.

Grab breakfast and brunch at the Lofts, a sleek place for serious coffee and tea drinkers and those who want quick bites like sandwiches, bagels, and pastries.

Scioto Ribber offers great hickory-smoked ribs, chicken, and all sorts of barbecued dishes with great sides.

The Malt Shop is the place for grilled burgers and hand-dipped ice cream, sundaes, shakes, banana splits, soft-serve yogurt, and Flavor Burst ice cream—from a machine that can add up to eight flavors all in one cone.

PLAY

Walk beside history at Flood Wall Murals, painted by award-winning artist Robert Dafford, which show the story of Ohio from 1730 to 2002 in scenes painted almost twenty feet high and stretching 2,090 feet long.

Ohio River, Charles Street

See the skies at the Clark Planetarium.

The Vern Riffe Center for the Arts, located on the campus of Shawnee State University, offers a variety of entertainment, such as jazz, bag band shows, dance, dramatic performances, and Broadway performances.

In the historic Boneyfiddle district of Portsmouth, one of the earliest European settlements in Scioto County, the Boneyfiddle Museum of Military History pays homage to all veterans and military people who defended our country.

The Southern Ohio Museum, housed in a former Beaux-Arts–style bank in Portsmouth's trending downtown, contains a plethora of exhibits and displays, including two permanent collections—that of Clarence Holbrook Carter, an American Scene painter who was born in the city, and the *Art of the Ancients*, showcasing ten thousand prehistoric Native American objects from the Charles and William Wertz Collection. Along with those are three other galleries displaying exhibitions of both group and solo famous and emerging works from regional artists. The one-hundred-seat theater presents music and performing arts, and a docent-center tour program offers tours.

Stop for ice cream, burgers, pizza, subs, and footers and stay to play a round of golf at Buckeye Ice Cream.

On the National Register of Historic Places, the Philip Moore Stone House is just one of a few remaining southern Ohio primitive homes. Moore, a Revolutionary War veteran, built the home for his wife and their four children in 1797. Also described as the "Cradle of Methodism" and currently open for tours, the home was the meeting place for Methodist Circuit Riders as they worked on plans for the future of their church.

The 1810 House, so called because that's when the home of Aaron and Mary Kinney was completed, is now a museum featuring furniture and memorabilia dating back to the 1700s. It is open for tours.

The Portsmouth Earthworks are a large prehistoric mound complex constructed by the Ohio Hopewell culture, Indigenous Mound Builder peoples of eastern North America (100 BCE to 500 CE). The site was one of the largest earthwork ceremonial centers constructed by the Hopewell. Of the remaining Portsmouth Earthworks, only Mound Park is open to the public, and it includes the Horseshoe Mound, a large horseshoe enclosure, one of several listed on the National Register of Historic Places.

Two-time Olympic gold medalist Jim Thorpe played for the Portsmouth Shoe Steels football team toward the end of his career.

Leonard Slye, later to be crowned King of the Cowboys and star in numerous movies and TV shows as Roy Rogers, was born in Cincinnati in 1911 but landed, literally, in Portsmouth a year later, when his father and uncle built a houseboat and traveled up the Ohio River to this river port.

James Ashley, an abolitionist and political activist, was twenty-four when he settled in Portsmouth in 1848. When young, he had seen slaves chained together, forced to march to the Deep South, and children who were his age being sold. His hatred of slavery was such that Portsmouth, which at the time had a large proslavery faction, became a dangerous place for him and his family to live. For safety they moved to Toledo, where there were more like-minded individuals. Elected to Congress during the Civil War, he was one of the proponents of the Thirteenth Amendment, which made slavery illegal.

79

Rockbridge

Named after a natural sandstone bridge stretching one hundred feet long and ten to twenty feet wide over a tributary of the Hocking River, Rockbridge is an unincorporated community in Hocking County with a population of less than two hundred.

STAY

The 140-acre Glenlaurel: A Scottish Inn and Cottages offers luxury rooms, suites, crofts, and cottages, spa, as well as six- to seven-course dinners, an epicurean brunch, and a Scottish links golf course.

If traditional Sioux Native American tipis are your thing, At Boulders Edge Tipi Retreat has two, each set in the woods and able to accommodate ten.

EAT

An old-fashioned metal-sided diner with a large neon sign, Chelle's 33 Diner, formerly Sandy Sue's, is an easy stop for some American-style comfort food, like homemade chicken and noodles, sloppy joes, pizza, and burgers.

Rock climbing

Hocking Hills Canopy Tours include a late-night Moonshine Zip, a Zip and Climb, Zip and Rappel, and X-Tour, an extreme professionally guided tour through a cave, across the river, using a series of lines and towers. They also offer an on-the-ground Segway trek.

A deep and narrow gorge, one of the deepest in Ohio, only one hundred feet wide in places with cliffs soaring more than two hundred feet tall, Conkle's Hollow State Nature Preserve has hiking trails leading to such beautiful sites as the twenty-five-foot Conkle's Hollow Falls and the Chapel Cave, sometimes known as 21 Horses Cave.

Flower power happens every July at Lilyfest, a three-day event featuring over seventy fine artists and crafts-people exhibiting and demonstrating their art, a plethora of plants—water plants, annuals, and perennials—and master gardeners to answer questions. The festival is held at Bishop Educational Gardens.

Hocking Hills Canopy Tours

Butterfly Ridge

80

Stockport

Yes, there really was a Captain Hook (we didn't know that either), but he wasn't a pirate. Instead, he was a riverboat captain named Isaac Newton Hook who during the Civil War ferried supplies for the Union army. A resident of Stockport, he lived to a great age, having been born in 1819 and dying in 1906, and during his time on earth, he spent most of it on the Muskingum River as both a ship captain and a boatbuilder. Now he rests in style at the Old Brick Cemetery, having designed his own tombstone—a barrel-like contrivance with a rounded top, shaped that way some say to keep his wife from dancing on his grave.

The story of Captain Hook is just one aspect of this charming village on the Muskingum River, the state's longest continually navigable river because of the series of locks and dams put in place in 1841. Located in Morgan County, Stockport was founded in 1839 and named after a town in England.

STAY

The last of the many mills once lining the banks of the Muskingum River, the four-story historic Stockport Mill Inn, in operation since 1906, is both an inn and a restaurant. Enjoy their Sunday brunch with items (though they can change) such as chicken with homemade noodles, pot roast, baked steak, roast pork with herb stuffing, Cuban pork, and both a salad and a dessert bar. There's also a gift shop and a spa in what was the original train bin on the second floor. Each of the rooms is named after a

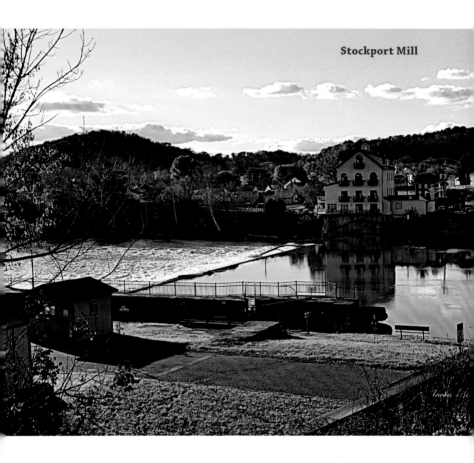

riverboat captain—and yes, Captain Hook's room accommodates eight, with a sitting room and stairs leading to a cupola. All the rooms have balconies with river views. This is definitely a bring-your-own-drink town because it's dry.

PLAY

Stockport is a birder's delight, with regular sightings of American bald eagles, pigeons roosting on the roof of the four-story post office, over forty species of songbirds, and an abundance of waterfowl. One great birding site is the Muskingum River State Park–Lock 6. The river is also great for fishing—think bass, saugeye, and shovelhead catfish. Muskellunge, those huge fish nicknamed muskies, were common once and still rarely might be spotted in the waters. Fishing is allowed from watercraft and at the locks on the Muskingum River.

Stockport Mill Inn

Big Bottom Memorial Park is a three-mile stretch of the Muskingum River flood plain commemorating the place where, in 1791, Lenape and Wyandot warriors tried to expel settlers from their lands, beginning what would become four years of warfare in the state. Approximately fourteen settlers were killed and several more captured. The park, listed on the National Register of Historic Places, has a twelve-foot marble obelisk, picnic tables, and informational signs depicting its history.

Enjoy fireworks, a parade, and homemade pies at the Fireman's Festival, which takes place the last weekend in July.

SOUTHWEST
OHIO

Clifton Mill

81

Clifton

Ohio wasn't yet a state in 1802 when Owen Davis, a veteran of the Revolutionary War, built a mill on a bluff overlooking the Little Miami River. Not only was it a beautifully scenic spot but more importantly, Davis chose a site where the Little Miami came crashing down twenty feet through a narrow gorge, creating a water powerhouse perfect for operating a mill.

When Davis's son-in-law, General Benjamin Whitehead, joined the family business, they built both a sawmill and a distillery nearby. If that sounds like an odd combination, consider this: drinking alcohol wasn't just a social occasion kind of thing back then. Water often carried dangerous and sometimes lethal bacteria. What were pioneers to do? Drink alcohol instead—something they did starting in the early morning until it was time for bed. Indeed, in the early 1800s, Americans guzzled over five gallons of pure alcohol per person on a yearly basis, compared to the average consumption of two gallons annually today. Millers like Davis and Whitehead who often paid in part by the grain they milled could turn around and distill it into whiskey and rye.

Other entrepreneurs were quick to erect their own mills along the river, and before long there were at least seven mills cutting lumber and producing linens, paper, and barrels within a mile of the Davis Mill.

Eight years after opening his mill, Davis sold the property to Colonel Robert Patterson, who sectioned the land into lots and changed the name from Davistown to Cliff Town, eventually shortened to Clifton. Patterson, a quartermaster during the War of 1812, obtained government contracts

Clifton Mill Gas Station Museum

to provide cloth from his woolen mill to make uniforms for the troops and cornmeal at his gristmill to feed them.

Times were good in other ways too as Clifton became a major stop on the Cincinnati, Lebanon, and Columbus Stagecoach Route, also known as the Accommodation Line, operating between 1827 to 1840. At its peak, the thriving village had a population three times as large as now, with blacksmith shops, weavers, shoemakers, papermakers, butchers, a hotel, a distillery, two grocers, a school, and two churches.

Technology was changing, and railroads began replacing stagecoaches, which were uncomfortable and very slow given the state of the roads. The fourteen miles between Springfield, Ohio, and Clifton could take five hours or more, and if the roads were bad or steep, often the passengers had to get out and walk.

The advent of the Little Miami Railroad at first looked like a boon for Clifton, which was a scheduled stop. But astute businessman William Mills, an attorney and judge who lived in nearby Yellow Springs, scored a loan to complete the railroad and had it rerouted through Yellow Springs, some three miles away, instead. No longer a transportation hub, Clifton experienced changing fortunes, but what's now the Clifton Mill continued to function.

In 1869, the Armstrong family built the mill still standing today, and it remained in operation longer than most, not closing until 1948 as the jobs mills did were replaced by factories. It was a common story. In the 1850s, there were more than one hundred thousand mills in America's thirty-one states.

Clifton might have met that fate except by chance and then hard work. Abandoned and forgotten, it was rediscovered by a hiker in 1962. Painstakingly restored, it is currently owned by the Satariano family.

For visitors, Clifton Mill, now the largest mill still operating in the US, offers a glimpse into this country's early pioneer history.

Clifton historical marker

EAT

The Restaurant at Clifton historic Clifton Mill, open for breakfast and lunch, serves homestyle meals and freshly made desserts, including cookies, pies, and such offerings as Chef Vinny's double chocolate ganache cake (a rich chocolate cake layered with velvety chocolate ganache) and flapjack cheesecake (with wild Maine blueberries and three tiers of maple cream and buttery cake).

PLAY

The Legendary Lights of Historic Clifton Mill, named in *USA Today*'s 10 Best Readers' Choice 2019 Travel Awards, is an extravaganza of sparkling lights—some four million. Running the entire month of December, the village attractions include a miniature village, Santa Claus, a toy collection, and a synchronized lights and music show on the covered bridge.

Take a stroll through the tiny village of Clifton. At center stage, the Old Clifton Schoolhouse, its bricks aged to a soft rose and its lawn dotted with flower beds and a gazebo, now houses the Shoebox Theatre. Side streets are lined with historic homes, and the Clifton Opera House, built in 1893, hosts live concerts and events on weekend evenings.

Located on a two-mile stretch of the Little Miami State and National Scenic River, the 268-acre Gorge State Nature Preserve, just west of the mill, is considered one of the most stunning dolomite and limestone gorges in Ohio. Known for its masses of wildflowers in the spring, the preserve has a nature center, trails, interpretative signs, and spectacular views of waterfalls and rapids.

SHOP

Weber's Antiques features one of the Midwest's largest collections of walnut and cherry early country furniture.

Artist Steve Robbins, owner of the Fish Decoy Company, hand carves wooden fish decoys.

NOTABLE

Football player and legendary coach Woody Hayes was born in Clifton in 1913. After serving in World War II, Hayes coached at Dennison and Miami University and then accepted the head coaching position at Ohio State University. He was among the first major college coaches to recruit and start African American players such as Jim Parker, who played both offensive and defensive tackle on Hayes's first national championship team. Hayes also filled assistant coaching positions with African Americans when he was at Ohio State University.

Isaac Kaufmann Funk, born in Clifton in 1838, cofounded the Funk and Wagnalls Company, publisher of *The Standard Dictionary of English Language* and the *Funk & Wagnalls Encyclopedia*.

82

Franklin

The Great Miami River flows through Franklin in Warren County, crossed by the Lion Bridge. The city, founded by General William C. Schenck in 1796, was named after Benjamin Franklin.

Twenty-nine years later, construction of the Miami and Erie Canal commenced. Following the Great Miami River, it brought prosperity, including a pork slaughterhouse, barrel-making factory, sawmill, and whiskey distillery to its two shores. Franklin had its racy side and was known in the 1850s for breeding racehorses, including Nightingale, a chestnut mare sired by Mambrino and Wood's Hambletonian, which in 1893 set a three-mile harness racing record of six minutes, fifty-five and a half seconds.

In an interesting aside, Dr. Absalom Death was elected as the city's first mayor at a tavern meeting in 1837 and later became director of a medical college in Cincinnati. In its history, two doctors in Franklin have been named Dr. Death. They also had a fire chief who in 1907 walked into the jail and shot a prisoner who supposedly had had a romantic liaison with the chief's wife. And the fortunes of the town plunged when a longtime bank teller absconded with a large sum of money, wiping out the fortunes of many of the town's businesses and citizens.

EAT

In business for more than three decades, Mom's Restaurant serves the type of food you'd expect with a place of that name—good old homestyle cooking like chicken and dumplings, country-fried steak, mashed potatoes, peas, and macaroni and cheese. They even have their own gravy maker—what could be more wonderful than that?

The Franklin Tavern has an open mic night, good sandwiches, burgers, an assortment of tavern dogs (no, not the kind that bark), brews, wines by the glass, and cocktails.

PLAY

Located on the western side of the Great Miami River, the Mackinaw Historic District is a stunning collection of well-curated and preserved homes. On the National Register of Historic Places, the homes span the decades between 1825 and 1925. A colonial revival mansion stands in the heart of the district.

The Spirituality Circle, which promotes spiritual knowledge, wisdom, inner peace, and tranquility, is home to both the Museum of Spiritual Art and the Oneness Harmony Center, which hosts open meditation sessions.

The Franklin Area Historical Society, dedicated to preserving the history of Franklin and Warren County, maintains museums at two historic sites: The Log Cabin Post Office, commissioned by Thomas Jefferson and built in 1805, is one of the oldest standing post offices in Ohio and displays relics from that era. The Harding Museum, a colonial revival mansion in the heart of the Mackinaw Historic District, is the former home of the late Major General Forrest Harding.

NOTABLE

Ronald Peters, a café owner in Franklin, was alleged to be the principal bookmaker for baseball player Pete Rose.

83

Germantown

Established in 1804, Germantown was founded by, as you would expect, German-speaking settlers from Berks County, Pennsylvania, only one of whom spoke English. That was Phillip Gunckel, who chose the spot between Little Twin and Big Twin Creeks as a perfect spot for his gristmill.

Let's just say it wasn't a healthy-living crowd, at least when it came to what they produced—whiskey and tobacco. Mudlick Distillery, founded in 1847, was considered to be the largest in the country, turning out thirty to forty barrels a day. The whiskey mash produced as waste annually fed twelve hundred hogs and four hundred heads of cattle and maybe produced a much-flavored meat. The distillery's inventory—around twenty thousand barrels of aging whiskey—was worth about $1 million. It all got wiped out in the Great Flood of 1913 when the Miami River overflowed, and the family decided not to rebuild.

As for cigars, well, what else can you say? At one time, Germantown had five cigar-manufacturing factories and twelve storage warehouses.

But there were healthy aspects to life in Germantown, the mineral springs—the same ones that added so much flavor to the whiskey—were said to be healthy, and people visited in hopes of curing what ailed them. Of course, with all that whiskey and all those cigars, maybe they went home more ill than when they started.

Florentine Hotel

EAT

Shortly after establishing Germantown, Philip Gunckel opened the Florentine Hotel around 1814. A stagecoach stop, the three-story brick building saw such famous people as Henry Clay and John Quincy Adams, to name a couple. Now one of the oldest inns in the state, the Florentine Hotel maintains much of its original charm, including the fireplace in the first-floor banquet room, where travelers on cold winter days would gather to keep warm, a magnificent staircase, and massive wood beams. One of their most popular dishes is the beer-battered, lightly fried orange roughy sandwich, and there are gourmet burgers on the menu, but this is also the place to get excellent cuts of chops and steaks.

The Creamery at Market and Main is a cozy space perfect for sipping your morning coffee, nibbling on a pastry, and gearing up for a new day. Their offerings include specialty coffees, Young's Jersey Dairy ice cream, smoothies, Piper and Leaf teas, doughnuts, pastries, and savories.

PLAY

We're all Germans during the Germantown Pretzel Festival, a free event held the last weekend in September for over forty years. Held in Veterans Memorial Park, the festival offers a lot of other foods, like ribs, funnel cakes, Chinese, and Cajun, but let's face it—it's all about the pretzel,

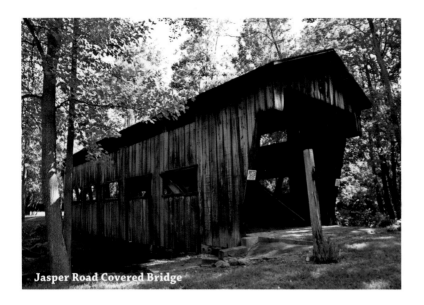
Jasper Road Covered Bridge

which includes those stuffed with jalapeño cheese, cheddar cheese, and cream cheese; pizza-flavored pretzels; and pretzel buns to kick your sandwiching game up a notch or two.

The By-Jo Theatre opened its doors at the beginning of the 1900s, and though it's gone through several low periods in which it was closed for several years at a time, it's restored and open today. Buy a ticket and some popcorn and settle down to watch a movie.

Crossing over Little Twin Creek and open only to pedestrian traffic, the Jasper Road Covered Bridge was built in 1870, and according to the Southern Ohio Covered Bridge Association, it's the only one built with an inverted bowstring truss, similar to that of suspension bridges.

At the Germantown Metropark, part of the Twin Valley Conservation Corridor, you can stand on the platform at the Overlook to view Twin Creek Valley, hike along the fifteen miles of trails through prairies and meadows, pass water-carved ravines, and immerse yourself in the largest swath of old-growth forest in Montgomery County. Before European settlers arrived, this is what forests were like: tall trees, dense foliage, and the feel of ancient natural wonders.

84

Greenville

A t one time Green Ville (that's how they spelled it back then, before the two words were merged) was truly considered the edge of the western frontier. Annie Oakley was born here, and in the Treaty of Green Ville, General "Mad" Anthony Wayne forced defeated Native Americans to sign a document ceding their lands to the ever-increasing number of settlers moving west.

Now this town of thirteen thousand in Southwest Ohio is definitely more Midwest than out West, but it is on the cutting edge as a destination for food, culture, and history. It's the only place in the world where KitchenAid's iconic stand mixer is made. And Greenville has over eighty buildings on the National Register of Historic Places, as well as four historic districts. The downtown is an enchanting blend of buildings dating back to the 1800s, restored and now eclectic restaurants, galleries, and shops. And, as befitting a town that has made KitchenAid stand mixers since 1941, it boasts a thriving culinary scene.

STAY

Enjoy goodies such as the butter crumb coffee cake at Wayman's Corner Bed and Breakfast, a restored 1925 American foursquare building. Decorated in Victorian styles but with twenty-first-century conveniences, the four-bedroom inn features three porches and a lovely corner garden blooming with roses, petunias, phlox, mums, and herbs.

The downtown has a dozen or so eateries offering menus ranging from down-home to upscale esoteric. So get your forks ready. It's time to dine.

Prime rib chili with a farmers' market salad; Detroit-style deep-dish pizzas; chicken and waffles made with bacon; macaroni, cheese, and walnuts; shrimp and grits; candied bacon; and banana pepper calamari are among the many offerings at the Merchant House, located in a historic building on Broadway. The owners completely renovated it, revealing brick walls, stained-glass windows, and glossy wood floors and adding a wall-sized photo of Greenville one hundred years ago that shows what Broadway, the city's main street, was like a century ago.

Get coffee any way you like it—frozen blended espresso, caramel brûlée latte, over-ice espresso, mochas, lattes, espressos, and creative café brews like the Squirrelly Pig latte (espresso and steamed milk with toasted marshmallow and raspberry syrups)—as well as noncoffee drinks at A&B Coffee.

Maid Rite Sandwich Shop, a small hole-in-the-wall diner that opened in 1934, is so ingrained in the city's culture that even though it is squat and nondistinctive, it has its own postcard for sale in the downtown Greenville's Welcome Center. It's a burger joint that's not really quite a burger place. Instead, they're famed for their loose meat steamed ground beef burgers. Yes, it's confusing, but try one and you'll understand. But get there early, as the line of cars gets extremely long around lunchtime. If you can score a seat inside, be sure to do so either at the chrome-lined counter, which stretches almost the width of the restaurant, or the line of tables opposite. It's not a big place by any means, which means you can watch big vats of meat being prepared for sandwiches. Is it worth the hassle? Definitely. Their burgers—ahem, let's say loose meat burgers—are moist and tender and covered with cheese and grilled onions.

Bathrooms are out back. It's that kind of place—even more so because what look like white and tan specks from a distance are in reality pieces of chewing gum, already chewed, on a wall specifically designated for just that. If that sounds less than appetizing, not to worry—it's on a brick wall outside the building.

Cinnamon rolls, peanut butter scotcharoos, chocolate twist cake, coffee streusel cake, turtle brownies, chocolate chip edible cookie dough, snickerdoodle cookies, chunky raspberry cheesecake, Highlander Grogg coffee, and more are all on the menu at All at Beanz Buttercream Bakery.

Follow the Darke County Whiskey, Wine & Ale Trail, a journey visiting charming towns and villages throughout the county with stops at three wineries, two breweries, and one distillery.

PLAY

The thirty-five-thousand-square-foot Garst Museum and National Annie Oakley Center includes the leading compendium of the life of the famed female sharpshooter, who was born in the area and supported her family by selling fur skins from the animals she shot. Her skills were such that she became a lead in Buffalo Bill's Wild West Show. See posters, photos of her husband, Frank Butler, and the long rifle she used in her shows. Other major exhibits include the Treaty of Green Ville and "Mad" Anthony Wayne, Tecumseh and Native Americans, and Lowell Thomas, as well as an extensive military collection, period American furnishings, county history, and agricultural artifacts. The museum is known for its well-staffed genealogy research library.

SHOP

Print out the floor-by-floor map of Bear's Mill from their website and take a self-guided tour of the fully functioning gristmill, which was built in 1844 and is on the National Register of Historic Places. Buy freshly ground flours and cornmeal at their small gift shop and admire the works of local and regional artists at the Art of Mill Gallery. The mill grounds have several walking paths following the Greenville River, the source of the mill's power; lookouts over the river; and a war memorial—designed using the dome from the old county courthouse—honoring Darke County veterans who died in Vietnam.

There are 118 acres of forest, wetlands, and prairie to wander through at the Shawnee Prairie Preserve and Nature Center. At the Nature Center, peruse the displays and visit the eighteenth-century log house and blacksmith shop.

Annual events include Greenville Farm Power of the Past, Hometown Holiday Horse Parade, Historic Bears Mill's Candlelight Walk Open House, and both a downtown and cemetery ghost walk.

85

Harveysburg

A Quaker village platted by William Harvey in 1829, Harveysburg almost immediately thrived with such commerce as a pork-packing plant, bank, tin shop, gristmills, hardware store, and blacksmith shop, as well as a dry goods store owned by Harvey. Like most Quaker communities, it was also staunchly abolitionist. For instance, Elizabeth Harvey and her husband, Dr. Jesse Harvey, established the Harveysburg Free Black School, the first free African American school in Ohio, open to any child no matter their race or heritage. The school closed in 1909, but the building remains and is now home to the Harveysburg Community Historical Society. As one might expect of a Quaker village, Harveysburg was an important stop on the Underground Railroad for freedom seekers on routes from Kentucky to Cincinnati and then north through Ohio to Detroit and then on to Canada.

PLAY

It doesn't take much imagination to believe you've stumbled into an authentic sixteenth-century English village at the annual Ohio Renaissance Festival held each year for nine weekends, starting on Labor Day weekend. Like the fairs of old, there's lot of entertainment—jousting knights in full amour, a presiding Queen Elizabeth I, and fifteen stages presenting around one hundred shows daily, with a full lineup of musicians, dancers, comedians, jugglers, sword fighters, storytellers, and hundreds of other performers dressed in Renaissance garb. More than 150 artisans

Ohio Renaissance Festival

demonstrate, display, and sell their wares, from blacksmiths to glass-blowers, weavers, and stone carvers. Who knows what you'll find to take home.

They ate big long ago—so look for authentic dishes such as giant turkey legs, bread-bowl stews, abundant ales and wines, and such modern fare as barbecue wings, wraps, and vegetarian offerings.

And who would want to miss sword fighting, tournaments, and acrobatic displays?

NOTABLE

Jennie McCowen, born in 1845 in Harveysburg, was a triple whammy—an American physician, writer, and medical journal editor as well as a lecturer and ardent supporter of women's right to vote. She spoke at the 1893 World's Columbian Exposition in Chicago, delivering an address on "Progress in Child-Saving Work" in the Congress on Social and Moral Reform. Among her many lectures, she covered such topics as "Preventing Insanity," "Prevention of Impurity among Children," and "The Relationship between Intemperance and Insanity."

86

Lebanon

Ichabod Corwin (you've got to love that name), the first European to settle in what now is Lebanon, built a cabin on the north branch of Turtle Creek in 1796. Six years later, Corwin, who was the uncle of Ohio governor Thomas Corwin, laid out the town along with Silas Hurin, Ephraim Hathaway, and Samuel Manning. Within the Cincinnati metropolitan area, Lebanon retains its small-town feel with a wide main street lined with historic buildings.

That it's not a major city is credited to the "Shaker curse." And no, we had never heard of it either, but it seems that the industrious but celibate Shakers, once a major cultural and religious movement in the United States but now almost extinct, started a community called Union Village near where Corwin's cabin had been. Some of the townspeople were incensed by this development, while Cincinnatians were kinder. The Shakers, shaken by the violence of those living in Lebanon, enacted the rare but maybe very effective Shaker curse on Lebanon and blessed Cincinnati. The latter flourished while Lebanon remained a small country town.

It may be a whole lot smaller than Cincy, but Lebanon is still an amazing destination for those who like history, great food, shopping, and a sense of time preserved in amber.

STAY

It cost Jonas Seaman, newly arrived from New Jersey, four dollars for a license to run a "house of Public Entertainment." We don't know how

Doc's Place

much for the sign of a golden lamb he hung outside what would be a stagecoach stop, inn, and restaurant, but it was necessary because many people couldn't read back then and recognized such signs instead.

More than two centuries later, the Golden Lamb, the state's oldest continually run restaurant and inn, is a standout magnificent red brick building overlooking Broadway (the main street in Lebanon), a major destination, and a who's who when it comes to famous people who have stayed there. That list includes twelve presidents, including Ulysses S. Grant and Warren G. Harding, as well as authors Mark Twain, Charles Dickens, and Harriet Beecher Stowe, author of *Uncle Tom's Cabin* and an avid abolitionist. We understand that Dickens, who arrived around 1:00 p.m. on Wednesday, April 4, 1842, after a five-hour trip by stagecoach from Cincinnati, wasn't happy to find that the inn was a temperance hotel at the time and so couldn't provide his favorite brandy or any other spirits. No worries about that anymore.

EAT

The Golden Lamb is famed for many of their menu items, including fried chicken, sauerkraut balls, Sister Lizzie's Sugar Shaker pie (from the aforementioned Union Village and named by *USA Today* as the Best Pie in Ohio), and yeast rolls made from a recipe first used in the early 1930s by Robert and Virginia Jones, whose family still owns the inn. Their turkey dinners at Thanksgiving are very popular and have been since Abraham Lincoln made it an official national holiday in 1863.

If you can't make it for Thanksgiving, not to worry—roast turkey and all the trimmings are on the menu year-round. Those are among the historic-dining menu options—dishes from the past like noodles and ale cheese, sauerkraut balls, fried chicken, and hickory-smoked prime rib. Burgers, salads, sandwiches, soups, and appetizers such as bacon jam and house-made biscuits give diners a wide range of delicious choices. In warm weather, there's dining on the veranda and sidewalk seating.

You can find the same menu items but in a more casual setting downstairs at the inn's Blackhorse Tavern, which serves a variety of casual dishes, like sauerkraut balls and fried chicken.

Since 1969, the Village Ice Cream Parlor and Restaurant, with its white tile floors, wrought-iron chairs, and a lengthy counter, has been serving ice cream in a number of flavors, house-made desserts, and frozen yogurts.

Golden Lamb

PLAY

Amazingly, Ichabod Corwin's cabin survives and is now on the grounds of Berry Intermediate School on North Broadway. It is marked with a monument erected by the Warren County Historical Society.

Hop aboard the Lebanon, Mason, and Monroe Railroad (LMM Railroad) for a one-hour scenic train ride through the countryside. Among the cars is one made by the Pullman Company in 1930 and said to have had a famous passenger—singer Frank Sinatra—on the Lackawanna in New Jersey. Throughout the year, LMM Railroad also offers special events and themed rides, including the Easter Bunny, Summer Steam Train, and Wine and Cheese Train.

Home to the single largest display of Shaker artifacts in the world as well as a nationally recognized research library housing Shaker journals, the stately three-story Harmon Museum and Art is housed in the twenty-eight-thousand-square-foot Harmon Hall.

The Shaker Museum located on the fourth floor of the Golden Lamb displays the lifestyle of the Shakers of Union Village in a series of rooms. In contrast to, say, De Witt Clinton, the governor of New York who stayed here for the opening of the Ohio Canal in a room with a lace-canopied four-poster bed, richly patterned wallpaper, and polished antique maple furniture, the Shakers lived austere lives. Nothing decorative here, just plain and simple, designed to get the job done.

Considered one of the finest examples of Greek Revival architecture in the Midwest, the Glendower Mansion was built in 1836 and is open for tours. The docents, knowledgeable about the home itself—all fourteen opulent rooms; the mid-nineteenth-century regal furnishings, including a silver sugar cellar with a lock, as that sweet stuff was very expensive back then; and the beautifully kept gardens—bring history alive during the tours.

Twice a year, Warren County Historical Society holds candlelight cemetery tours. It also hosts other events, such as Music at the Museum, garden tours, antique shows, art exhibits, and teas.

Celebrate! The annual Lebanon Country Music Festival is for stomping in the street and is held in June. The three-day Blues Fest held in downtown Lebanon is an annual summer winner.

SHOP

Local food producers—beekeepers, orchardists, farmers, and others—bring their wares to the Jam and Jelly Lady, who almost magically transforms them into delicious preserves, chutneys, jams, and jellies. You can sign up for classes and learn to make your own or show up for one of their Girls' Nights Out, a food-centric event held regularly (check out their website for dates: https://jamandjellylady.com/) with gourmet food items and nibbles.

If you love popcorn, then Anna's Gourmet Popcorn is for you. Besides traditional flavors like caramel and cheddar, there are flavors of the month, which in the past have included Neapolitan (a mix of strawberry, vanilla, and chocolate popcorn) and loaded baked potato—butter, cheddar, sour cream, and chives with bacon.

Burlap and Burch has a great selection of home goods.

Check out Hidden Valley Orchards, in business for over sixty years, for a wide range of fresh produce and such home decor items as Stoneworks Pottery, Candleberry Candles, farm gifts, freshly baked pastries and breads, local jams and jellies, and seasonal butters. Take a break from shopping for such sips as hard cider, bubble tea, fruit slushies, lattes, or lemonade at the Unique Taprooms at Hidden Valley Orchards, or stop by the barn for soft-serve ice cream.

87

Loveland

We're going to hazard a guess that Loveland is the only small town in Ohio with a real castle. But even without the Historic Loveland Castle and Museum Chateau Laroche, this pretty village, once known as the "Little Switzerland of the Miami Valley" because of its beauty, is a special spot. Located on the Little Miami River, the historic downtown bustles with an eclectic mix of shops, restaurants, a community theater, an art gallery, and, no matter the time of year, plenty of outdoor activities for those so inclined.

Settled in 1795 by Colonel Thomas Paxton, the village was ultimately named after general-store owner and postmaster James Loveland in the mid-1800s. The advent of the railroad caused a boom in population and prosperity. But that wasn't the only mode of transportation.

Its location on the banks of the 111-mile Little Miami River, which flows through five Southwest Ohio counties before joining the Ohio River east of Cincinnati, made Loveland an important stopping point for freedom seekers on the Underground Railroad. Now the Little Miami, a National Scenic River, attracts kayakers and paddlers. For those who like traveling on dry land, there's the Loveland Bike Trail, part of the Little Miami Scenic Trail, which, at 78.1 miles, is the third-longest paved trail in the United States.

STAY

The twenty-eight-acre Lake Isabella is great for fishing, and the canoe and kayak launch located on the lake offers access to the Little Miami River. There are also boat rentals and twenty-four primitive camping spots.

Loveland Candies

EAT

The downtown has a plethora of places to eat, many within walking distance of or right on the trail. Depending on what you have a hankering for, there's Narrow Path Brewing Company, a five-barrel brewing house; the dog-friendly Wicked Pickle; brick-oven pizzas at the Works, located in a 1905 water filling station for steam engines; and patio dining during warm weather at Paxson's Grill, located in one of the oldest buildings in the downtown and right on the Little Miami Scenic Trail.

Not to be missed, Graeter's has been making ice cream for a century and a half. Indulge your literary side during poetry teatime, order breakfast and lunch or coffee and pastries, and stock up on locally made food items at Hometown Café Loveland.

The three-story Bishop's Quarter offers multiple levels of fun and New Orleans–style food, bourbon, craft brews, live music, and great views of the trail and downtown.

Enjoy Cappy's Hour on Tuesdays through Saturdays at Cappy's Wine and Spirits. It's just one of their many weekly events, such as Wine Wednesday, a weekly wine tasting; Monday through Wednesday's Kick the Keg, with discounts on select kegs; and Pint Night on Thursdays, featuring a different brewery each week.

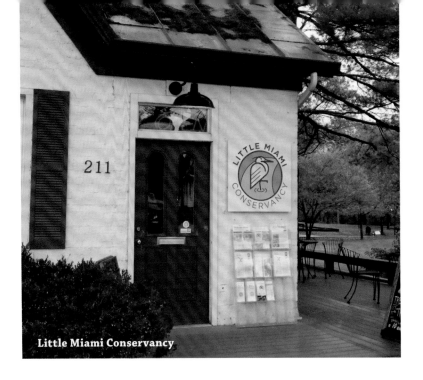

Little Miami Conservancy

You can't go wrong whatever your choices at the family-owned Holtman's Donuts, in business for more than eighty years. But may we make suggestions? Consider such diet busters as their yeast doughnuts with toppings like maple icing with bacon or pecans or the white icing topped with Lucky Charms; cake doughnuts like their red velvet topped with cream cheese icing; and buckeye doughnuts because, well, this is Ohio, the Buckeye State.

PLAY

Harry D. Andrews believed that the world would be a much better place if we could go back in time to the days of yore when chivalry and knighthood defined society. A medic during World War I, he attempted to do his part. He started constructing the Historic Loveland Castle and Museum Chateau Laroche in the 1920s and devoted the rest of his long life to this heroic effort, creating the Knights of the Golden Trail. For a nominal entrance fee, visitors can view Harry's superb collection of ancient weaponry, explore the castle's architecture, picnic on the castle grounds and elaborate gardens, and participate in games designed to test the mettle of the stouthearted and brave.

Check out the Little Miami Scenic Trail Visitor's Center in Nisbet Park for information and amenities like restrooms, picnic tables, an amphitheater, and a free primitive campground. The seventy-eight-mile trail, once the railroad bed for the Pennsylvania Railroad, follows the Little Miami River and passes through such historic towns as Lebanon, Milford, and Newtown. Loveland Canoe and Kayak and Loveland Bike Rental make it easy for those who don't own their own to explore both the trail and the river.

Bring a swimsuit, as there's a small sandy beach in Nisbet Park for cooling off in the river.

For the arts, there's Loveland Stage Company, an award-winning community theater; the annual Loveland Art Show; Loveland Art Studios on Main; and the Greater Loveland Historical Society Museum.

SHOP

Plaid Room Records offers over twenty thousand vinyl records to choose from and also functions as home to the Coleman Records label and live music venue.

Grab a bag full of candies at Loveland Sweet Shoppe, an adorable confectionery full of house-made treats.

Every Tuesday evening from 3:00 p.m. to 7:00 p.m., the Loveland Farmers' Market is the place to meet and shop for local produce as well as wares made by regional artisan and cottage industry vendors.

For antiques, check out Memento Mori.

NOTABLE

Salmon P. Chase, chief justice of the Supreme Court, had a summer place here; professional golfer Bob Lohr is from Loveland, as are Broadway star Wendy Barrie-Wilson and TV host and former Cincinnati mayor Jerry Springer.

88

Morrow

Valley Vineyards Winery and Brewery, the second-largest winery in the state of Ohio, isn't in a big city or a popular tourist destination but is instead located in Morrow, a small village (population around twelve hundred) in Warren County named after former state governor Jerome Morrow. Part of the Ohio River Valley American Viticulture Area (AVA), it is here that fertile limestone soil and moderate temperatures along the Ohio River create a rich growing region for wine grapes. That's one of the reasons that Valley Vineyards, in business for a half century, produces award-winning wines. Valley Vineyards is one of the many wineries that are part of the Ohio River Valley AVA, where Nicholas Longworth planted native varieties of Alexander and Isabelle grapes in 1823 after his European grapes failed to mature. Two years later, he planted catawba grapes, and they flourished—so much so that Longworth, an attorney, quit his practice after tasting the first wine made from his grapes and became a full-time winemaker.

Flash forward. The Ohio River Valley AVA is the second-largest in the US, covering 16,640,000 acres in a large swath of land that also includes sections of Indiana, Ohio, Kentucky, and West Virginia. The largest is the Upper Mississippi Valley.

EAT

Growing over twenty-eight grape varietals, Valley Vineyards also makes microbrews and has weekend cookouts where guests can grill their own

Valley Vineyards Winery and Brewery

Valley Vineyards Winery and Brewery

steak or salmon to enjoy with sides the restaurant offers, such as their pizza salad or green beans almandine, and made-on-site beverages.

Valley Vineyards also teams up with Morgan's Canoe and Kayak on select dates to offer a "Twilight Canoe & Dinner for Two" package, which features a canoe float trip down the Little Miami Scenic River and a Valley Vineyards cookout

Born Goldie Merie Ireland on May 13, 1889, in Morrow, Merie Earle played Maude Gormley from 1972 to 1979 in the TV series *The Waltons*. She also guest starred on such popular sitcoms as *Petticoat Junction*, *Green Acres*, *The Beverly Hillbillies*, *Bewitched*, *The Bob Newhart Show*, and *All in the Family* and appeared frequently on *The Tonight Show Starring Johnny Carson*.

89

Oregonia

Europeans first settled here in 1802, establishing a mill on the Little Miami River. By 1820, the settlement had become known as Freeport. Around 1845, the Little Miami Railroad arrived; a year later, a post office opened and was known by the name Oregon. Almost forty years later, in 1882, the name of the village officially became Oregonia. That seems like a long time to come up with a name.

It's a small hamlet with a lot happening, from history to outdoor adventures.

STAY

Terrapin Village is a bed and breakfast and music venue.

Morgan's Riverside Campground is a family-oriented campground with riverside camping spots, group camping, and Amish-built cabins on the Little Miami River and next to the Little Miami Bike Trail.

EAT

Become a Double Donk Champ (let's just say it means eating a lot of food) and win a T-shirt at the Little River Bar and Grill. Located just off the Little Miami Bike Trail and the Little Miami River in downtown Oregonia, it offers a beer garden and dishes made from family recipes. It's a great place for bikers, bicyclists, and paddlers, but if you come by car or foot, that's OK too.

Morgan's Outdoor Adventure

Caesar Creek State Park

PLAY

Zip your way through history through and above the canopy of the Little Miami River Valley. Designed as an adventurous and educational canopy tour, Ozone Zipline Adventures features a course of twelve zip lines as high as two hundred feet in the air. It's educational as well, offering an overview of the valley's early history, including its Native American earthworks, fossils dating back five hundred million years, and local flora and fauna. And, seriously, don't miss their Zipping from Zombies.

Rising 260 feet above the Little Miami River, the Fort Ancient Earthworks and Nature Preserve, listed on the National Register of Historic Places, is an important part of Ohio's prehistory—a term

Ozone Zipline Adventures

referring to the time before the development of written records, which in Ohio was around the mid-1600s. Enclosed by embankment walls ranging from five to twenty-three feet high (they were made by a multitude of people filling and dumping baskets of dirt over and over again), the 126-foot plateau represents over two thousand years of Hopewell Native American history.

Visit the nine-thousand-square-foot Museum at Fort Ancient for its introduction of the various stages of history, including outside gardens where crops from one to two millennia ago are again growing.

Morgan's Canoe and Outdoor Adventures at Fort Ancient is located in the Fort Ancient Gorge of the Little Miami River, where the water ranges from calm, making it perfect for swimming, to easily negotiable rapids.

The challenging Silver Moccasin Trail is a rehabbed hiking trail that once stretched fourteen miles between Fort Ancient and Lebanon, Ohio, and now comprises three miles of rugged walking through the Little Miami River Gorge.

At 239 feet tall and spanning 2,252 feet across the Little Miami River, the Jeremiah Morrow Bridge (named after an Ohio governor) is the tallest bridge in the state, connecting Fort Ancient earthworks to the village of Oregonia.

90

Oxford

When George Washington crossed the Delaware River, a sturdy white oak, already two hundred years old, stood near Harkers Run, a meandering stream flowing through what was then an uninhabited wildness. Flash forward twenty years or so, President Washington's signature on an act of Congress led to the founding of Miami University. More than two centuries later, you can stroll along Harkers Run Trail in Miami University Natural Areas and pass by this ancient oak, now the site of a geocache, one of many located nearby.

Oxford, with its Victorian-era downtown and Georgian-style university buildings, still retains much of its outdoor charm, offering places to explore both forest and city, perfect for shaking off the winter cobwebs and enjoying the best of spring, summer, and fall.

STAY

The Victorian-style White Garden Inn, a nine-thousand-square-foot bed and breakfast snuggled in the hilly landscape surrounding Oxford, is conveniently situated between Hueston Woods State Park and Miami University. The house, designed to fulfill the owners' dreams of owning a bed and breakfast, is surrounded by a lush white garden.

A full-service hotel, the Elms is conveniently located in uptown Oxford, within walking distance of many of the shops, green spaces, and restaurants as well as the University of Miami.

Black Covered Bridge

PLAY

Download the walking-tour maps of Oxford's University Historic District, a collection of thirty-three stately nineteenth- and twentieth-century homes grouped around three sides of University Square, including the Lottie Moon Home, a majestic Italianate. Maybe most interesting is the house's backstory: both Lottie and her sister Ginny were Confederate spies.

As long as you're downloading, the Miami University Natural Areas comprise one thousand acres with seventeen miles of trails and lots to explore. In the springtime, take a guided tour or just a walk on your own to see the extensive wildflower garden—more than sixty species—at Silvoor Biological Sanctuary. Visit the log cabin built in 1805 by Zachariah Price DeWitt, an early settler who came with his wife and seven kids from Kentucky for the cheap land and ended up village treasurer, a captain during the War of 1812, co-owner of the Mansion House Hotel, and founder of the Masonic Lodge.

Dating back to 1868, the Black Covered Bridge is one of just a few reminders of Southwest Ohio and is the only covered bridge in Butler County on its original site. The bridge offers a charming peek into rural agricultural history.

EAT

Mahlzeit, German for good eating, is what Steinkeller, modeled after a German bier hall, is all about. Done in a Bavarian style with highly polished dark wood, the eatery offers such menu items as bratwursts, spaetzle, Reuben sandwiches, and sides like Münchner pickles—dill wedges hand dipped in beer batter.

Check out the daily specials at Bodega or go for such popular staples as their chili mac, a creative dish consisting of a cup of chili topped with layers of their signature spicy macaroni and cheese, sour cream, and shredded cheese.

With Giant muffins, yummy cinnamon rolls, chai lattes, sun-kissed lavender tea blend, and Skinny Piggy Kombucha, Kofenya, an independent coffee shop, is the place to go for a cup of joe.

SHOP

You'll love the eclectic gifts, women's clothing and accessories, and home decor at the Apple Tree.

Check out Bird House Antiques for a long list of collectibles and vintage, hard-to-find-antiques, including primitives and Hummels. Unique objects include both Miami University Redhawks and the scarcer Redskins collectible items. There's more, including glassware; Coca-Cola memorabilia; hunting, fishing, and other sporting gear; turquoise and coral Native American jewelry; and a lot more.

For works by local artists, stop by the Art Shop. Or become an artist yourself: choose a clay object of your choice and create your own work of art at You're Fired.

91

Ripley

A small village (population under two thousand) overlooking the Ohio River, Ripley is a stop on the Ohio River Scenic Byway—the longest National Scenic Byway in the country. Almost two centuries ago, it was a major stop on the Underground Railroad as well. That history is still present in the buildings that served as stations for escaping slaves. Ripley's fifty-five-acre historic district, most likely the largest in the state for a village its size, showcases its history through the years, starting from before it was platted in 1812.

Founded by Revolutionary War colonel James Poage, a staunch abolitionist, Ripley soon drew in other like-minded folks. Two of those were John Rankin, a Presbyterian minister, and Dr. Alexander Campbell, Ripley's first doctor and the state's first abolitionist, who freed his slaves after moving to Ohio in 1803. Hatred for the two was so intense that slaveholders offered rewards for their abduction or murder.

Ripley's Historic District is considered the best-preserved antebellum river town in Ohio.

STAY

When the riverbanks were all clear of slave hunters and owners, as well as their tracking hounds, the owners of what is now called the Signal House sounded the all clear for passengers on the Underground Railroad. The mansion, circa 1830, is a marvelous bed and breakfast; all of its rooms

John Rankin House

offer views of the river, and its three porches and two parlors are perfect for quiet time.

The Amish-built Eagle Creek Country Cabins offer privacy, as they're situated on 1.5-acre wooded lots fronted with eighteen- to twenty-foot-deep stretches of Eagle Creek.

Logan's Gap Camping Resort has both RV sites and primitive camping, as well as such amenities as a pool, playground, fishing dock, and miniature golf course. There are also camping sites at the Ripley Boat Club.

EAT

A restored 1840s building with fantastic views of the Ohio River, Cohearts Riverhouse offers a sense of history, lovely views—from both the screened-in upstairs porch and the first floor—and good food: steaks, ribs, salads, and desserts.

Enjoy watching the boats move down the river and race at the Ripley Boat Club, known for their burgers and broasted chicken.

Dairy Yum-Yum, a family-style diner, serves big portions of country food, such as biscuits and gravy, mushroom steak, chicken livers, and blackberry cobbler. They're open for breakfast, lunch, and dinner.

Union Township Library

PLAY

The award-winning Kinkead Ridge Winery, a stop on the Oho River Valley Wine Trail, gets its name from William Kinkead, who settled on this land toward the very end of the eighteenth century. The current winery property includes a Gothic Revival home built in 1880 and vineyards, as well as an indoor tasting room and outdoor patio.

Once the farm belonging to Kinkead's great-great-grandfather, the Meranda-Nixon Winery produces premium wines in what was one of the largest grape-growing regions in the country during the 1800s. On the second Saturday of the month, the winery hosts a steak and salmon dinner featuring a bottle of their wine that pairs well with the meal. They also offer wine tours and tastings.

In 1828, Rankin founded Ripley College, and many of its students, often hailing from Ohio, Kentucky, and southern states, had antislavery beliefs. This school became a meeting ground for many other individuals who were against slavery. A decade later, a student named Ulysses S. Grant enrolled in Ripley College.

The red brick home of John and Jean Rankin, built in 1828, sits atop Liberty Hill overlooking seven bends (on a clear day) of the Ohio River. A National Historic Landmark and Underground Railroad station, the house still has the original woodwork as well as items belonging to the Rankin family, including the family Bible.

There are numerous other historic sites, including that of famous Civil War rear admiral Joseph Fyffe Ripley, commander of a wooden gunboat, and the Kirker House, where Grant stayed while a student at Ripley College. The Ohio Tobacco Museum, located in the 1850s two-story Federal Georgian–style home once owned by the Espery family, relays the history of Ripley's agricultural history.

A marker in front of the home of Thomas McCague reads, "This tablet marks the home of Thomas McCague, an ardent anti-slavery advocate. On one occasion, John Parker, as underground conductor, being pursued, brought a party of slaves to this house at break of day. McCague said, 'It's daylight, don't stop.' His wife, Aunt Kitty, said, 'Daylight or no daylight, Parker, bring them in.'"

Another story has it that when Parker was helping two slaves escape, McCague, a cabinetmaker and woodworker, helped hide them in some empty coffins he had (furniture makers often made coffins as well).

Friday through Sunday, the John P. Parker Historical Society offers tours of his Federal-style home. Parker, one of the more than three hundred members in the Ripley Antislavery Society, was a former slave who had been able to purchase his freedom. He knew how to read (having been illegally taught by the children of one of his "owners") and did foundry work during the day, and he often crossed the Ohio River at night, bringing fugitives back with him. To stop him, a $1,000 bounty was offered for his capture, but to no avail. A major recruiter for the Twenty-Seventh Ohio Volunteer Infantry (Colored) Regiment, after the war he held patents for two of his agricultural inventions—the earliest granted to an African American.

One mile north of Ripley, visit the North Pole Road Covered Bridge, built in 1875 and spanning Eagle Creek.

NOTABLE

Aunt Jemima wasn't just an image. Over the years there were many women who represented syrup and pancake products made by Quaker Oaks, and third one was Rosa Washington Riles (1901–69), who is buried in the Red Oak Presbyterian Church Cemetery in Ripley, which also was a stop on the Underground Railroad. Her photo is on her tombstone.

92

Springboro

Though it looks a dream town from a romantic painting, Springboro is more than just a collection of nineteenth- and early twentieth-century homes with pretty gardens and tree-lined streets. It's also a heroic sort of place, a major stop on the Underground Railroad, one where citizens united to do the right thing no matter the risk in helping freedom seekers.

Settled around 1796, Springboro was founded in 1815 by Jonathan Wright, as Springborough. Wright had some background in town planning; his father, Joel, was a surveyor who plotted Columbus and Dayton, Ohio and Louisville, Kentucky. Predominantly Quaker in the early 1800s, Springboro was named after its many springs, which is why by the 1830s it had two mills and a wool factory.

History is so intertwined in today's Springboro that even a cup of coffee can be enjoyed in a building once a safe place on the Underground Railroad. Indeed, historic tours take you not through dusty old sites but into wonderfully preserved buildings now serving as boutiques, homes, restaurants, and shops.

STAY

Built in 1815 and listed on the National Register of Historic Places, the Wright House Bed and Breakfast is the oldest home in Springboro. A documented Underground Railroad site with one of the most authentic slave hiding places in the state of Ohio, this wonderful home, decorated

Rotary Park

with period antiques, combines gourmet breakfasts, teatimes, and tours of the Underground Railroad.

EAT

Heather's Coffee and Café is a charming eatery serving wraps, salads, soups, and specialty coffees, making it a delightful place to meet friends. But its past is even more spectacular. Once an active safe house, the basement still has an underground tunnel system used to help freedom seekers make their way under the city's streets.

The Ambiance Wine Bar Café, known for its romantic and artistic atmosphere, offers a nice selection of beers and wines; menu items like pan-seared salmon, cabbage rolls, chicken parmesan, turkey tetrazzini, and apple strudel; and a list of events ranging from adult and children painting nights to live music.

The fourth-largest dinner theater in the state, La Comedia is the place to go for a wonderful dinner and Broadway-style theatrical evening.

Mr. Boro's is all about locally sourced and scratch cooking, including house-made smoked chicken, craft beer and cocktails, and, of all things, wood painting classes—just for the fun of it.

For over three decades, the Donut Haus has been selling their freshly baked apple cinnamon fritters, sour cream doughnuts, and yeast rings.

Crooked Handle Brewing offers fourteen draft taps plus a selection of premium spirits, signature cocktails, cider, and wine, along with live music. If you're hungry, they host food trucks and delivery options from local restaurants as well as a small menu of snacks of their own.

PLAY

The Springboro Historical Society and Chamber of Commerce have curated an excellent interactive self-guided Underground Railroad tour showcasing twenty-seven sites that were hideouts, escape routes, and

Downtown shops

safe houses for those escaping from slavery. There are also guided tours. For more information, stop by the Springboro Historical Society, housed in the 1810 home built by Griffin "Griffy" Griffis. It's one of forty of Springboro's original brick buildings still standing.

Celebrate the holidays in style during the three-day Springboro Christmas Festival with all the fun trappings, including holiday foods, storytelling, a parade, music, horse-drawn carriage rides, children's activities, and Mr. and Mrs. Claus.

Get your bike out and hit the Great Miami Riverway Alternate, a bikeway that travels through Springboro as well as many other scenic villages and towns.

SHOP

Founded in 1894, Friesinger's Candy Factory sells an assortment of chocolates made using techniques garnered over more than a century.

Once the M & J Wright General Store, circa 1854, the two-story building boasts second-story porches and is a vital architectural part of the historical district of South Main Street. Now Magnolias on Main is a boutique store selling clothing, jewelry, and accessories.

Shoppe Smitten is a giddy shopping experience where you can find unique clothing, jewelry, and gifts. Best of all, they specialize in goods that give back both locally and globally.

Paintbrush Pottery is a contemporary ceramics studio for painting your own.

A Federal-style house going back to 1831 and on the National Register of Historic Places, Lamplight Antiques was a stop on the Underground Railroad.

Arts and crafters will like Wooly Bully Yarn Company, with its great selections of brands in wonderful colors as well as the necessary tools for knitting, darning, weaving, and crocheting, among others.

NOTABLE

Tommy Kessler, guitarist for the rock band Blondie, was born in Springboro.

93

Tipp City

Tipp City, voted one of the Five Best Hometowns in Ohio by *Ohio Magazine*, was founded in 1840 along the developing Miami and Erie Canal. Originally Tippecanoe City, it was named in honor of General William Henry Harrison, who won the Battle of Tippecanoe in 1811 and used the slogan "Tippecanoe and Tyler too" in his run for president. Tyler, in case you're wondering, was John Tyler, who became the tenth president following Harrison's death thirty-one days after he took office.

Somehow, we don't think Tipp and Tyler too would have worked quite as well.

The tree-lined main thoroughfare, with planters brimming with flowers during warm weather and patios set for outdoor dining, are what make this historic town so appealing. The shops, housed in nineteenth-century brick buildings, are eclectic, filled with trendy shops and restaurants. Where the downtown dwindles to an end, the 1839 Tipp City Roller Mill is situated on what was once Lock 15 of the Miami and Erie Canal. But more about that later.

EAT

A former bank building, Coldwater Café may be in the historic downtown of a midwestern town, but its heart and soul is also partly European, including Provence, France, in everything from the furnishings to a menu replete with offerings such as brie pasta, lobster crab cakes, green curry, and, of course, quiche. The extensive wine list has something for every

Scratch Bakery by Justin Tyler

pocketbook, including a wide selection of by-the-glass reds, whites, sparkling, and rosés.

At Grounds for Pleasure, a coffee shop that sources from small farms, like the El Carmelo farm in Colombia that provides the red and yellow bourbon coffee cherries or the inactive volcano on Uganda's border with Kenya where beans for their Uganda Mt. Elgon Italian Roast grow. Order a cup of joe and savor the world.

PLAY

The Tipp City Mum Festival is a great weekend event in fall to celebrate the beauty of these brightly colored blooms. Besides pageants and a parade, the festival, going on sixty years, features the largest car show in the Miami Valley.

Fed by underground springs, Charleston Falls cascades thirty-seven feet down, and then its waters continue on to the Great Miami River. Often compared to Niagara Falls given the similarity of their rock strata, the Charleston Falls Preserve is a standout on its own for its stunning beauty. Follow walking trails paralleling the rapids and wander through caves, prairies, meadows, and woods.

Three stories high, the rambling red Tipp City Roller Mill was built in 1837 along the banks of the Miami and Erie Canal. The cut and stacked stones outside show how water was channeled through the canal, and an old white and blue canal boat sits dry-docked nearby at what was Lock 15. Now a venue for the Tipp Roller Mill and Theater, the old mill features live entertainment on Saturday night.

Downtown mural

SHOP

The Golden Leaf Tea and Herb sells bagged and loose-leaf teas, herbs, spices, and coffee beans and will also craft special blends suited to your taste or needs. They also offer mixtures to help soothe such ailments as the flu and achy joints.

Not your usual jumbo of used books, Browse Awhile Books is four thousand square feet and two stories with over 150,000 books (plus another 50,000 online), all categorized, alphabetized, and easy to access.

Bodega Wine and Specialty Foods Market is a cornucopia of wonderful foods. Gather up what looks good—cheese, crackers, wine, spreads, whatever else looks yummy—and have a picnic, dinner, or lunch or stock your pantry. The staff is well versed in their product lines.

NOTABLE

In 1849, Peter Bohlender, who had immigrated from Bavaria with his family when he was six, started a small garden company in Dayton, Ohio. In 1889, he moved the business to Tipp City, renaming it Spring Hill Nurseries because of its new location, at the top of a hill near a spring. Now one of the oldest and largest nurseries in the country, Spring Hill produces enough chrysanthemums to earn Tipp City the designation of "Mum Capital of the World."

94

Versailles

When General "Mad" Anthony Wayne and his army marched through here, his troops noticed the rich soil of the Miami Valley, and some returned to farm. First known as Jacksonville after President Andrew Jackson when founded in 1819, less than twenty years later, the village was called Versailles, in honor of the many French immigrants who moved here. But like its Indiana counterpart, its name is pronounced "ver-sales," and if you say it the French way, people will either not know what you're talking about or instantly recognize you as a stranger—which is OK because it's a friendly kind of place.

STAY

Located on a beef farm with a century-old barn, the French House Bed and Breakfast provides its guests with access to a great room, kitchen, and outdoor patio. Continental breakfast is included.

EAT

In a small village with a population of around twenty-eight hundred, a traveler might hope, at best, to find a wonderful mom-and-pop restaurant serving American diner classics. But hardly anyone expects to discover a restaurant that reviewers call world class. But so it is at the corner restaurant located in the Versailles Hotel in the downtown, which is open for breakfast, lunch, and dinner. The chef-driven menu focuses on fresh ingredients and locally sourced ingredients.

Voted Best Winery in Ohio 2016, 2017, 2018, 2019, and 2020 by *Ohio SIP* magazine Reader's Poll as well as the Best Winery in Darke County by the *Daily Advocate* Reader's Poll, the Winery at Versailles is all pastoral sophistication. With more than thirty wines and such menu offerings as starters, wraps, and designer pizzas, they also feature special events—just check their website (see "Destination Information").

One of three parks in Versailles, Ward Park has lots of recreational opportunities, including a swimming pool, tennis court, playground, and concession stand.

Twelve life-size bronze figures dominate the brick walkways at the Sculptural Village of Versailles, located in the downtown. Beautiful all the time, they're particular stunning when lit up at night.

Endless Pint Brewery in the downtown offers pizza, artisan brews, and good fun.

Opened in 1933, Versailles Gas and Oil has morphed into Gus's Coffee, Creamery, and Bakery. Now a place to get hand-brewed coffees, panini, sandwiches, soups, and pastries, it is a sleek glass-and-metal "cool" kind of place, fun to hang out, read emails, and catch breakfast, lunch, or dinner.

95

Washington Court House

Though it might seem like an unusual name for a town, Washington Court House follows a longtime Virginia tradition of naming the county seat—in this case for Fayette County—using the town's name followed by Court House. It all makes sense since the area was settled by veterans of the Revolutionary War who hailed from Virginia and were granted Ohio lands as payment for their service. The city itself was settled in 1810 by Edward Smith Sr., who drowned after returning home from serving in the War of 1812, leaving his widow with ten children to raise. She must have done an exceptionally good job indeed—the Smith family remained prominent in Washington Court House for over a century.

The city has many sites listed on the National Register of Historic Places; the Court House Square was designated as a historic district.

EAT

Known for their homestyle cooking, the Willow serves up comfort food, including entrées like prime rib, steaks, fried perch, and even fried liver; sides like twice-baked mashed potatoes, green beans, and buttered corn; and of course, homemade pies, such as that Midwest specialty sugar cream, as well as pecan cream, peanut butter, Dutch apple, and blackberry.

PLAY

Washington Court House has some outstanding architecture, but probably the most talked-about place is the three-story Second Empire–style

Fayette County Courthouse

county courthouse. Both inside and out, it's a marvel—and unique. That's because of the interior murals and frescoes completed by Ohio artist Archibald Willard in 1882. Willard, whose *The Spirit of '76*, commissioned for the 1876 US Centennial, is probably one of the most famous paintings in the country. The three murals, all of which incorporate the image of a winged woman and measure ten by fourteen feet, are *The Spirit of the U.S. Mail*, *The Spirit of Electricity* (remember that electricity was pretty new back then), and *The Spirit of Telegraph*.

Once the Dayton and Southeastern Railroad, the thirty-four-mile Paint Creek Recreation Trail is an easy ride—or walk—connecting Washington Court House to Chillicothe.

In 1875, Morris Sharpe built a spectacular Victorian Italianate home designed to be "the Showplace of Washington Court House." Now the Fayette County Museum and on the National Register of Historic Places, the house has fourteen rooms filled with exhibits, artifacts, and displays about the county's history. The tower of the house, accessible by a winding staircase, offers a stunning panoramic view of the city.

The Fayette County Fair is held each July in Washington Court House. The three-day annual Scarecrow Festival is held the third weekend in September in downtown Washington Court House and features music,

Fayette County Museum

food, rides, games, craft vendors, a 5K Walk and Run, classic cars, and children's activities.

SHOP

Sweetwater Bay Boutique sells a wide range of fashionable women's clothing and accessories for all sizes, as well as wine and spirits. For antiques, check out Memories Gate, Northshore Primitives, and Harry and Annie's, just to start. Simply Home sells home furnishings and decor, primitives, candles, linens, seasonings, and dried flower arrangements.

96

Waynesville

Founded in 1897, making it older than the state of Ohio, Waynesville was designed by its founders in the typical fashion of an English village, with formal parks and squares bordering a central public square. Starting in 1801, Quaker families began arriving from the south wanting to get away from the repression of slave states and to create a community where fugitives could be safe as they continued their journey north to freedom. Four years later, Waynesville was home to the largest Friends meeting in the country.

STAY

The quaint two-bedroom and two-bath Cranberry Cottage Bed and Breakfast is located on Waynesville's historic Main Street within walking distance of its many shops and restaurants. A delightfully cozy place, it also has lovely gardens and a patio.

EAT

The Stone House Tavern in downtown Waynesville is known for their hot and sticky burgers made with bacon, peanut butter, pepper jack cheese, and pepper jelly. Also on the menu are steaks, peanut butter pie, citrus crab cakes, and mushroom ragù crepes.

Hand-curated furniture and decor reflect the eclectic, French-influenced approach to menu items and ambience at the popular Cobblestone Café.

Caesar's Creek Pioneer Village

The lovely Remember When Tea Room, located in a whimsically painted Victorian-style house with white accents and large front porch, is the place to go for peace, beauty, and a good cup of tea accompanied with such delights as their house-made macaroons, freshly baked scones with Chantilly cream (the only way to eat scones, we say), and petite tea sandwiches, including adorable heart-shaped pimento cheese.

Just down the street, the Hammel House Inn opened in 1822 as a stagecoach stop. Now a restaurant and inn, it's right in the hub of downtown Waynesville and within walking distance of more than fifty antique and specialty shops. It's also just half a mile from the Little Miami Bike Trail staging area. But please note, some say it's the most haunted place in Waynesville.

PLAY

Built in 1905, the Museum at the Friends Home (its legal name is the Waynesville Area Heritage and Cultural Center) has art exhibits, ghost tours, local history displays, and rooms done in period decor, including some set with the same china pattern President Richard Nixon used in the White House. As an aside, his great-grandparents, the Millhouses, were Quakers and are buried at Caesar's Creek Cemetery, behind the meetinghouse near Caesar Creek Lake. The museum also holds an annual Christmas tour of historic homes in the village.

Caesar's Creek Pioneer Village

Caesar's Creek Pioneer Village features authentic Quaker buildings from the 1700s to the 1800s and is always a popular stop for history buffs. Buildings include the Bullskin Inn, named for the old animal and Native American trail from the Ohio River to Detroit that ran just east of Harveysburg; the toll house for the Waynesville-Wilmington Pike; a Friends meetinghouse built in 1849; and both a two-story home built in 1808 and a barn erected two years later belonging to the Lukens family.

Waynesville is also the site of Caesar Creek State Park, an enormous outdoor area with a recreational lake, miles of hiking trails, terrific fossil hunting, a thirteen-hundred-foot public beach, and fishing for a variety of bass—smallmouth, largemouth, white, and Kentucky spotted—as well as bluegill and crappie. As if that wasn't enough fish, saugeye and muskellunge are stocked annually. There are numerous boat ramps on the 2,830-acre lake, designated swimming areas, and a marina with 112 seasonal and 10 transient slips.

Regarded as the most haunted village in the entire state of Ohio, Waynesville hosts a lot of great Halloween-time offerings. For more information, contact the Museum at the Friends Home, which offers ghost tours of the village all throughout October.

During the second full weekend in October, heads of cabbage dot farmers' fields, and so why not support the pickling process that made this oversized veggie last throughout long pioneer winters? That's right— Waynesville has been hosting the annual Ohio Sauerkraut Festival for more than a half century. If you're thinking sauerkraut festival—really?—know that it attracts more than 450 vendors from over half the United States, more than 350,000 visitors who consume seven tons of sauerkraut, including the festival's famous sauerkraut pizza (and yes, it's really good), as well as almost sixty other food offerings. Imaginative and must-sample dishes include sauerkraut doughnuts, hot dogs topped with kraut, and pulled pork and kraut potato skins. Oh, and don't be fooled by the name: German sundaes are not ice cream but instead consist of a bowl filled with chopped potatoes, sauerkraut, cheddar cheese, sour cream, bacon, and an olive.

SHOP

Known as the "Antique Capital of the Midwest," Waynesville is also home to sixty or so unique shops. Popular stops include the Looking Glass, featuring garden art and home boutique items; American Pie, with custom-made furniture and handcrafted home decor; and the Kindred Nest, a specialty gift shop selling handbags, jewelry, scarves, home decor, and entertainment-serving pieces.

97

Yellow Springs

Offbeat with a friendly, what's-happening vibe, Yellow Springs is a crazy quilt of eclectic shops housed in historic buildings, vegan restaurants and house-made sauerkraut balls, biking paths and walking trails, the state's oldest tavern, and even a raptor center.

There's a hippy-dippy look to many of the storefronts, some of which are drenched in a plethora of eye-catching color combos. The Village Herb Shop has a vivid pink, lavender, orange, and red front. Yellow Springs Toy Company opted for blue stairs and a front façade of bright green. But none is more colorific than the exterior of the Tie-Dyed Gift Shop, which is painted with oversized curlicues of green, red, yellow, orange, blue, and pink. Going beyond colors in making a statement, Asanda Imports has large foo dogs flanking its entrance. This artistic vibe is also reflected in the public art installations along the main thoroughfares.

The name Yellow Springs comes from the many springs bubbling up from the ground in the surrounding landscape; the yellow is the residue of golden orange left on the cliffsides by the iron in the water of the cascading waterfalls. A century or more ago, the springs, thought to be restorative, attracted visitors seeking their curative powers. It's still a destination spot, but now visitors take to the streets not for the waters but to enjoy Yellow Springs's sixty-five-plus funky and fun shops, restaurants, and galleries, many housed in historic buildings as well as the recreational activities in the surrounding woodlands.

Birch Creek Falls

STAY

Even though it was the town's jail from 1878 until 1929, staying at the Jailhouse Suites doesn't mean doing hard time. Luxe rooms, modern amenities, and a location just a block from the downtown make this a good choice for overnight stays.

Want the feel of something grand? With its wide veranda, second-story balconies, oak floors, and plantation shutters, the Mills Park Hotel looks like one of the grand resorts from a century or so ago, a forever fixture on Xenia Street. But it's all new, modeled after the nineteenth-century home of William Mills, who financed the first railroad line to Yellow Springs.

First built in 1811 and then rebuilt several times, the current Grinnell Mill Bed and Breakfast is filled with period furniture and original items from the days when it was an operating mill. Other amenities include a freshly prepared continental breakfast, a patio overlooking the old mill wheel, and a grill for outdoor dinners.

EAT

Once a stagecoach stop, Ye Olde Trail Tavern opened in 1827 and is Ohio's oldest tavern. The menu is eclectic, but if you like German fare, try the house-made sauerkraut balls and their loaded bier cheese fries.

Grinnell Mill

At Young's Jersey Dairy, you can go for the Buffalo chicken melt or the burgers topped with their farmstead cheddar cheese, made on their farm, as are the cheese curds used to top the Philly cheesesteaks. But for most people, the big draw is their house-made ice cream. You can choose from always-on-the-menu scoops of smores, cotton candy, and cow patty (well, it is a real dairy farm, but in this case expect dark chocolate ice cream with pieces of chocolate cookie, chocolate-covered toffee, and chocolate chips).

Or go for specialties, like Wooly Wonka, available only one week in September, as it's made especially for the Fiber Festival going on then. Want to see how they make their ice cream? Tours are available. The family also hosts such annual special events as the Young's Ice Cream Charity Bike Tour and *Vintage Truck* Magazine—Young's Truck Show, which draws about one hundred antique trucks.

In the fall, wander through the corn maze, try some pumpkin ice cream, and pick a pumpkin or two to take home.

A farm-to-table restaurant before the term was even coined, the Winds Café's upscale and creative cuisine uses locally sourced ingredients as much as possible. Open since 1977, it offers a great wine list as well as wine classes and tastings.

Old Union School

Ye Olde Trail Tavern

PLAY

Fresh cider on a fall day—well, it doesn't get much better than that. But you don't have to wait until autumn to enjoy fresh fruit, baked goods, local honey, and maple syrup at Peifer Orchards.

There's lots to see and do at the one-thousand-acre Glen Helen Nature Preserve, a living sanctuary and nature classroom. Twenty-five miles of walking trails wander through woodlands and meadows, along cliffsides, and to the Yellow Springs that gave the town its name. There's also the 1885 Glen Helen Covered Bridge and Raptor Center (and yes, you can adopt one if you want). The nature preserve allows visitors to observe four-hundred-year-old trees, limestone cliffs with waterfalls and over-hangs, and more.

The spectacular 286-acre Clifton Gorge State Nature Preserve is best known for its dolomite and limestone chasms carved out over the centuries by the Little Miami River. Lovely at any time of the year, it's considered one of the premier spots in the state for wildflowers come springtime.

In June, there's the not-to-be-missed Yellow Springs Street Fair.

SHOP

From the foo dogs standing at the entrance to their brick patio fronting the door of this wonderfully eclectic shop, it's all about the unique at Asanda Imports, a delightful collection of clothing, jewelry, rich materials, scarves, and home decor—all at reasonable prices.

For almost forty years, Yellow Springs Pottery has created one-of-a-kind (no two pieces alike) made-by-hand pottery, mostly designed for practical use. Think plates, bowls, teapots, vases, covered casseroles, flowerpots, and more in a variety of colored glazes to go with your decor.

NOTABLE

Comedian Dave Chapelle is from Yellow Springs and continues to live there with his wife and children.

Coretta Scott King attended Antioch College in Yellow Springs and did her student teaching in the public school there.

Actor John Lithgow also attended Antioch, and King often babysat him when he was a child.

To add to other well-known folks, there's Rock and Roll Hall of Fame member Paul Richard Furay, founder of the band Buffalo Springfield, and the great educator Horace Mann.

Destination Information

NORTHEAST OHIO

ALLIANCE

Beech Creek Botanical Garden and Nature Preserve
https://www.beechcreekgardens.org/

Feline Historical Museum
http://www.felinehistoricalfoundation.org/

Glamorgan Castle
https://www.glamorgancastle.com/

Haines House Underground Railroad Museum
http://www.haineshouse.org/

Heggy's Confectionery
https://heggysalliance.com/

Papa Gyros
https://www.papagyros.com/

Troll Hole Museum
https://www.thetrollhole.com/

ASHLAND

Ashland BalloonFest
http://ashlandohioballoonfest.com/

Ashland University Theatre
https://www.ashland.edu/cas/departments
/theatre-department

Ashley's Candy and Nut Shoppe
https://www.ashleyscandyandnutshoppe.com/

Audubon Wetlands Preserve
https://ashlandcountyparks.com/index.php
/parks/audubon-wetlands-preserve

Eva's Treats
https://evas-treats.business.site/

Fig and Oak
https://figandoakshop.com/

Grandpa's Cheesebarn
https://www.grandpascheesebarn.com/

Kelley's Vinyl Record Store
https://www.facebook.com/KelleysRecords/

Myers Memorial Band Shell
https://www.ashland-ohio.com/departments
/parks-and-recreation/guy-c-myers-band
-shell-2

Uniontown Brewing Company
https://uniontownbrewing.com/

Yoder's Red Barn Ice Cream
https://www.facebook.com/YodersIceCream/

ASHTABULA

Ashtabula Arts Center
https://ashtabulaartscenter.org/

Ashtabula Maritime and Surface Transportation Museum
http://www.ashtabulamaritime.org/

Bridge Street Art Works
https://bridgestreetartworks.wixsite.com
/bridgestreetartworks

Briquettes Smokehouse
https://www.briquettessmokehouse.com/

Carlisle's Home in the Harbor
https://www.facebook.com
/carlisleshomestory/

Edge-O-Town Motel
https://www.ashtabulamotel.com/

Geneva State Park
https://ohiodnr.gov/go-and-do/plan-a-visit
/find-a-property/geneva-state-park

Harbor Perk
https://www.harborperk.com/

Heartmade Boutique and Bitchy Bath Co.
https://heartmadeboutique.square.site/

Hubbard House
https://hubbardhouseugrrmuseum.org/

Marianne's Chocolates
https://www.marianneschocolates.com/

Michael Cahill Bed and Breakfast
http://www.cahillbb.com/

North Coast Outpost
http://www.thenorthcoastoutpost.com/

Rennick Meat Market
http://www.rennickmeatmarket.com/

Saybrook Township Park
https://www.saybrookpark.org/

Walnut Beach Park
https://visitashtabulacounty.com/things
-to-do/lake-erie-recreation/parks-beaches
/walnut-beach/

BERLIN

Berlin Cottages
https://www.amishcountrylodging.com
/berlin-cottages

Berlin Farmstead Restaurant
https://www.dhgroup.com/restaurants
/berlin-farmstead-berlin-oh?fbclid
=IwAR2pz1yWbuZsbTOrX_5ZuBDkMG
x6eo1K8j63wfpW8AxN4cqog6a3lLddXzI

Berlin Village Antique Mall
http://www.berlinvam.com/

Berlin Village Gift Barn
https://www.sheiyahmarket.com/

Berlin Village Inn
http://www.berlinvillageinn.com/

Boyd and Wurthmann
https://boydandwurthmann.com/

Der Bake Oven
https://www.derbakeoven.com/

Donna's Premier Lodging
https://www.donnasofberlin.com/

Heini's Cheese Chalet
https://www.yelp.com/biz/heinis-cheese
-house-berlin-4

Helping Hands Quilt Shop
https://helpinghandsquilts.com/

Jake and Ivy's Bed and Breakfast
https://www.jakenivyslodging.com/

Pottery Niche
https://www.thepotteryniche.com/

Troyer Country Market
https://troyerscountrymarket.com/

CARROLTON

Algonquin Mill Complex
http://carrollcountyhistoricalsociety.com
/Mill/MillComp.htm

Algonquin Mill Fall Festival
http://carrollcountyhistoricalsociety.com
/Mill/Millfest.htm

Ashton House Museum
http://ashtonhousemuseum.com/

Betty Kaye Bakery
https://bettykayebakery.com/

Bluebird Farm Park
http://www.ccparkdistrict.org
/bluebirdfarmpark.html

Donna's Deli
http://donnas-deli.edan.io/

**The McCook House Civil War Museum and
the Historical Society of Carroll County**
https://hsccmd.org/

CHAGRIN FALLS

17 River Grille
https://www.17rivergrille.com/

Art by the Falls
https://www.valleyartcenter.org/abf.html

Blossom Time Carnival
https://www.cvjc.org/blossom-time/

Blush Boutique
https://blushcle.com/

Chagrin Arts
https://www.chagrinarts.org/

Chagrin Valley Little Theatre
https://cvlt.org/

Chagrin Falls Popcorn Shop
https://www.chagrinfallspopcorn.com/

Chagrin Falls Historical Society and Museum
https://www.chagrinhistorical.org/

Chagrin Hardware and Supply
https://www.facebook.com/Chagrin-Hardware
-Supply-Co-153090558038669/

Chestnut Hill House
https://www.facebook.com/chestnuthill
homechagrin

Crooked Pecker Brewing Company
https://www.crookedpeckerbrewing.com/

Cru Uncorked
https://www.cruuncorked.com/

Chuck's Fine Wines
https://chucksfinewines.com/

Fireside Book Shop
https://www.firesidebookshop.com/

Frohring Meadows
https://www.geaugaparkdistrict.org/park
/frohring-meadows/

Jeni's Splendid Ice Cream
https://jenis.com/scoop-shops/chagrin-falls/

Dave's Cosmic Subs
https://www.davescosmicsubs.com/locations
/chagrin-falls-ohio/

Paris Room Bistro
https://www.parisroombistro.com/

The Inn of Chagrin Falls
https://www.innofchagrin.com/

River Run Park
https://chagrin-falls.org/parks-chagrin-falls/

CHARM

Amish Country Riding Stables
https://amishcountryridingstables.com/

Chalet in the Valley
http://www.chaletinthevalley.com/

Charm Family Restaurant
https://www.facebook.com/Charm-Family
-Restaurant-1525695027704691/

Charm General Store
https://charmohio.com/Shopping.html

Charm Sweet Shoppe and Pizzeria
https://www.visitcharmohio.com/charm
-pizza-co

Guggisberg Cheese
https://www.babyswiss.com/

Guggisberg Swiss Inn
http://www.guggisbergswissinn.com/

Hershberger's Farm and Bakery
https://hershbergersfarmandbakery.com/

Keim Lumber
https://www.keimlumber.com/

CONNEAUT

Buccia Vineyards
http://bucciavineyards.com/

Centennial Inn Bed and Breakfast
https://www.centennialinnbandb.com/

Grandpa's Castles
https://www.grandpascastles.com/

White Turkey Drive-In
https://whiteturkey.com/

DOVER

Breitenbach Wine Cellars
https://www.breitenbachwine.com/

Broad Run Cheesehouse
http://www.broadruncheese.com/

Crowe's Nest Bed and Breakfast
https://www.innsite.com/inns/F020385.html

Dandelion May Fest
https://www.facebook.com
   /DandelionMayFest/

Dough Co. Doughnuts and Coffee
https://www.facebook.com
   /doughcodoughnuts/

Ernest Warther Museum and Gardens
https://thewarthermuseum.com/

Mindy's Diner
https://www.facebook.com/mindysdiner/

Reeves Victorian Home and
   Carriage House Museum
http://www.doverhistory.org/

School House Winery
https://www.schoolhousewine.com/

Silver Moon Winery
https://www.silvermoonwinery.com
   /Default.asp

GENEVA

Barrels and Bridges Tours
https://barrelsandbridgestours.com/

Breakwater Beach
https://www.visitgenevaonthelake.com
   /Businesses/Geneva-State-Park
   -(Breakwater-Beach)

Broadway Antiques
https://broadway-antiques-collectibles
   .hub.biz/

Catherine's Christmas
https://catherineschristmas.com/

Deer's Leap Winery
https://www.deersleapwine.com/

Earth's Natural Treasures
https://earthsnaturaltreasures.com/

Ferrante Winery and Ristorante
https://www.ferrantewinery.com/

Geneva State Park
https://ohiodnr.gov/wps/portal/gov/odnr
   /go-and-do/plan-a-visit/find-a-property
   /geneva-state-park

Hundley Cellars
http://www.hundleycellars.com/

Kosicek Vineyards
https://www.kosicekvineyards.com/

Laurello Vineyards
https://www.laurellovineyards.com/

Maddie's Place
https://www.facebook.com/maddiesplacelr

M Cellars
https://www.mcellars.com/

Moonshine Manor Cabin
https://www.facebook.com/Moonshine
   -Manor-Cabin-2032413827036100/

Old Mill Winery
https://www.theoldmillwinery.com/home

Red Eagle Distillery
http://www.redeaglespirits.com/

Sawdust Park
https://www.facebook.com
   /sawdustfarmcamp/

South River Vineyard
http://southrivervineyard.com/

Vines and Wines Wine Trail
https://www.ohiowines.org/vines-wines
   -wine-trail

Virant Family Winery
http://www.virantfamilywinery.com/

Warner-Concord Farms
https://www.warner-concordfarms.com/

The Winery at Spring Hill
https://thewineryatspringhill.com/

GENEVA-ON-THE-LAKE

Eagle Cliff Inn
https://eaglecliffinn.com/

Eddie's Grill
http://eddiesgrill.com/

Frank's Toybox
https://toyboxantiques.com/

The Gift Shop at the Lodge
https://www.thelodgeatgeneva.com/?utm
   _source=googlemaps&utm_medium
   =local&utm_campaign=lodge?utm
   _source=google&utm_medium=Yext

Goblin Wine and Ale House
https://www.facebook.com/Goblin-Wine-Ale
   -House-190293261610693/

GOTL Brewing Company
http://www.gotlbrewing.com/

Lodge at Geneva-on-the-Lake
https://www.thelodgeatgeneva.com/?utm
_source=googlemaps&utm_medium
=local&utm_campaign=lodge?utm
_source=google&utm_medium=Yext

L. Taylor Glass Studio
No website

Madsen Donuts
https://www.madsendonuts.com/

Mary's Kitchen
https://maryskitchengotl.com/

Pucker Up Candy Shoppe
https://www.facebook.com/puckerup
candyshoppe/

Sandy Chanty Seafood Restaurant
http://www.sandychanty.com/

GREENVILLE
A&B Coffee
https://abcoffeeshop.square.site/

Beanz
https://www.beanzbuttercreambakery.com/

Bear's Mill
https://www.bearsmill.org/

Darke County Whiskey, Wine, and Ale Trail
https://www.whiskeywineandaletrail.com/

Garst Museum and National Annie Oakley Center
https://www.garstmuseum.org/

Greenville Welcome Center/Visit Darke County
https://www.visitdarkecounty.org/

Maid Rite Sandwich Shoppe
https://www.maidrite-greenville.com/

Merchant House
https://www.tmhgreenville.com/

Shawnee Prairie Preserve and Nature Center
http://www.darkecountyparks.org
/shawnee-prairie-preserve-nature-center

Wayman's Corner Bed and Breakfast
https://waymanscorner.com/

HANOVERTON
Spread Eagle Tavern
http://spreadeagletavern.com/

JEFFERSON
Ashtabula County Covered Bridge Festival
http://www.coveredbridgefestival.org/

Ashtabula County Historical Society
https://ashtcohs.com/?fbclid=IwARokBsx
1El5TFF82I-KDhVtoFm_yppMEJae_xeCsUi
MokpF4RxYeDJK9t_g

Emerine Estates Winery
https://emerineestates.com/

Herb Garden
https://hgschoolofcooking.com/

Jefferson Depot Village
http://www.jeffersondepotvillage.org/

Victorian Perambulator Museum
https://www.ohiotraveler.com/victorian
-perambulator-museum/

Wall Street Coffee Company
https://wallstreetcoffeecompany.com/

LISBON
Courthouse Inn and Restaurant
https://thecourthouseinnandrestaurant.org/

Dulci-More Festival
https://www.dulcimore.org/

Guilford Lake State Park
https://stateparks.com/guilford_lake_state
_park_in_ohio.html

The Lake House on Guilford Lake
Website no longer up

Marks Landing
https://sites.google.com/site/markslanding
restaurant/

Mary's Pizza
https://www.themaryspizzashop.com/

MAGNOLIA
Canal Country Wine Trail
https://www.ohiowines.org/

Creekside Cottage Winery
http://www.creeksidecottagewinery.com/

Crossroads Restaurant
http://crossroads-magnolia.edan.io/

Magnolia Area Historical Society
https://www.facebook.com/groups
/1543115649233711/about

Magnolia Flouring Mills
https://starkparks.com/parks/magnolia
-flouring-mills/

Magnolia Market
https://www.facebook.com/MagnoliaMarket

Nest Café and Ice Cream Parlor
https://xn--thenestcafandicecreamparlor
-koc.com/

Tozzi's Restaurant
https://www.facebook.com/TozzisofMagnolia/

MILLERSBURG
Amish Country Century Ride
https://www.bikede.org/amish-country
-bike-tour/

Farmhouse Frocks
https://www.farmhousefrocks.com/

Hipp Station
https://www.holmestrail.com/images
/Millersburg_Detail-FINAL.pdf

Holmes County Trail
https://www.holmestrail.com/

Hotel Millersburg
https://hotelmillersburg.com/

Jackson Street Antiques
https://www.facebook.com/JacksonStreet
AntiquesMillersburg/

The Jenny Wren
https://thejennywrenhc.com/

Miller Country Bakery
https://www.facebook.com/Millers
-Bakery-214862078536382/

Millersburg Brewing Company
https://www.millersburgbrewing.com/

Millersburg Glass Museum
https://www.holmeshistory.com/glass
-museum

Three Feathers Pewter
https://www.threefeatherspewter.com/

Troyer Country Market
https://troyerscountrymarket.com/

Victorian House Museum
https://www.holmeshistory.com
/victorian-house

Village Toy Shop
https://www.facebook.com/VillageToyShop1/

Yoder's Amish Home
https://yodersamishhome.com/

MINERVA

Alpaca Spring Valley Farm
https://www.alpacaspringvalley.com/

Hart Mansion Restaurant
https://hartmansionrestaurant.com/

Market Street Art Spot
https://www.marketstreetartspot.com/

Minerva Classic 57
http://minerva57.com/

Minerva Dairy
https://minervadairy.com/

Normandy Inn
https://www.facebook.com/tomandraefry/

Off the Beaten Path Gift Shop
https://www.facebook.com/OffTheBeaten
PathGiftShop/

Sandy Springs Brewing Company
https://www.sandyspringsbrewery.com/

MOUNT HOPE

Homestead Furniture
https://homesteadfurnitureonline.com/

Kauffman's Country Bakery
http://kauffmanscountrybakery.com/

Mt. Hope Auction
http://www.mthopeauction.com/

Mrs. Yoder's Kitchen
https://mrsyoderskitchen.com/

MOUNT PLEASANT

Abram Dilworth House
https://www.airbnb.com/rooms/20495204
?source_impression_id=p3_1654272729
_oGVf%2BF%2BztdNnAZtZ

Black Sheep Vineyard
https://blacksheepvineyard.com/

Farm Restaurant and Pub
https://www.facebook.com/TheFarm
RestaurantAndPub/

Historical Society of Mount Pleasant
https://www.facebook.com/MPAHistorical
Society/

Quaker Meeting House
https://www.ohiohistory.org/visit/museum
-and-site-locator/quaker-yearly-meeting
-house

NEW PHILADELPHIA

Broadway Brewhouse
https://www.broadwaybrewhouseohio.com/

Dee's Restaurant
https://www.facebook.com/Dees-Restaurant
-205521549465587/

J-N-G Grill
https://jnggrill.com/

Schoenbrunn Inn
https://theschoenbrunninn.com/

Tuscora Park
https://www.tuscorapark.com/

Woods Tall Timber Resort
https://woodstalltimberresort.com/

OBERLIN

Allen Memorial Art Museum
https://amam.oberlin.edu/

Apollo Theatre
https://www.clevelandcinemas.com/apollo

Ben Franklin Store
https://www.benfranklinoberlin.com/

Common Ground Canopy Tours
http://commongroundcenter.org/zipline
-canopy-tour/

Gibson's Bakery and Candy
https://www.gibsonsbakeryandcandy.com/

Gingko Gallery and Studio
https://www.facebook.com/Ginko-Gallery
-Studio-186896992769/

Hallauer House Bed and Breakfast
https://hallauerhousebnb.com/

Hotel at Oberlin
https://thehotelatoberlin.com/

Mad Cow Curiosity Shop
https://www.facebook.com/madcowcuriosities

North Coast Inland Trail
https://www.loraincountymetroparks.com
/north-coast-inland-trail

Oberlin Heritage Center
http://www.oberlinheritagecenter.org/

Ratsy's Store
https://ratsysstore.com/

Workshop Art Gallery
https://www.facebook.com/TheWorkshopArt
Gallery/

PENINSULA

Boston Mills / Brandywine Ski Resort
https://www.bmbw.com/

Bronson Memorial Church
https://www.facebook.com/Bronson-Church
-365915480127598/

Century Cycles
https://www.centurycycles.com/about
/peninsula-pg2844.htm

Cuyahoga Valley Historical Museum
http://cuyahogafallshistory.com/

Cuyahoga Valley National Park
https://www.nps.gov/cuva/index.htm

Cuyahoga Valley Scenic Railroad
https://www.cvsr.org/

Dilly's Drive-In
http://www.doubledilly.com/

Fisher's Café and Pub
https://www.fisherscafe.com/

Peninsula Art Academy
https://www.peninsulaartacademy.org/

Spicy Lamb Farm
https://thespicylamb.com/

Stanford House
https://www.conservancyforcvnp.org
/experience/plan-your-visit/retreats
-lodging/

Szalay's Sweet Corn Farm
https://szalaysfarm.com/

Trail Mix Peninsula
https://www.conservancyforcvnp.org/park
-stores/

Yellow Creek Trading Company
https://yellowcreektrading.com/

SEBRING

Ashton's 5 and 10
https://www.facebook.com/ashtons5and10
sebringohio/

JP's Snacks and Sodas
https://www.facebook.com/JpsSnacksand
Sodas/?ref=br_rs

Sebring Historical Society Strand Museum
https://www.facebook.com/sebringohio
historicalsociety/

Sebring Mansion
https://www.sebringmansion.com/

Sweet Bunz Donuts and Such
https://www.facebook.com/Sweet-Bunz
-donuts-such-532582600111479/

STEUBENVILLE

Bayberry House Bed and Breakfast
Victorian Guest Houses
https://www.facebook.com/BayberryHouse/

Drosselmeyer's Nutcracker Shoppe
https://www.steubenvillenutcrackervillage
.com/shop.html

Fort Steuben
https://www.ftsteubenmall.com/

Garrett House
https://www.bayberryproperties.com/Rooms
.htm

Scaffidi's Restaurant and Tavern
https://www.scaffidirestaurant.com/

Steubenville Nutcracker Village
https://www.steubenvillenutcrackervillage
.com/

Steubenville's Historic Union Cemetery
https://unioncemeterysteubenville.com/

Ville Restaurant and Bar
https://thevillerestaurant.com/

Westfall House
https://www.bayberryproperties.com/Rooms
.htm

SUGARCREEK

Age of Steam Roundhouse
https://www.ageofsteamroundhouse.org/

Alpine Hills Historical Museum
https://www.alpinehillsmuseum.org/

Carlisle Inn Sugarcreek
https://dhgroup.com/inns/carlisle-inn
-sugarcreek

Collectors Decanters and Steins
http://www.collectorsdecanterssteins.com/

David Warther Carvings and Gift Shop
https://warther.org/

Der Spinden Haus
https://www.facebook.com/derspinden.haus/

Dutch Host Inn
https://dutchhostinn.com/

Dutch Valley Restaurant and Bakery Valley
Restaurant
https://www.dhgroup.com/restaurants/dutch
-valley-sugarcreek-oh

Esther's Home Bakery
https://visitsugarcreek.com/visit-esthers
-home-bakery.html

Honey Bee Café
https://www.facebook.com/Honey-Bee-Cafe
-554318841254396/

Ohio Star Theater
https://www.dhgroup.com/theater

Ohio Swiss Festival
https://ohioswissfestival.com/

Swiss Country Lawn and Crafts
http://swisscountrylawn.com/

Swiss Village
https://swissvillagebulkfoods.com/

WALNUT CREEK

Amish Country Theater
https://amishcountrytheater.com/

Andre's Primitive Crafts and Furniture
No website

Carlisle Gifts
https://www.facebook.com/CarlisleGifts
WalnutCreek/

Carlisle Inn
https://www.facebook.com/CarlisleInn
WalnutCreek/

Der Dutchman
https://www.facebook.com/DerDutchman
WalnutCreek/

German Culture Museum
http://cometowalnutcreekohio.com
/portfolio-view/german-culture-museum/

Mudd Valley Café and Creamery
https://walnutcreekcheese.com/

New Grounds Café and Diner
https://newgroundscafe.wixsite.com/mysite

Walnut Creek Cheese
https://walnutcreekcheese.com/

ZOAR

Benson's Marketing and Catering
http://bensonsmc.com/

Canal Tavern of Zoar
http://www.canaltavernofzoar.com/

Cobbler Shop Antiques
http://cobblershop.com/

Donnie's Tavern
https://www.donniestavern.com/

Historic Zoar Village
https://historiczoarvillage.com/

Keeping Room Bed and Breakfast
http://thekeepingroombandb.com/

Maifest
http://historiczoarvillage.com/

Ohio and Erie Canal Towpath Trail
https://www.ohioanderiecanalway.com/

Tin Shop Coffee House
https://www.tinshopcoffeehouse.com/

Weaving Haus
http://www.weavinghaus.com/

Zoar Market
https://www.facebook.com/ZoarMarket

Zoar School Inn Bed and Breakfast
https://www.facebook.com/ZoarSchoolInn

Zoar Wetland Arboretum
http://www.zoarwetland.org/

NORTHWEST OHIO

ARCHBOLD

Al-Meda Chocolates
https://www.al-meda.com/

Home Restaurant
https://thehomerest.com/

Koelsch Farm
https://www.koelschfarmhomestead.com/

Sauder Village
https://saudervillage.org/

BELLEVUE

Bierkeller Pub and Restaurant
http://bierkellerpub.com/

Gotta Getaway RV Park
https://www.gottagetawayrvpark.com/

Historic Lyme Village
https://lymevillage.org/

Mad River and NKP Railroad Society Museum
http://www.madrivermuseum.org/

Miller's Drive-In
https://www.millersdriveintogo.com/

Seneca Caverns
https://senecacavernsohio.com/

BRYAN

Frankie's
https://website-706039420487681610027
-restaurant.business.site/

Jumpin' Beanz Coffee
https://www.facebook.com/Jumpin-Beanz-A
-Coffee-House-1527983720584820/

Kora Brew House and Wine Bar
https://www.korabrewandwine.com/

Spangler Factory Dum Dum Trolley Tour
https://www.spanglercandy.com/

Stoney Ridge Farm and Winery
https://www.stoneyridgewinery.com/

DEFIANCE

Andrew L. Tuttle Memorial Museum
https://www.facebook.com/TuttleMuseum/

Auglaize Village Museum
https://www.facebook.com/defiancecounty
historicalsociety/

Bud's Restaurant
https://www.budsrestaurantdefiance.com/

Cabin Fever Coffee
http://www.cabinfevercoffee.com/

Eclectic Wallflower Boutique
https://eclecticwallflowerboutique1
.godaddysites.com/

Fort Defiance Market Antiques
https://www.facebook.com/Fort-Defiance
-Antiques-187890252420/

Inn on Third
https://www.facebook.com/innonthird/

Kissner's
https://m.facebook.com/kissners1928/

A Little Slice of Heaven
https://www.facebook.com/alittleslice
defiance/

Meek's Pastry Shop
https://www.cakes.com/us/bakeries/oh
/defiance/meeks-bakery

Pontiac Park
No website

Second Story on Clinton Street
https://www.secondstorydefiance.com/

FORT LORAMIE

Brucken's Neighborhood Pub
http://bruckenspub.com/

Buckeye Trail
https://www.facebook.com/buckeyetrail/

Fort Loramie State Park
https://ohiodnr.gov/go-and-do/plan-a-visit
/find-a-property/lake-loramie-state-park

Fort Loramie Trading Post
https://www.facebook.com/FortLoramie
TradingPost/

Morrie's Landing
https://www.facebook.com/Morries-Landing
-516693248475308/

St. Michael Catholic Church
https://www.nflregion.org/

Small Town Boutique
https://shopsmalltownboutique.com/

Wilderness Trail Museum
https://www.facebook.com/pages/Wilderness
%20Trail%20Museum/111596302211892/

FOSTORIA

Flippin' Jimmy's
https://www.facebook.com/flipjims/

Fostoria Area Historical Society
https://www.facebook.com/fostoriahistory/

**Fostoria Iron Triangle Visitor Center and
Viewing Area**
http://www.fostoriairontriangle.com/

Fostoria Rail Festival
https://www.facebook.com/events/d41d8cd9
/fostoria-rail-festival/317692715501268/

Glass Heritage Gallery
http://www.glasspass.org/glassheritate.htm

Hancock Hotel
https://www.hancockhotel.com/?gclsrc=aw.ds

KemoSabes Roadhouse Grill
http://www.kemosabes.com/index.html

Midwest Sculpture Initiative Walking Tour
https://www.facebook.com/MidwestSculpture
Initiative/

UrbanWoody Brewery
https://www.theurbanwoody.com/

Whippy Dip
https://www.facebook.com/Whippy-Dip
-103543047898124/

GRAND RAPIDS

Angelwood Gallery
https://www.angelwoodgallery.com/

Applebutter Fest
https://www.applebutterfest.org/

Canal Experience at Providence Metropark
https://metroparkstoledo.com/features-and
-rentals/canal-experience/

Gilead Side-Cut Canal
https://metroparkstoledo.com/media/3621
/maumee-waterway-brochure-031318-web
.pdf

Grand Kerr House
https://www.thegrandkerrhouse.com/

Isaac Ludwig Mill
https://metroparkstoledo.com/explore-your
-parks/providence-metropark/

Just for You Riverfront Consignment
https://www.facebook.com/shopjust4yougr/

Knucklehead's Kafé
https://www.facebook.com
/Knuckleheadskafe/

LaRoe's Restaurant
https://www.laroesgrandrapids.com/

Library House Books and Art
https://libraryhousegallery.com/

**Majestic Oak Winery and Neon Ground Hog
Brewery**
https://www.majesticoakwinery.com/

Mary Jane Thurston Park and Marina
https://ohiodnr.gov/go-and-do/plan-a-visit
/find-a-property/mary-jane-thurston-state
-park

Mary's Apple Orchard
https://www.carsonblockshoppes.com/villa-
georchard.html

Mill House Bed and Breakfast
https://themillhouse.com

Miss Lily's
https://www.facebook.com/Miss-Lilys
-288846091149209/

Wild Side Brewing
https://wildsidebrewing.com/

KELLEYS ISLAND
Caddy Shack Bar and Grill
https://www.facebook.com/caddyshack419/

Charles Herndon Galleries and Sculpture Gardens
http://www.charlesherndon.com/

Crooked Tree Winery
https://www.crookedtreevineyard.com/

Docker's Waterfront Bar and Restaurant
https://www.facebook.com/Dockers
-Waterfront-Bar-and-Restaurant
-150324821645829/

Glacial Grooves Geological Preserve
https://www.ohiohistory.org/visit/museum
-and-site-locator/glacial-grooves

Island Fudge Shoppe
https://kelleysisland.com/listing/island
-fudge-shoppe/

Kelleys Island General Store
https://www.kigeneralstore.com/

Kelleys Island State Park
https://www.facebook.com/KelleysIsland
StatePark/

Kelleys Island Wine Co.
https://www.kelleysislandwineco.com/

Taste by the Lake
https://facebook.com/Taste-by-the-Lake
-1648562948705579/?fref=ts

Water's Edge Island Retreat
https://watersedgeretreat.com/

MARBLEHEAD
Canoe Club Wine Company
https://www.canoeclubwinebar.com/

East Harbor State Park
https://ohiodnr.gov/wps/portal/gov/odnr/go
-and-do/plan-a-visit/find-a-property/east
-harbor-state-park

Ferguson Gallery
https://www.fergusongallery.com/

Hidden Beach Bar
https://hiddenbeachbar.com/

Jamestown Tavern
https://www.facebook.com/JTTavern/

Lakeside Daisy State Nature Preserve
https://ohiodnr.gov/wps/portal/gov/odnr
/go-and-do/plan-a-visit/find-a-property
/lakeside-daisy-state-nature-preserve

Marblehead Lighthouse Historical Society Museum
https://www.facebook.com
/marbleheadlighthouse/

Marblehead Soap Company
https://www.marbleheadsoap.co/

Ottawa National Wildlife Refuge
https://www.fws.gov/refuge/ottawa/

Rocky Point Winery
https://www.rockypointwinery.com/

Skipper's Marina and Resort
http://www.skippersresort.com/

MARIA STEIN
Korner Kafe
https://www.kornerkafe.net/

Marie Stein Country Fest
http://www.mscountryfest.com/

Maria Stein Shrine of the Holy Relics
https://mariasteinshrine.org/

Moeller Brew Barn
https://www.moellerbrewbarn.com/

Precious Blood
http://www.marioncatholiccommunity.org
/precious-blood.html

St. John
http://www.marioncatholiccommunity.org/

St. Rose (or St. Rosa)
http://www.marioncatholiccommunity.org/

MAUMEE
Baker's Kitchen
https://www.thebakerskitchen.net/

Clara J's Tea Room
http://www.clarajsat219.com/

Dale's Bar and Grill
https://www.dalesbarandgrill.com/

Fort Meigs
https://fortmeigs.org/

Maumee Valley Chocolate and Candy
https://valleycandy.com/

Shops at Fallen Timbers
https://theshopsatfallentimbers.com/

Side Cut Metropark
https://metroparkstoledo.com/explore-your
-parks/side-cut-metropark/

Towpath Park
https://metroparkstoledo.com/trails
/towpath-trail/

MILAN
Alto Inn
https://altoinn.com/

Angel Welcome Bed and Breakfast
https://www.angelwelcome.com//?utm
_source=google&utm_medium=GMB

Milan Coffee Station
http://milancoffeestation.com/

Milan Inn-tiques
https://www.milaninn-tiques.com/

Milan Museum
https://www.facebook.com/milanmuseum/

Milan Wine Post Pub and Bar
https://m.facebook.com/Milanwinepost/

Old Tobacconist Inn
https://oldtobaconistinn.com/

Thomas Edison Birthplace and Museum
https://tomedison.org/

White Dog Bed and Breakfast
https://whitedogbandb.wpcomstaging.com/

MINSTER

Community Lanes Bowling Alley
https://communitylanes.com/

Fort Loramie State Park
https://ohiodnr.gov/go-and-do/plan-a-visit
/find-a-property/lake-loramie-state-park

Miami Erie Bed and Breakfast
https://miamieriebb.wixsite.com/

Minster Historical Society and Museum
https://www.minsterhistoricalsociety.com/

St. Augustine Catholic Church
http://www.staugie.net/

Oktoberfest
https://www.minsteroktoberfest.com/

Olde Dutch Mill
https://www.oldedutchmill.com/

Wooden Shoe Inn
https://www.thewoodenshoeinn.com/

MONTPELIER

Churn Handcrafted Ice Cream
https://www.churnohio.com/

Cookies on Demand
https://www.facebook.com/CookiesOn
DemandMontpelierOhio/

Drop Tine Winery and Tap House
https://drop-tine-winery-and-tap-house
.business.site/

Hay Jay One Room Schoolhouse
https://walkerhomeschoolblog.wordpress
.com/2021/06/12/hay-jay-one-room
-schoolhouse-district-no-3-edon-oh/

Lake La Su An Wilderness
https://ohiodnr.gov/wps/portal/gov/odnr/go
-and-do/plan-a-visit/find-a-property/lake
-la-su-an-wildlife-area

Williams County Community Theatre
https://www.williamscountycommunity
theatre.com/

Williams County Historical Society's Museum
https://www.williamscountyhistory.org/

NEW BREMEN

Bicycle Museum of America
http://www.bicyclemuseum.com/

Kuenning-Dicke Natural Area
https://newbremen.com/historical-sites
-museums/

New Bremen Coffee Co.
https://nbcoffee.com/

17 West
https://www.17west.com/

William Luelleman House
https://newbremenhistory.org/en/content
/78-new-bremens-historical-museums

PERRYSBURG

Carriage House Antiques and More
https://www.facebook.com/perrysburg
antiques/

Guesthouse
https://the-guesthouse-perrysburg.booked
.net/

Marsha's Homemade Buckeye Chocolates
https://marshashomemadebuckeyes.com/

Perrysburg Symphony
http://www.perrysburgsymphony.org/

Rose and Thistle
http://www.roseandthistlepub.com/

Sheffield Road
https://www.sheffieldroad.com/

Spafford House Museum
https://www.facebook.com/auroraspafford/

Swig
https://swigrestaurant.com/

PUT-IN-BAY

Forge
http://theforgepib.com/

Heineman's Winery
https://heinemanswinery.com/

Island Tour Train
https://www.putinbaytrans.com/public/island
_transportation/

Miller Marina
https://millermarinapib.com/

Park Place Boat Club at the Boardwalk
http://parkplaceboatclub.com/

Put-in-Bay Resort
https://www.putinbayresort.com/

Put-in-Bay Wine Festival
https://putinbay.com/events/annual-island
-wine-festival/

Put-in-Bay Winery
https://www.facebook.com/putinbaywinery/

ST. MARY'S

Belle of St. Marys Canal Boat
https://www.tripadvisor.com/Attraction
_Review-g50935-d12581730-Reviews-Belle
_of_St_Mary_s_Canal_Boat-Saint_Marys
_Ohio.html

Grand Lake St. Marys
https://www.facebook.com
/GrandLakeSaintMarys/

Grand Lake St. Marys State Park
https://www.facebook.com/glsmstatepark/

JT's Brew and Grill
https://www.jtbrewandgrill.com/stmarys
banquets

K. C. Geiger Park
https://www.cityofstmarys.net/Facilities
/Facility/Details/KC-Geiger-Park-5

Matt Tuttle Guide Service
http://matttuttlefishing.co/

Memorial Park
https://cityofstmarys.net/departments/parks
/memorial-park

Romer's Westlake Hotel Villas
https://westlakevillas.com/

St. Marys Canal House
No website

West Bank Inn
https://www.westbankinn.com/

Xcaret Restaurant
https://xcaretrestaurant.com/

VAN WERT

Antique Farm Museum
https://sites.google.com/historicalvanwert
.com/historicalvanwertcom/home

Bob's Bargain Barn
https://www.facebook.com
/BobsBargainBarnLLC/

Brewed Expressions
https://brewedexpressions.com/

Brumback Library
https://brumbacklib.com/

Collins Fine Foods
http://vanwert.com/collins/

Flour Loves Sugar
https://www.facebook.com/FlourLovesSugar/

Landeck Tavern
https://www.facebook.com/SK-Landeck
-Tavern-120037074823368/

Niswonger Performing Arts Center
https://www.vanwertlive.com/

Olde Barn
https://www.facebook.com/Olde-Barn
-680326465644806/

Sycamore of Van Wert
https://www.facebook.com/sycamorevw/

Van Wert County Courthouse
https://www.vanwertcountyohio.gov
/government/courts/common_pleas_court
/index.php

Van Wert County Fair
https://www.vanwertcountyfair.com/

VERMILION

Ancient Celtic Shop
https://ancientcelticshop.com/

Big Ed's Main Street Soda Grill
https://www.facebook.com/BigEdsSodaGrill/

Brownhelm Heritage Museum
https://www.brownhelm.org/museums/

Brummer's Homemade Chocolates
https://brummers.com/

Burning River Boutique
https://burningriverboutique.wordpress.com/

Chez Francois
https://chezfrancois.com/

Chez Riverfront Café
https://chezfrancois.com/

Dick Goddard Woollybear Festival
https://www.facebook.com/vermilionchamber
Woollybear/

Festival of the Fish
https://www.facebook.com/Festival-of-the
-Fish-104199688001659/

Granny Joe's Ice Creamatorium
https://www.facebook.com/people/Granny
-Joes-Ice-Creamatorium/100057589572504/

Lee's Landing
https://www.facebook.com/Lees-Landing
-Nautical-Gift-Shop-Art-Gallery-Video
-Transfers-647193408638587/

Lucky Duck Charters
https://www.luckydcharters.com/

Main Street Beach
https://www.shoresandislands.com/things
-to-do/main-street-beach?id=12724

Moe's Marine Service
https://www.moesmarineservice.com/

Old Vermilion Jailhouse Bed and Breakfast
http://jailbed.com/

Romp's Dairy Dock
https://romps.com/

Silly Goose
https://www.facebook.com/sillygoosegifts/

Swan Creek Candle
https://www.facebook.com/swancreekcandle
vermilion/

Szabo Apparel
https://www.szaboapparel.com/

Old Prague Restaurant
https://oldprague.com/

Olive Scene
https://theolivescene.com/

Trolling Eye Charters
https://trollingeyecharters.com/

Vermilion Farm Market
https://www.vermilionfarmmarket.net/

Vermilion-Lorain Water Trail
https://www.facebook.com/108664362534220
/posts/the-vermilion-lorain-water-trail-is
-a-truly-unique-paddling-experience
-featuring/4206089032791712/

Vermilion River Reservation
https://www.loraincountymetroparks.com
/vermilion-river-reservation

West River Paddling Co.
http://westriverkayak.com/

WAPAKONETA
Alpha Café
https://www.alpha-cafe.biz/

Fort Amanda Memorial Park
https://www.jampd.com/parks-facilities/fort
-amanda-park/

J. Marie's Wood-Fired Kitchen and Drinks
https://www.facebook.com/woodfiredwapak/

Neil Armstrong Air and Space Museum
https://www.armstrongmuseum.org/

Temple of Tolerance
https://www.facebook.com/events/raymond
-thunder-sky/jim-bowsher-and-the-temple
-of-tolerance/387958241699537/

**Venture Out! Resorts' Arrowhead
Lakes Resort**
http://ventureoutresorts.com/arrowhead
-lakes/

WATERVILLE
Dale's Diner
https://www.dalesbarandgrill.com/dales
-diner/

Fallen Timbers Monument
https://www.nps.gov/places/fallen-timbers
-battlefield-and-fort-miamis-national
-historic-site.htm

Garden Smiles by Carruth Studios
https://carruthstudio.com/

Roche de Boeuf Festival
https://www.facebook.com/rochedeboeuf
festivalwaterville/

Rue des Artistes
No website

Side Cut Metropark
https://metroparkstoledo.com/explore-your
-parks/side-cut-metropark/

Smoke and Fire Company
https://www.smoke-fire.com/

Waterville Historic Society
https://www.watervillehistory.org/location/

WHITEHOUSE
Blue Creek Recreational Area
https://whitehouseoh.gov/having-fun/parks
-recreation-2/

Fayette County Museum
https://www.facebook.com/Fayettecounty
museum/

Generals Ice Cream
https://www.generalsicecream.com/

Local Thyme Restaurant and Bar
https://www.localthyme.pub/

Share Our Grounds
https://www.facebook.com/shareourgrounds/

Village of Whitehouse
https://whitehouseoh.gov/having-fun
/tree-tour/

Wabash Cannonball Trail
https://www.wabashcannonballtrail.org/

Wheeler Farms
https://www.wheelerfarms.com/

Whitehouse Inn
https://thewhitehouseinn.net/

CENTRAL OHIO
ALEXANDRIA
Alexandria Museum
https://www.facebook.com/alexandria
museumonmain/

Lobdell Reserve
https://lickingparkdistrict.com/parks-trails
/lobdell-reserve/

Matchmade Designs
https://matchmadedesigns.com/

Ragamuffins Coffee
https://www.ragamuffinscoffeealexandria
.com/

Sunbear Studio and Gallery
http://sunbearstudio.com/

WillowBrooke Bed 'n Breakfast
https://www.willowbrooke.com/

BELLEFONTAINE
City Sweets and Creamery
https://www.facebook.com/citysweets
bellefontaine/

Four Acre Clothing Co.
https://fouracreclothingco.com/

Holland Theatre
http://thehollandtheatre.org/

Just U'NeeQ
https://www.facebook.com/JustUNeeq/

Logan County History Center
https://www.loganhistory.org/

Nest 1896
https://www.nest1896.com/

Olde Mint Antiques
https://www.facebook.com/oldemintantiques/

PeachTree
https://www.peachtreeboutique.com/

Rise Bakehouse
https://www.risedoughjo.com/

Six Hundred Downtown
https://600downtown.com/

Sweet Aromas
https://www.sweetaromascoffee.com/

CANAL FULTON

Canal Boat Lounge
https://www.facebook.com/canalboatlounge/

Canal Fulton Canoe Livery
https://www.cfcanoe.com/

Canal Fulton Glassworks
https://www.facebook.com/CanalFulton
Glassworks/

Cherry Street Creamery
https://business.facebook.com/CherryStreet
Creamery/?ref=py_c

Deliciously Different Candies
https://www.facebook.com/pages/category
/Candy-Store/Deliciously-Different
-348605328590/

Dragonfly Tea Room
https://www.dragonflyontheriver.com
/tea-room/

Dragonfly Winery
https://www.dragonflyontheriver.com/

Oberlin House Museum
https://www.facebook.com/oberlin
heritagecenter/

Ohio and Erie Canalway Hike/Bike Path
https://www.ohiotoerietrail.org/

Peace, Love and Little Donuts
https://www.facebook.com/PeaceLoveAnd
LittleDonutsOfCanalFulton

Yankee Peddler Festival
https://www.yankeepeddlerfestival.com/

Sisters Century House Restaurant
http://www.canalfultoncenturyhouse.com/

Sluggers and Putters Amusement Park
https://www.sluggers-putters.com/

St. Helena III
http://cityofcanalfulton-oh.gov/departments
/canal-boat-operations/

St. Helena Heritage Park–Canal
http://cityofcanalfulton-oh.gov/locations
/st-helena-heritage-park/

CANAL WINCHESTER

Barrel and Boar BBQ Gastropub
https://www.barrelboar.com/

Canal Winchester Area Historical Society
https://www.cwhistory.org/

CornerSmiths
https://www.cornersmiths.com/

Georgie Emerson Vintage
https://www.georgieemerson.com/

Loose Rail Brewing
https://looserailbrewing.com/

Motts Military Museum
https://mottsmilitarymuseuminc.com/

National Barber Museum
https://www.nationalbarbermuseum.org/

Nom Nom Nom
http://www.nomnomnomfordogs.com/

Old Town Tavern
https://m.facebook.com/Old-Town-Tavern
-121136977917202/

Shade on the Canal
https://www.shaderestaurants.com/

Slate Run Metropark
https://www.metroparks.net/parks-and-trails
/slate-run-historical-farm/

Sticks and Stones
https://www.sticksandstonesstudiooh.com/

Ugly Mug Bar and Grill
http://www.theuglymugbarandgrill.com/

CIRCLEVILLE

A. W. Marion State Park
https://ohiodnr.gov/wps/portal/gov/odnr
/go-and-do/plan-a-visit/find-a-property
/a-w-marion-state-park-campground

Castle Inn Bed and Breakfast
http://www.castleinn.net/

Creative Chaos
https://www.facebook.com/creativechaos
circleville/

Goodwin's Family Restaurant
http://goodwinsfamilyrestaurant.com/

Lindsey's Bakery
https://www.facebook.com/LindseysBakery/

Maggie and Me
https://www.facebook.com/profile.php?id
=100057353354379

Manchester Hill Winery
http://manchesterhill.com/

Ted Lewis Museum
https://www.tedlewismuseum.org/

Watt Street Tavern
https://wattstreettavern.com/

Wittich's Candy Shop
https://wittichscandyshop.com/

GRANVILLE

Alligator Effigy Mound
http://touringohio.com/history/alligator
-mound.html

Avery-Downer House
http://www.robbinshunter.org/

Bryn Du Mansion
https://www.bryndu.com/

Buxton Inn
https://www.eventvenuegranville.com/

Dawes Arboretum
https://dawesarb.org/

Granville Inn
https://granvilleinn.com/

Lynd Fruit Farm
https://lyndfruitfarm.com/

Mai Chau Kitchen
https://maichaukitchen.com/

Newark Earthworks
https://www.ohiohistory.org/visit/museum
-and-site-locator/newark-earthworks

River Road Coffeehouse
http://www.riverroadcoffeehouse.com/

Snapshots Lounge
https://www.facebook.com/Snapshots
-lounge-208134212530883/

Three Oaks Vineyard
https://threeoaksvineyard.com/

Three Tigers Brewing Company
https://threetigersbrewing.com/

Whit's Frozen Custard
https://whitscustard.com/

HEATH

Coffee Shack Coffee Roasters
https://coffeeshackroasters.com/

Dizurts Custom Cakes and More
https://www.facebook.com/dizurtscustom
cakesandmore/

Finders Keepers Village
http://www.finderskeeperscrafts.com/

Sand Hollow Winery
https://sandhollowwine.com/

JOHNSTON

Antiques for Home and Garden
https://www.facebook.com/TimberTunes
Johnstown/

Antiques on Main
https://antiques-on-main.square.site/

Autumn Rush Vineyard
https://www.autumnrushvineyard.com/

Ghostwriter Public House
https://ghostwriterph.com/

Heart of Home
https://www.facebook.com/Heartof
HomeJTown/

Johnstown Town Hall and Opera House
https://explorelc.org/directory/johnstown
-town-hall-and-opera-house

My Soaps
https://www.my-soaps.com/

Timber Tunes Gifts
https://www.facebook.com/TimberTunes
Johnstown/

Whit's Frozen Custard
https://whitscustard.com/

LOUDONVILLE

Alabaster Mouse
https://www.facebook.com/thealabaster
mouse/

Blackfork Marken Inn Bed and Breakfast
https://www.blackforkmarkeninn.com/

Cleo Redd Fisher Museum
https://www.crfmuseum.com/

Creative Outlet Indian Crafts and Jewelry
https://www.creativeoutlet.net/

Landoll's Mohican Castle
https://landollsmohicancastle.com/

Loudonville Canoe Livery
https://www.facebook.com/Loudonville
Canoe/

Mohican State Park
https://www.facebook.com/MohicanState
Park/

Ohio Theatre
https://www.theohiotheatre.com/

River Room Lounge
https://www.facebook.com/riverroomlounge/

Ugly Bunny Winery
https://uglybunnywinery.wpcomstaging.com/

Wally Road Scenic Byway
https://www.facebook.com/wallyroadscenic
byway/

Wally World River Resort
https://www.facebook.com/WallyWorld
Resort/

LUCAS

AngelWoods Hideaway B&B
http://mohicancountry.org/members
/Angelwoods_Hideaway.html

Johnny Appleseed Historic Byway
https://www.destinationmansfield.com
/johnny-appleseed-historic-byway/

Malabar Farm
https://malabarfarm.org/

Malabar Farm Restaurant
https://www.facebook.com/TheMalabarFarm
Restaurant/

Open Door Café
https://www.opendoorcafemenu.com/

Rainbow Gardens
https://www.restaurantji.com/oh/lucas
/rainbow-gardens-/

MOUNT VERNON

The Alcove
https://www.restaurantmountvernonoh.com/

Ariel-Foundation Park
https://arielfoundationpark.org/

Butcher Family
https://www.butchermaple.com/

Half Baked Cafe
https://www.hbcafeohio.com/

Happy Bean
https://happybeancoffeeshop.com/

Harmony Salt Spa
https://harmonysaltspa.com/

Kokosing Gap Trail
http://www.kokosinggaptrail.org/

Makery on Main
https://www.themakery.shop/our-shop/

Mazza's
https://www.mazzas.com/

Mount Vernon Downtown District
https://www.facebook.com/MVDA98273/

Mount Vernon Inn
https://www.themountvernoninnohio.com/

On the Square
https://www.facebook.com/On-The-Square
-Antiques-230330317524082/

Paragraphs Bookstore
https://paragraphsbookstore.indielite.org/

Walk Eat Mount Vernon
https://www.facebook.com/walkeatmount
vernon/

Woodward Opera House
https://thewoodward.org/

Y-Not Cycling
https://www.ynotcycling.com/

ORRVILLE

Cobblestone Hotel and Suites
https://www.staycobblestone.com/oh/orrville/

Dravenstott's Restaurant
http://www.dravenstotts.com/

Jerry's Café
https://www.jerrysinorrville.com/

J. M. Smucker Company Store
https://www.jmsmucker.com/smucker
-cafe-store

Johnson Woods State Nature Preserve
https://ohiodnr.gov/wps/portal/gov/odnr/go
-and-do/plan-a-visit/find-a-property
/johnson-woods-state-nature-preserve

Michael's Bakery
https://www.michaelsbakeryorrville.com/

Mrs. J's
https://www.facebook.com/Mrs-Js
-102962253077450/

Orrville Historical Museum
https://www.facebook.com/OrrvilleHistory/

Shisler's Cheese House
https://cheesehouse.com/

Sure House Coffee Roasting Co.
https://www.surehousecoffee.com/

UTICA

Branstool Orchards
https://www.branstoolorchards.com/

Legend Hills Orchard
https://www.legendhillsorchard.com/

River's Edge Grill
https://www.facebook.com/RiversEdgeUtica/

Velvet Ice Cream
https://www.velveticecream.com/

Watt's Restaurant
https://www.facebook.com/pages/Watts
%20Restaurant/348422958526450/

SOUTHEAST OHIO
ALBANY

Albany Café
http://albanycafe.com/

Lake Snowden Camping
https://lakesnowden.hocking.edu/camping

Ohio Paw Paw Festival
https://www.ohiopawpawfest.com/

Ray's Harvest House
https://www.facebook.com/rdnkray/

ATHENS

Athens Belpre Chillicothe
https://www.facebook.com/athensbelprerail
trail/

Athens Central Hotel
https://athenscentralhotel.com/

Athens Underground Furniture
https://www.facebook.com/Athens
Underground/

Beads and Things
https://www.facebook.com/athensbeads
andthings/

Bodhi Tree Guesthouse and Studio
http://www.bodhitreeguesthouse.com/

Dairy Barn Arts Center
https://dairybarn.org/

Dutch Creek Winery
http://dutchcreekwinery.com/

Figleaf
https://figleafboutique.com/

International House and Artifacts Gallery
No website

Kismet
https://www.iluvthatstore.com/

Larry's Dawg House
https://larrysdawghouse.com/

Little Professor Book Center
https://sites.google.com/view/littleprofessor
    bookcenter/home

Miller's Chicken
https://www.facebook.com/millerschicken/

Moonville Rail Trail
https://www.facebook.com/MoonvilleRail
    Trail/

O'Betty's Hot Dog Museum
http://www.obettys.com/

Pleasant Hill Vineyards
https://www.pleasanthillvineyardsllc.com/

Ridges
No website

Strouds Run State Park
https://ohiodnr.gov/wps/portal/gov/odnr/go
    -and-do/plan-a-visit/find-a-property
    /strouds-run-state-park

Zoe Fine Dining
http://www.zoefinefood.com/

BEAVER

Dogwood Pass Old West Town
https://www.facebook.com/dogwoodpassold
    westtown/

Roy Rogers Museum
https://www.facebook.com/RoyRogers
    MuseumandFestival/

BELPRE

Belpre Historic Society
https://www.facebook.com/Belpre
    -Historic-Society-641758756246558/

Belpre Multi-use Trail
No website

Civil War Cemetery
No website

McHappy's Bake Shoppe
http://www.mchappys.com/

A Touch of Charm Mercantile
https://www.facebook.com/aTouchofCharm
    Mercantile/

Unicorn Wine Guild
https://www.unicornwineguild.com/

CAMBRIDGE

**Cambridge Guernsey County Tourist
    Information Center**
https://visitguernseycounty.com/

Cambridge Wooden Toy Company
http://cambridgewoodentoyco.com/

Colonel Taylor Inn
http://www.coltaylorinnbb.com/

Dickens Victorian Village
https://dickensvictorianvillage.com/

Ellie's Cottage Candles
https://www.facebook.com/ElliesCottage
    CambridgeOhio/

Georgetown Tavern on the Hill
https://www.georgetowntavern.com/

Kennedy's Bakery
https://kennedysbakery.com/

Ladder's Coffee Bar
https://www.facebook.com/ladderscoffeebar

Mosser Glass Factory
https://www.mosserglass.com/

National Museum of Cambridge Glass
https://cambridgeglassmuseum.org/

Nothing but Chocolate
https://nothingbutchocolate.com/

Salt Fork State Park
https://ohiodnr.gov/wps/portal/gov/odnr/go
    -and-do/plan-a-visit/find-a-property/salt
    -fork-state-park

CHILLICOTHE

Adena Mansion
https://www.adenamansion.com/

American Vintage Warehouse
https://www.facebook.com/groups
    /308523789286987/

Carl's Townhouse
https://m.facebook.com/Carls-Townhouse
    -120991834581381/

Cross Keys Tavern
https://thecrosskeystavern.com/

Grandpa Joe's Candy Store
https://grandpajoescandyshop.com/

Guest House Bed and Breakfast
No website

Highland Ice Creamery
https://highlandsicecreamery.com/

Hopewell Culture National Historical Park
https://www.nps.gov/hocu/index.htm

Junction Earthworks / Arc of Appalachia
https://arcofappalachia.org/junction
    -earthworks/

Lucy Hayes Heritage Center
https://www.facebook.com/Lucy-Webb-Hayes
    -Heritage-Center-113641638669868/

Majestic Theatre
https://www.majesticchillicothe.net/

Old Canal Antiques and Primitives
https://www.facebook.com/groups
    /2077305535826945/

Old Canal Smokehouse
https://www.oldcanalsmokehouse.com/

Porch Swing Days
https://www.facebook.com/porchswingday
chillicothe/

Pour House at Machinery Hall
https://www.pouronchillicothe.com/

Sugarloaf Mountain Amphitheater
https://tecumsehdrama.com/

COSHOCTON

Apple Butter Inn
https://www.facebook.com/RoscoeVillage
Coshocton/

McKenna's Market
https://mckennasmarket.com/

Monticello III
https://www.facebook.com/watch/?v
=927158564801688

Roscoe General Store
https://theroscoegeneralstore.com/

Roscoe Hillside Cabins
https://www.facebook.com/Roscoehillside
cabins/

Roscoe Village Sweets and Treats
http://roscoesweetsandtreats.com/

Roscoe Visitor Center
https://roscoevillage.com/

Warehouse Steak n' Stein
https://www.warehouserestaurants.com/

GALLIPOLIS

Bob Evans Farm
https://www.facebook.com/BobEvans
Gallipolis/

French Art Colony Museum
http://www.frenchartcolony.org/

Gallia County Hike and Bike Trail
https://www.traillink.com/trail/gallia-county
-hike--bike-trail/

Laurel Valley Creamery
https://www.laurelvalleycreamery.com/

Mound Hill Cemetery
https://ohio.org/wps/portal/gov/tourism
/things-to-do/destinations/mound-hill
-cemetery

Our House Tavern
https://www.ohiohistory.org/visit/museum
-and-site-locator/our-house-tavern

IRONTON

Armory Smokehouse
http://thearmorysmokehouse.com/

Lake Vesuvius Recreation Area
https://www.fs.usda.gov/recarea/wayne
/recarea/?recid=6204

Lawrence County Museum
https://www.facebook.com/LawCoHS/

Melini Cucina
https://www.facebook.com/melinicucina
ironton/

Peddler's Home Cooking
https://www.facebook.com/Peddlers-home
-cooking-1408957815994403/

LOGAN

Brewery 33 Hocking Hills
http://www.brewery33.com/

Christmas Treasures
https://www.windchimeshopsales.com/

Columbus Washboard Museum
https://columbuswashboard.com/

Hocking Hills Canoe and Livery
https://www.hockingriver.com/

Hocking Hills Inn and Coffee Emporium
https://www.hockinghillsinnandcoffee
emporium.com/

Hocking Hills Moonshine
http://www.hockinghillsshine.com/

Hocking Hills Visitor Center
https://www.explorehockinghills.com/

Hocking Hills Winery
https://www.hockinghillswinery.com/

Inn and Spa at Cedar Falls
https://innatcedarfalls.com/

John Glenn Astronomy Park
https://jgap.info/

Midwest Glassware Outlet
https://www.facebook.com/Midwest
-Glassware-Outlet-249732788551282/

Millstone BBQ
https://www.themillstonebbq.com/

The Olde Dutch Restaurant
https://www.theoldedutchrestaurant.com/

Paul A. Johnson Pencil Sharpener Museum
https://www.explorehockinghills.com
/things-to-do/arts-museums/museums
/pencil-sharpener-museum/

Pearl's Diner
https://www.facebook.com/Pearls-Diner
-454776697893144/

Penny's Pastries
https://www.facebook.com/PennysPastries
LoganOH/

Rockside Winery and Vineyards
https://www.rocksidewinery.com/

Shade Winery
https://shadewinery.com/

Treehouse Treats and Treasures
https://www.facebook.com/TreehouseTnT

White Pillars Inn
https://www.facebook.com/White-Pillars-Inn
-115285987965/?ref=page_internal

MALTA

Blue Rock State Park
https://ohiodnr.gov/wps/portal/gov/odnr/go
-and-do/plan-a-visit/find-a-property/blue
-rock-state-park

Burr Oak State Park
https://www.stayburroak.com/?utm_source
=GMBlisting&utm_medium=organic

Dillon State Park
https://ohiodnr.gov/wps/portal/gov/odnr/go
-and-do/plan-a-visit/find-a-property/dillon
-state-park

Sandstone Retreat
https://www.facebook.com/Sandstone-Retreat
-1450739091729027/

Morgan County Historic Society
https://historicalmorgancounty.com/

Wilds
https://thewilds.columbuszoo.org/

MARIETTA

Adelphia Music Hall
https://www.theadelphia.com/

Buckley House
https://www.facebook.com/buckleyhouse
restaurant/

Castle
https://mariettacastle.org/

Cook's Shop
https://www.thecooksshop.com/

Harmar Tavern
https://www.facebook.com/HarmarTavern/

Lafayette Hotel
http://www.lafayettehotel.com/

Marietta Adventure Company
https://www.mariettaadventurecompany.com/

Marietta Brewing Company
https://mbcpub.com/

Marietta Earthworks
https://ohioriverscenicbyway.org/?page_id
=1071

Ohio River Museum
https://mariettamuseums.org/ohio-river
-museum/

Parkview House
https://www.facebook.com/ParkviewHouse/

People's Bank Theatre
https://peoplesbanktheatre.com/

Putnam Chocolates
https://www.facebook.com/PutnamChocolate/

Riverside Artists Gallery
https://www.riversideartistsgallery.com/

Valley Gem Sternwheeler
https://www.valleygemsternwheeler.com/

Wayne National Forest
https://www.waynenationalforest.com/

Wildroot
https://www.wildrootflowerco.com/

Wit and Whimzy
http://www.witnwhimzy.com/

McCONNELSVILLE

Boondocks BBQ and Grill
https://theboondocksinmoco.business.site
/?utm_source=gmb&utm_medium=referral

Little Dog Deli
https://www.seethemenu.net/

Morgan County Cabin in the Woods
http://cabinwoods.net/

Morgan County Historical Society Museum
http://morganmomuseum.org/

Old Bridge Brewing Company
https://www.oldbridgebrewing.com/

Repo Kafe Roasters
https://www.facebook.com/rkroasters/

Twin City Opera House
http://www.operahouseinc.com/

NELSONVILLE

Hockhocking Adena Bike Path
https://www.traillink.com/trail/hockhocking
-adena-bikeway/

Hocking Valley Scenic Railway
https://www.hvsry.org/

Nelsonville Emporium
https://launch.newleafmarketplace.org/

Nelsonville Quilt Company
https://www.facebook.com/Nelsonville
-Quilt-Company-202620289806298/

Rhapsody Restaurant
https://rhapsody.hocking.edu/

Robbins Crossing
https://robbinscrossing.hocking.edu/

Stuart Opera House
https://stuartsoperahouse.org/

PORTSMOUTH

Bonneyfiddle Museum of Military History
https://www.facebook.com/boneyfiddle
militarymuseum/

Buckeye Ice Cream
https://www.facebook.com/Buckeye-Dairy-Bar
-Miniature-Golf-166451746787194/

Clark Planetarium
https://www.facebook.com/SSUClark
Planetarium/

1810 House
https://www.1810house.org/

Malt Shop
https://www.maltshops.com/

Patsy's Inn Restaurant
https://www.facebook.com/Patsys-Inn
-Restaurant-175420916824/

Philip Moore Stone House
http://www.sciotoheritagetrail.com
/philip-moore-stone-house.html

Portsmouth Brewing Company
http://portsmouthohbrewing.com/

Portsmouth Earthworks
https://ohiohistorycentral.org/w/Portsmouth
_Earthworks

Scent from Heaven Bakery
https://www.facebook.com/Scent-From
-Heaven-Bakery-176839332364210/

Scioto Ribber
https://m.facebook.com/thesciotoribber/

Shawnee State Park
https://ohiodnr.gov/wps/portal/gov/odnr/go
-and-do/plan-a-visit/find-a-property
/shawnee-state-park

Southern Ohio Museum
https://somacc.com/information/

Vern Riffe Center for the Arts
https://vrcfa.com/

ROCKBRIDGE

Boulders Edge Tipi Retreat
https://www.atbouldersedge.com/

Chelle's 33 Diner
https://www.facebook.com/Chelles-33-Diner
-1687925594622562/

Glenlaurel: A Scottish Inn and Cottages
https://www.glenlaurel.com/

Hocking Hills Canopy Tours
https://www.hockinghillscanopytours.com/

STOCKPORT

Big Bottom Memorial Park
https://www.ohiohistory.org/visit/museum
-and-site-locator/big-bottom-memorial
-park

Stockport Mill Inn
http://www.stockportmill.com/

SOUTHWEST OHIO
CLIFTON

Clifton Opera House
https://www.villageofclifton.com/clifton
-opera-house/

Fish Decoy Company
https://decoypedia.com/index.php/2016/05/17
/robbins-steve-clifton-ohio/

Gorge State Nature Preserve
https://www.facebook.com/CliftonGorge/

Historic Clifton Mill
https://cliftonmill.com/

Shoebox Theatre
https://www.facebook.com/The-Shoebox
-Theatre-1512857095656959/

Weber's Antiques
https://www.facebook.com/Webers-Antiques
-338689766621735/

FRANKLIN

Franklin Area Historical Society
https://www.facebook.com/FranklinArea
HistoricalSocietyFranklinOh/

Franklin Tavern
http://hhufo.com/franklintavernohio/

Mackinaw Historic District
https://remarkableohio.org/index.php
?/category/1481

Mom's Restaurant
https://www.facebook.com/Moms-Restaurant
-1521911834726876/?rf=173872112635469

Spirituality Circle
https://www.spiritualitycircle.com/museum
.html

GERMANTOWN

By-Jo Theatre
https://byjotheatre.tripod.com/

Creamery at Market and Main
http://thecreamery.coffee/

Florentine Hotel
https://www.theflorentinerestaurant.com/

Germantown Metropark
https://www.metroparks.org/places-to-go
/germantown/

Germantown Pretzel Festival
https://www.facebook.com/PretzelFestival/

HARVEYSBURG

Harveysburg Community Historical Society
https://www.facebook.com/Harveysburg
CommunityHistoricalSociety/

Ohio Renaissance Festival
https://www.renfestival.com

LEBANON

Anna's Gourmet Popcorn
https://www.annasgourmetpopcorn.com/

Burlap and Burch
https://www.myburlapandbirch.com/

Glendower Mansion
https://www.wchsmuseum.org/glendower
.html

Golden Lamb
https://www.goldenlamb.com

Harmon Museum and Art
https://www.wchsmuseum.org/

Hidden Valley Orchards
https://www.hiddenvalleyorchards.com/

Jam and Jelly Lady
https://jamandjellylady.com/

Lebanon Country Music Festival
https://www.mainstreetlebanon.org/event
-info/lebanon-country-music-festival

Lebanon, Mason, and Monroe Railroad
https://lebanonrr.com/

Village Ice Cream Parlor and Restaurant
http://www.villageparlor.com/

Warren County Historical Society
https://www.wchsmuseum.org/

LOVELAND

Bishop's Quarter
https://www.bishopsquarterbar.com/

Cappy's Wine and Spirits
https://lovelandcappys.com/

Greater Loveland Historical Society Museum
https://www.lovelandmuseum.org/

**Historic Loveland Castle and Museum
  Chateau Laroche**
https://lovelandcastle.com/

Holtman's Donuts
https://www.holtmansdonutshop.com/

Hometown Café Loveland
https://www.hometowncafeloveland.com/

Loveland Art Studios on Main
https://studiosonmain.com/

Loveland Bike Rental
http://www.lovelandbikerental.com/

Loveland Bike Trail
https://lovelandbiketrail.com/

Loveland Canoe and Kayak
https://www.lovelandcanoe.com/

Loveland Farmers' Market
https://www.facebook.com/CityofLoveland
FarmersMarket/

Loveland Stage Company
http://lovelandstagecompany.org/

Loveland Sweet Shoppe
https://www.lovelandsweetshoppe.com/

Memento Mori
http://www.mementomorioohio.com/

Narrow Path Brewing Company
http://www.narrowpathbrewing.com/

Nisbet Park
https://www.lovelandoh.gov/Facilities/Facility
/Details/Nisbet-Park-Amphitheater-2

Paxton's Grill
https://www.paxtonsgrill.com/

Plaid Room Records
https://www.plaidroomrecords.com/

Works
http://theworkspizza.com/

MORROW

Morgan's Canoe and Kayak
https://www.facebook.com/morganscanoe/

Valley Vineyards Winery and Brewery
https://valleyvineyards.com/

OREGONIA

Fort Ancient
http://www.fortancient.org

OXFORD

Apple Tree
https://www.theappletreeoxford.com/

Bird House Antiques
https://www.facebook.com/thebirdhouse
antiques/

Black Covered Bridge
https://www.oxfordmuseumassociation.com
/black-covered-bridge

Hueston Woods State Park
https://www.facebook.com/HuestonWoods
StatePark/

Kofenya
https://www.kofenyacoffee.com/

Miami University Natural Area
https://miamioh.edu/student-life/natural
-areas/

Oxford's University Historic District
https://www.enjoyoxford.org/article-archive
/exploring-oxfords-history/

Steinkeller
https://www.steinkellercircle.com/

RIPLEY

Eagle Creek Country Cabins
http://www.eaglecreekcountrycabin.com/

Logan's Gap Camping Resort
https://www.logansgap.com/

Ripley Boat Club
https://www.facebook.com/ripleyboatclub/

Cohearts Riverhouse
http://cohearts-riverhouse.edan.io/

Dairy Yum-Yum
http://dairy-yum-yum-ii.edan.io/

John and Jean Rankin House
https://www.facebook.com/John-Rankin
-House-Historic-Site-470341046414955/

John P. Parker Historical Society
http://johnparkerhouse.net/

Kinkead Ridge Winery
https://www.kinkeadridge.com/

Kirker House
https://www.hmdb.org/m.asp?m=135536

Meranda-Nixon Winery
http://www.meranda-nixonwinery.com/

North Pole Road Covered Bridge
https://bridgehunter.com/oh/brown/north
-pole/

Ohio Tobacco Museum
http://www.ripleyohio.net/htm/museums.htm

Red Oak Presbyterian Church Cemetery
https://en.wikipedia.org/wiki/Red_Oak
_Presbyterian_Church

Signal House
https://www.facebook.com/The-Signal-House
-Bed-Breakfast-116566381700983/

SPRINGBORO

Ambiance Wine Bar Café
https://www.facebook.com/ambiancewine
barcafe/

Crooked Handle Brewing
https://crookedhandle.com/

Donut Haus
https://m.facebook.com/DonutHausBakery/

Friesinger's Candy Factory
https://www.candyandnutstore.com/

Great Miami Riverway Alternate
https://www.greatmiamiriverway.com/?fbclid
=IwAR0IyaE7l4SM2LU55VdL9vLfrlBk
241kTZ_R1rHZbuwWfMQD10exVHpmofo

Heather's Coffee and Café
http://www.heatherscafe.com/

La Comedia
https://lacomedia.com/

Lamplight Antiques
http://www.lamplightantiques.com/

Magnolias on Main
https://www.magnoliasonmainspringboro
.com/

Springboro Christmas Festival
https://springborofestivals.org/?fbclid
=IwAR3R3rWC5EBBKfZnSIuldxzmBoEVS
oJ2QQHKy7II5v_ng20DkgdjF5-CspI

Wooly Bully Yarn Company
https://m.facebook.com/woolybullyyarn
company/

Wright House Bed and Breakfast
https://www.facebook.com/WrightHouseBB

TIPP CITY

Bodega Wine and Specialty Foods Market
https://www.bodegatippcity.com/

Browse Awhile Books
https://www.browseawhilebookshop.com/

Charleston Falls
https://www.facebook.com/Charleston
FallsPreserve/

Coldwater Café
https://coldwater-cafe.com/

Golden Leaf Tea and Herb
https://www.thegoldenleafonline.com/

Grounds for Pleasure
https://groundsforpleasurecoffeehouse.com/

Spring Hill Nurseries
https://www.springhillnursery.com/?fbclid
=IwAR10PkmcsaZCuJsIcZSLs6slM-lCNd
-Cb1E9vaeU2TQYT5Ak2HAE4xlCGb8
Temporarily closed

Tipp City Mum Festival
https://tippmumfestival.org/

Tipp City Roller Mill and Theater
https://www.tipprollermill.com/

VERSAILLES

Endless Pint Brewery
http://www.endlesspintbrewing.com/

French House Bed and Breakfast
http://www.frenchhousebnb.com/directions
.php

Gus's Coffee, Creamery, and Bakery
https://www.gusscafe.net/

Versailles Hotel
https://www.hotelversaillesohio.com/

Sculptural Village of Versailles
https://www.visitdarkecounty.org/culture

Ward Park
https://versaillesoh.com/residents-visitors
/parks-recreation

Winery at Versailles
https://wineryatversailles.com/

WASHINGTON COURT HOUSE

Fayette County Courthouse
No website

Harry and Annie's
https://www.facebook.com/HarryAndAnnies/

Sweetwater Bay Boutique
https://sweetwaterbayboutique.com/

Willow
http://www.thewillowrestaurant.com/

WAYNESVILLE

American Pie
http://www.americanpiestore.com/

Caesar Creek State Park
caesarcreekstatepark.com

Caesar's Creek Pioneer Village
https://www.ccpv.us/

Cobblestone Café
https://www.facebook.com/Cobblestone
VillageCafeandGifts/

Cranberry Cottage Bed and Breakfast
https://m.facebook.com/Cranberry
-Cottage-Bed-Breakfast-697832670271962/

Hammel House Inn
https://www.hammelhousebb.com/

Kindred Nest
http://thekindrednest.com/

Looking Glass
https://thelookingglass.mobi/

Museum at the Friends Home
https://www.friendshomemuseum.org/

Ohio Sauerkraut Festival
https://sauerkrautfestival.waynesvilleohio
.com/home/

Remember When Tea Room
https://www.rememberwhentea.com/

Stone House Tavern
http://shtavern.com/

**Waynesville Area Heritage and Cultural
Center at the Friends Home**
https://www.friendshomemuseum.org/

YELLOW SPRINGS

Asanda Imports
https://www.asandaimports.com/

Clifton Gorge State Nature Preserve
https://www.facebook.com/CliftonGorge/

Glen Helen Nature Preserve
https://www.glenhelen.org/

Grinnell Mill Bed and Breakfast
http://www.grinnellmillbandb.com/

Jailhouse Suites
https://www.jailhousesuites.com/

Little Miami Scenic Trail
https://www.miamivalleytrails.org/trails
/little-miami-scenic-trail

Mills Park Hotel
https://www.millsparkhotel.com/

Peifer Orchards
https://www.peiferorchards.com/

Winds Café
http://www.windscafe.com/ezh41u26zmh80
audfcsjg1gvkojfrp

Yellow Springs Pottery
http://www.yellowspringspottery.com/

Yellow Springs Street Fair
https://www.facebook.com/YellowSprings
StreetFair/

Yellow Springs Toy Company
https://ystoyco.com/

Ye Olde Trail Tavern
https://www.oldetrailtavern.com/

Young's Jersey Dairy
https://youngsdairy.com/

Photo Credits

ALBANY

Ohio Pawpaw Festival. Courtesy of the Ohio Pawpaw Festival.

Ohio Pawpaw Festival. Courtesy of the Ohio Pawpaw Festival.

ALEXANDRIA

Alexandria Museum. Photo by author.

ARCHBOLD

Barn Restaurant. Photo by Councilman Collection, Flickr, https://www.flickr.com/photos/counselman/8051727093/in/photostream/, CC BY-SA 2.0.

Sauder Heritage Inn. Councilman Collection, Flickr, https://www.flickr.com/photos/counselman/8051729669/in/photostream/, CC BY-SA 2.0.

ASHLAND

Fig and Oak. Courtesy John and Julie Mitchell.

Uniontown Brewing Company. Courtesy Uniontown Brewing Company.

ASHTABULA

Ashtabula Harbor Light. Courtesy Ashtabula County Visitors Bureau.

Ashtabula Harbor. Courtesy Ashtabula County Visitors Bureau.

ATHENS

Dairy Barn Arts Center. Photo by Ed!, Wikimedia Commons, https://commons.wikimedia.org/wiki/File:ASH_Cow_Barn_Athens_OH_USA.JPG. CC BY-SA 3.0.

Wayne National Forest. Photo by Dan Molter, Wikimedia Commons, https://commons.wikimedia.org/wiki/File:2011-06-17_Hygrocybe_cantharellus_69428_cropped.jpg, CC BY-SA 3.0.

BEAVER

Dogwood Pass Old West Town. Courtesy Mike Montgomery.

BELLEFONTAINE

Bellefontaine Courthouse. Photo by Derek Jensen, Wikimedia Commons, https://commons.wikimedia.org/wiki/File:Bellefontaine-ohio-courthouse-fountain.jpg, released to public domain.

Holland Theatre. Photo by Derek Jensen, Wikimedia Commons, https://commons.wikimedia.org/wiki/File:Bellefontaine-ohio-holland-theatre.jpg released to public domain.

BELLEVUE

Sorrowful Mother Shrine. Photo by Nheyo, Wikimedia Commons, https://commons.wikimedia.org/wiki/File:Saint_Joseph_and_the_Child_Jesus_Grotto_(Sorrowful_Mother_Shrine).jpg, CC BY-SA 4.0.

BELPRE

Charles Rice Ames Home. Photo by BWSmith84, Wikimedia Commons, https://commons.wikimedia.org/wiki/File:Charles_Rice_Ames_House.jpg, CC BY-SA 3.0.

BERLIN

Amish buggy. Photo by author.

Kettle corn vendor. Courtesy Holmes County Chamber of Commerce & Tourism Bureau.

CAMBRIDGE

Guernsey County Courthouse. Photo by Paula R. Lively, Flickr, https://www.flickr.com/photos/29621494@N02/8308126062/in/photolist-dEaeSm-cgJ31E-dEajqN-dE4XX4-dE4VUZ-dE4TQr-dEaktE-dE4Vqz-dEafoQ-dEahVb-dE4WW2-dEamuY-dEaghW-dE4SQP-dEamXE-dE4ZkR-dE4ZLi-dE4Um2-5ZPk78-5ZTxtU, CC BY 2.0.

CANAL FULTON

St. Helena Heritage Park–Canal. Photo by Tom Bower, Flickr, https://www.flickr.com/photos/zuikosan/8844989554/in/photostream/, CC BY 2.0.

Lock 4. Photo by Tom Bower, Flickr, https://www.flickr.com/photos/zuikosan/6906296098, CC BY 2.0.

CANAL WINCHESTER

O. P. Chaney Elevator and Caboose, Historical Society Complex. Photo by author.

Fall Festival. Photo by author.

CARROLLTON

Algonquin Mill. Courtesy Carroll County Historical Society.

Algonquin Mill Fall Festival. Courtesy Carroll County Historical Society.

CHAGRIN FALLS

Main Street Bridge. Photo by Jon Dawson, Flickr, https://www.flickr.com/photos/jmd41280/5850607566/in/photostream/lightbox/, CC BY-ND 2.0.

Bell Street Park. Photo by Jon Dawson, Flickr, https://www.flickr.com/photos/jmd41280/5850607120/in/album-72157627018045812/, CC BY-ND 2.0.

CHARM

Guggisberg Cheese. Photo by author.
Guggisberg Swiss Inn. Photo by author.

CHILLICOTHE

Second Street. Photo by David Wilson, Flickr,
https://www.flickr.com/photos/david
wilson1949/49811193893/in/photolist
-2iTDoxP-zg3APK-AcW5iD-zVjExy
-2mkEsUi-AaARTu-zVqAHg-zfUwtC
-2nEeBgw-zVqATX-AdU5Ca-zg3CtM-AaAS7q
-AbKQP7-3SQZg5-zVqCk4-AcW4Dn
-2nE9A8a-zVjEGS-2nE9zXA-9bxLVh
-2dcaBhy-dyyBQ8-9ee7rT-2TujJn-2dbqCSK
-267WGKy-4VVoF7-LzaimQ-Mw8tr4
-Lq4uM8-2eMBBTs-24cmwSY-L2ikNa
-dz6zwJ-2ipc2Dy-2iuA1Gt-25Rvt83
-2eMBBUu-MehQsU-9abj4J-JPfQ4N
-24ckRGo-Ltk68X-n2EMRU-24ckMK5
-zVm93j-zfUwUs-FB6REe-24cmmKJ,
CC BY 2.0.
Lake Ellensmere Covered Bridge. Photo by Jer-
rye & Roy Klotz MD, Wikimedia Commons,
https://commons.wikimedia.org/wiki/File
:LAKE_ELLENSMERE_COVERED_BRIDGE
,_CHILLICOTHE.jpg, CC BY-SA 3.0.

CLIFTON

Clifton Mill. Photo by author.
Clifton Mill. Photo by author.
Clifton historical marker. Photo by author.

CONNEAUT

Conneaut Township Park. Courtesy Ashtabula
County Visitors Bureau.

COSHOCTON

Shops at Roscoe Village. Photo by author.
Historic water wheel, Roscoe Village. Photo by
author.

DOVER

Breitenbach Wine Cellars. Photo by author.
Ernest Warther Museum and Gardens. James
St. John, Flickr, https://www.flickr.com
/photos/jsjgeology/27086960234/in
/photolist-HgzKzL-H3YnX7-HeRbKy
-HBcZe5-Hi2PYh-J7x6wi-HpCKjx-J3RqJW
-HvxFwx-J6bmta-HMb9cd-HNxLWs-J7xjyk
-HgzPry-HizG9n-Hi2SsA-J7xeKn-HMd8of
-J5evbG-J5eCR1-HMd7Z9-HgzJxf-HgDYm9
-GZotom-HxWCSX-J6bmQc-J67FTk-J67KS2
-JbcEXs-HMc1j7-HMd789-HNxW45
-HrmnqT-JcHCUn-J3RrqA-HNxKMU
-HeS5y3-J5etio-Hi6Zuo-Higcoe-H7jSJf
-HcuvML-GGdwkt-J9JHMq-HNMSLW
-JcHdfn-JcHkZa-J67zoX-HeRTUN-HeRYi7,
CC BY 2.0.
Dover Dam. Photo by Huntington District, US
Army Corps of Engineers, https://commons
.wikimedia.org/wiki/File:Dover_Dam
_(Ohio)_in_winter.jpg, Public Domain.

FORT LORAMIE

Gazebo in Canal Park. Photo by author.
Erie Canal Mile Stone Historical Marker. Photo
by author.

GALLIPOLIS

Our House Tavern. Photo by Nyttend, Wikimedia Commons, https://commons.wikimedia
.org/wiki/File:Our_House_in_Gallipolis
.jpg#file, public domain.
Gallipolis from Mound Hill. Photo by Mike
Tewkesbury, Flickr, https://www.flickr.com
/photos/7687126@N06/10743649084/in
/photolist-hno123-2boipAb-WcsJg-d8YeME
-29XCZZ-3yDNPA-3yztnk-hxAgYX-3yzryZ
-7pKku8-3yDM8y-5ayXmD-p6BLTQ
-7pPdHW-2jtgnmF-2nznqRT-cPYkEU
-5tQ3bN-4ujqDn-oeYXi7-hnnXaQ-owXrEe
-9Npzqb-own3Cc-7pPdgo-4uovB9-uRWjLq
-6UsvBb-2kSzXnR-5ABAqx-bmhsAi, CC
BY-ND 2.0.

GENEVA

South River Vineyard. Courtesy Ashtabula
County Visitors Bureau.
Geneva State Park. Courtesy Ashtabula County
Visitors Bureau.
Geneva State Park. Courtesy Ashtabula County
Visitors Bureau.

GENEVA-ON-THE-LAKE

Eddie's Grill. Courtesy Ashtabula County
Visitors Bureau.
Old Firehouse Winery. Courtesy Ashtabula
County Visitors Bureau.

GERMANTOWN

Florentine Hotel. Photo by Pjsham, Wikimedia
Commons, https://commons.wikimedia.org
/wiki/File:Gunckel%27s_Town_Plan
_Florentine_Hotel.JPG, CC BY-SA 3.0.
Jasper Road Covered Bridge. Photo by Niag-
ara66, Wikimedia Commons, https://
commons.wikimedia.org/wiki/File:
Jasper_Road_Covered_Bridge_01.jpg, CC
BY-SA 4.0.

GRAND RAPIDS

Gilead Side-Cut Canal. Photo by author.
Isaac Ludwig Mill. Photo by author.
Front Street. Photo by author.

GRANVILLE

Buxton Inn. Photo by author.
Robbins Hunter Museum. Photo by author.

HANOVERTON

Spread Eagle Tavern. Photo by Roseohioresi-
dent, Wikimedia Commons, https://
commons.wikimedia.org/wiki/File:
Packard_1938_Convertible_Victoria
_Darrin.JPG, CC BY-SA 4.0.
Spread Eagle Tavern. Photo by Roseohioresi-
dent, Wikimedia Commons, https://
commons.wikimedia.org/wiki/File:Spread
_Eagle_Tavern_(Hanoverton,_Ohio).JPG,
CC BY-SA 4.0.

HARVEYSBURG

Ohio Renaissance Festival. Courtesy Warren
County Convention & Visitors Bureau.

JEFFERSON

Jefferson Historical Society. Photo by Doug Kerr, Flickr, https://www.flickr.com /photos/dougtone/7974745515/in/photolist -d9GE1k-d9GCKi-d9GDwb-d9GEwR -d9GDL5-d9GFTU-d9GFZa-d9GGbX -d9GFjG-d9GF2r-d9GDiC-d9GDJk-d9GE1w -d9GCSx-d9GERJ-d9GEqA-d9GFBt-d9GEsg -d9GFhx-dReoYK-dRjXxf-dRepze-dRephg -dRjY4J-dRjYE5-d9GEZy-pXAZ2L-dRjYaG -dRepG6-dRjXAQ-dRjXU3-dRjYsh-dRjYL7 -dRjYWU-dRjYRE-dRjYz3-pVnsg9-ds7AsA -ds7Aa5-ds7rkv-ds7rq4-ds7rxK-ds7Af3 -ds7rBt-dRjXKs-pXAZyh-pF6Xat-pF3kwT -pF6XWZ-6cSrND, CC BY-SA 2.0.

Caine Road Bridge. Photo by Doug Kerr, Flickr, https://www.flickr.com/photos/dougtone /4713392638/in/photolist-8bvnqj-8bs6A8 -8bvfaY-qh8vpF-qhizPX-8bs6FT-8bvnBh -8bvnwd-8bvnyN-8bvnsf-d9imXE-d9imKu -d9iofC-d9inzJ-d9ineW-d9inWm-7fsHBN -8tfDsi-8bvAS1-7foSZc-7foRw8-7foRvB -7foS4R-7fsK5y-7foRtT-7foRur-8tf56H -5dwyTM-7foRL8-7fsKud-7fsHEw-7foSCM -7foRx6-7foRUK-7fsHXA-7fsKih-8tf5kr -8tfp6T-7fsHLC-7foRxz-7foSyD-7fuRv8 -7foSSF-7fsHFA-7fsHNL-7foRzT-7foRqe -7foRNB-7fsJY3-7foRrp, CC BY-SA 2.0.

Netcher Road Covered Bridge. Courtesy Ashtabula County Visitors Bureau.

KELLEYS ISLAND

Kelleys Island. Courtesy Lake Erie Shores & Islands.

Glacial Grooves Geological Preserve. Courtesy Lake Erie Shores & Islands.

Lake Erie. Courtesy Lake Erie Shores & Islands.

LEBANON

Doc's Place. Photo by author.

Golden Lamb. Photo by author.

LISBON

Teegarden-Centennial Covered Bridge. Photo by and courtesy of Jimmy Emerson, DVM, Flickr, https://www.flickr.com/photos /auvet/17213502066/in/photolist-se6Gso -sgoLyn-sgoKBT-dkvmxR-2Ym3ay-gw5RJp -cRV2Eb-cRV3dL-cRV3Cf-cRV4rW-pMbgkW -p79V4n-HtBBJ-HtL28-ZfiqMC-HuNYF -pLNvg5-dLCp6q-dLCoUw-Zfioky-HuNWD -HuHVG-YeNWzC-HuJ1A-HuNPz-YeNW3W -34qGbU-HuJ4A-vdNgMJ-gw5MLV-YijHP8 -2YgB3r-YeNYDY-YeNXEJ-vvnM8c-YeNX3G -YeNXp3-vuQA2o-vuQwCQ-YeNYkw-ZfioMf -YeNY7q-5ZRsnf-2nsR7kq-aEoPzY-bDW6xX -2gXnW15-2gXnW7c-MKssgd-rX4B8M.

The Fighting McCooks historical marker. Photo by and courtesy of Jimmy Emerson, DVM, Flickr, https://www.flickr.com/photos /auvet/17021142077/in/photolist-ouhqRi -5AukGY-owidTZ-oukmBJ-owhw1M -rW6NwR-NHYboj-ovGedC-ow7vNR -tEQwSM-ouuUPu-xGEmYp-77uo7V-toftQJ -vtfcLj-xq3PaW-otP1tQ-oeEP36-owiK3r -qtDVSz.

LOGAN

Ash Cave at Hocking Hills State Park. Courtesy Weirick Communications.

Inn and Spa at Cedar Falls. Courtesy Weirick Communications.

LOUDONVILLE

Landoll's Mohican Castle. Photo by Angela Leezer, Flickr, https://www.flickr.com /photos/angela_leezer/7623620794/in /photolist-cBF3RQ-6BgFp5-5C9jVC-6wNjHX -SJNEmb-6BgvC3-5C9j4s-SNp7EM-8DHgvN -6BguRo-5C9jHo-ffig6T-4nPacG-4nK6B6 -4nK6J2-4nPakd-S6C2Ua-4nPafW-5C52kZ -4YfbU9-6V9tPE-5C521p-5C9jhm-5C51RM -5C9jD3-5C9jum-5C51D4-5C51MF-4nPa8o -5Ko4nh-6MFaXX-4nPa79-anAffQ-5C51pg -5C9iYw-w2Hbg-4nPa1d-w2GU2-4nK6vT -w2Hbi-uUyGn-w2GU1-4nPa55-uUDxs -uUDvP-uUDxK-w2Hbk-uUDui-w2GU5 -uUDym/, CC BY-ND 2.0.

Landoll's Mohican Castle. Photo by Angela Leezer, Flickr, https://www.flickr.com /photos/angela_leezer/7623620794/in /photolist-cBF3RQ-6BgFp5-5C9jVC-6wNjHX -SJNEmb-6BgvC3-5C9j4s-SNp7EM-8DHgvN -6BguRo-5C9jHo-ffig6T-4nPacG-4nK6B6 -4nK6J2-4nPakd-S6C2Ua-4nPafW-5C52kZ -4YfbU9-6V9tPE-5C521p-5C9jhm-5C51RM -5C9jD3-5C9jum-5C51D4-5C51MF-4nPa8o -5Ko4nh-6MFaXX-4nPa79-anAffQ-5C51pg -5C9iYw-w2Hbg-4nPa1d-w2GU2-4nK6vT -w2Hbi-uUyGn-w2GU1-4nPa55-uUDxs -uUDvP-uUDxK-w2Hbk-uUDui-w2GU5 -uUDym/, CC BY-ND 2.0.

LOVELAND

Loveland Candies. Photo by author.

Little Miami Conservancy. Photo by author.

LUCAS

Malabar Farm State Park. Photo by Niagara66, Wikimedia Commons, https://commons .wikimedia.org/w/index.php?curid =51585678, CC BY-SA 4.0.

Malabar Farm State Park. Photo by Niagara66, Wikimedia Commons, https://commons .wikimedia.org/wiki/File:Malabar_Farm, _The_Big_House_15.jpg, CC BY-SA 4.0.

MAGNOLIA

Magnolia Flouring Mills. Courtesy Stark Parks.

Magnolia Flouring Mills. Courtesy Stark Parks.

MALTA

Wildcat Hollow Trail. Forest Service photo by Kyle Brooks, Flickr, https://www.flickr.com /photos/waynenf/52308190454/in/photolist -2mKqv2h-2nGiaB8-2nGi9CE, public domain.

McConnelsville Dam. Photo by Mike Tewkesbury, Flickr, https://www.flickr.com/photos /7687126@N06/4567520298/in/photolist -7XBJDY-Y1F3qB-XXVTNA-XXVUuL -rqLgZW-WXi2m5-r6ACya-r7vsZp-robdws -r8tZvK-rapmRE-rpV7mK-rqi2sH-r8EQYS -rqMomz-w4C3x8-Y1EuTD-Ye1c7P-Y1F22V -r9bq3R-r8h9eu-XXVWvu-ay5JmS-rpXibh

-ouCNFS-u3HMah-ovyukD-64ouhh-7eEDPL
-oeS6WK-7eAJMk-JWhzj3-3kTy4D-ou2mJL
-ow9FpT-7eDZdd-7eDYK3-nwaBmp-ow3jrK
-nNEfk8-7eDYZY-PyaqqZ-8CCcCF-roDt2a
-oe9TAq-7XMbLM-nNuHcS-nwayJ9-x3tEGB
-nwaND, CC BY-ND 2.0.

MARBLEHEAD

Marblehead Lighthouse. Courtesy Lake Erie Shores & Islands.

MARIETTA

Muskingum River. Courtesy Marietta-Washington County Convention and Visitors Bureau.

Williamstown Bridge. Courtesy Marietta-Washington County Convention and Visitors Bureau.

Ohio River Museum. Courtesy Marietta-Washington County Convention and Visitors Bureau.

MCCONNELSVILLE

Mail Pouch Barn. Photo by and courtesy of Jimmy Emerson, DVM, Flickr, https://www
.flickr.com/photos/auvet/1408101653/in
/photolist-39qTyH-fP8Vw-7z8rKt-7fqafz
-9HhfSM-nTYfmf-2aAqVJW-2bJ9neX
-dGXKBU-39xeFs-FFb9w-rjpSaQ-5JXCf4
-Ayx7Zg-5u7d3R-be9LwP-5K2g9s-aRozBa
-c6DFGd-5adjh3-w61yLE-81YSTQ-DDBymw
-e7ragT-c6DFx5-6k5fQf-6gMyMc-9zENPn
-4fo1d6-eh7PhC-n45Ep-c6DG65-s2Np6H
-Jvizry-e7wPZs-oaMnqf-6iF5EN-6gRKcY
-6Mp65Q-2vuUkQ-8mcCj3-5K2gd7-8riu8N
-EpGZ1-c6DFTC-xeYfqq-4nhBWQ-oKQhfe
-GXhjAL-7EVkLP.

Twin City Opera House. Photo by Mike Tewkesbury, Flickr, https://www.flickr.com/photos
/7687126@No6/4569214745/in/photolist
-7XLqmz-6pFGAR,CC BY-ND 2.0.

MILAN

Thomas Edison Birthplace Museum. Photo by and courtesy of Bill Badzo, Flickr, https://
www.flickr.com/photos/onasill
/16627378564/in/photolist-rkiEmL-CFksmj
-rBySqB-23FiUyF-T7HGw8-2aUynTm
-BLMuLs-APW9Nt-DGM3ci-2mHkkeT
-2mVe6Ta-26fmJk7-2kSvdJ5-2kSNdq4
-26fmHWS-Bm97tG-9kigJD-27r1vs6
-27DoDoR-26fmJDJ-81PJNT-rBySdT-3eoST7
-3ep9fd-3epbvQ-3eoSYW-3epau1-81ST1f
-3epbSo-3ep9cb-nE3Jvr-3epjs1-3ep9P3
-3ejMvn-81STgA-8dJHNg-3epa2L-3epany
-8dMYfd-3ep9rY-3epj1L-3eoTds-3epcx9
-81PJxx-3ejUQ6-8dJHHe-avzbP4-3ejLHt
-3ejLRX-8dMYaw.

MILLERSBURG

Yoder's Amish Home. Courtesy Holmes County Chamber of Commerce & Tourism Bureau.

Hotel Millersburg. Courtesy Holmes County Chamber of Commerce & Tourism Bureau.

Yoder's Amish Home. Courtesy Holmes County Chamber of Commerce & Tourism Bureau.

MINERVA

Market Street. Photo by Roseohioresident, Wikimedia Commons, https://commons
.wikimedia.org/wiki/File:Market_Street_
Minerva_Ohio001.jpg, released to public domain.

MINSTER

Canal mural. Photo by author.

Minster Historical Society Garden. Photo by author.

MORROW

Valley Vineyards Winery and Brewery. Courtesy Warren County Convention & Visitors Bureau.

Valley Vineyards Winery and Brewery. Courtesy Warren County Convention & Visitors Bureau.

MOUNT PLEASANT

1804 log cabin. Courtesy Historical Society of Mount Pleasant, Ohio.

Mt. Pleasant Historic District. Photo by Bwmith84, Wikimedia Commons, https://
commons.wikimedia.org/wiki/File:Mount
_Pleasant_Historic_Site.jpg, CCBY 3.0.

MOUNT VERNON

Knox County Courthouse. Photo by Mark Spearman, Wikimedia Commons, https://
commons.wikimedia.org/wiki/File:Knox
_County,_Ohio_Courthouse_(14516804607)
.jpg, CC BY 2.0.

Woodward Opera House. Photo by Mark Spearman, Wikimedia Commons, https://
commons.wikimedia.org/wiki/File:Mount
_Vernon-Woodward_Opera_House_and
_Cooper_Building_(OHPTC).jpg, CC BY 2.0.

OBERLIN

Oberlin College. Photo by and courtesy of Bill Badzo, Flickr, https://www.flickr.com
/photos/onasill/17146925715.

OREGONIA

Morgan's Outdoor Adventure. Courtesy Warren County Convention & Visitors Bureau.

Caesar Creek State Park. Courtesy Warren County Convention & Visitors Bureau.

Ozone Zipline Adventures. Courtesy Warren County Convention & Visitors Bureau.

ORRVILLE

J. M. Smucker Company Store and Café. Photo by and courtesy of Joanna Poe, Flickr, https://www.flickr.com/photos/jopoe
/7221465958.

OXFORD

Black Covered Bridge. Photo by Ron Hautau. Courtesy Enjoy Oxford.

Downtown. Photo by Ron Hautau. Courtesy Enjoy Oxford.

PENINSULA

Kendall Lake. Photo by Steve @ the Alligator Farm, Flickr, https://www.flickr.com

/photos/bowwowbeach/2933335733/in
/album-72157608030004028/, CC BY-SA 2.0.

Cuyahoga Valley National Park. Peninsula
fall by Steve @ the Alligator Farm, Flickr,
https://www.flickr.com/photos
/bowwowbeach/3999619312/in/album
-72157608030004028/, CC BY-SA 2.0.

PORTSMOUTH

Turkey Creek Lake. Courtesy Portsmouth-
Scioto County Visitors Bureau.

Ohio River, Charles Street. Courtesy
Portsmouth-Scioto County Visitors Bureau.

PUT-IN-BAY

Brig Niagara. Photo by Lance Woodworth,
Wikimedia Commons, https://commons
.wikimedia.org/wiki/File:Brig_Niagara
_full_sail.jpg, CC BY 2.0.

The Boardwalk. Courtesy Lake Erie Shores &
Islands.

Jet Express. Courtesy Lake Erie Shores &
Islands.

RIPLEY

John Rankin House. Photo by Christopher L.
Riley, Wikimedia Commons, https://
commons.wikimedia.org/wiki/File:John
_Rankin_House_%E2%80%94_Ripley,
_Ohio.jpg, CC BY-SA 4.0.

Union Township Library. Photo by Nyttend,
Wikimedia Commons, https://commons
.wikimedia.org/wiki/File:Union_Township
_Library_in_Ripley.jpg, released to public
domain.

ROCKBRIDGE

Hocking Hills Canopy Tours. Courtesy Weirick
Communications.

Rock climbing. Courtesy Weirick Communications.

Hocking Hills Canopy Tours. Courtesy Weirick
Communications.

Butterfly Ridge. Courtesy Weirick Communications.

SEBRING

Sebring Mansion. Photo by Nyttend, Wikimedia Commons, https://commons.wikimedia
.org/wiki/File:Frank_Sebring_House.jpg,
released to public domain.

SPRINGBORO

Rotary Park. Photo by author.

Downtown shops. Photo by author.

STEUBENVILLE

Jefferson County Courthouse. Photo by
Nyttend, Wikimedia Commons, https://
commons.wikimedia.org/wiki/File:
Jefferson_County_Courthouse_in
_Steubenville.jpg, released to public
domain.

Carnegie Library. Photo by Nyttend, Wikimedia Commons, https://commons.wikimedia
.org/wiki/File:Steubenville_Carnegie
_library.jpg, released to public domain.

ST. MARYS

Grand Lake St. Marys Lighthouse. Photo by
Nyttend, Wikimedia Commons, https://
commons.wikimedia.org/wiki/File:Grand
_Lake_St._Marys_Lighthouse.jpg, released
to public domain.

Belle of St. Marys Canal Boat. Photo by author.

STOCKPORT

Stockport Mill. Photo by Mike Tewkesbury,
Flickr, https://www.flickr.com/photos
/7687126@N06/10662820964/in/photolist
-hfeKbL-6bviuq-6bBCG7-7XytUr-e3YLjp
-6eWvLy-6eSfA3-7XBJbC-6eLAMj-6eQWuP
-6eTyBp-hfeV4y-7XGXgn-6eLg53-7YaT7U
-6eGsAk-6bwa7S-7XKYDq-6eKX8y-6eLtvs
-6eLoa3-7XGazV-hfeR2f-6eR9Qv/, CC BY-ND
2.0.

Stockport Mill Inn. Photo by Mike Tewkesbury,
Flickr, https://www.flickr.com/photos
/7687126@N06/10662840596/in/photolist
-hfeKbL-6bviuq-6bBCG7-7XytUr-e3YLjp
-6eKX8y-6eLtvs-6eLoa3-7XGazV-6eWvLy
-6eSfA3-7XBJbC-6eLAMj-6eQWuP-hfeR2f
-6eTyBp-hfeV4y-6eR9Qv-7XGXgn-6eLg53
-7YaT7U-6eGsAk-6bwa7S-7XKYDq, CC
BY-ND 2.0.

SUGARCREEK

David Warther Carvings and Gift Shop. Photo
by author.

World's Largest Cuckoo Clock. Photo by author.

TIPP CITY

Scratch Bakery by Justin Tyler. Photo by
author.

Downtown mural. Photo by author.

UTICA

Velvet Ice Cream. Courtesy Weirick Communications.

Water wheel, Velvet Ice Cream. Photo by
author.

VAN WERT

Downtown Wall Mural. Photo by and courtesy
of Bill Badzo, Flickr, https://www.flickr.com
/photos/onasill/30322078771/in/photolist
-FhAn4H-FsZP4a-L5vsLp-29q7CmZ-EkdLr6
-2krDgsV-GbYYk4-2krRBVG-2krRBLD
-2krAzuu-GbYYbB-NcszBz-CLFsWY
-MTpPqu-2aNuwmp-2aHt8iy-CLFsaN
-2kDmMTs-2gRqnXJ-NCxi8y-PE7Ctc
-2aMoxFa-2cba6gn-GhQb1K-LUrMBP
-2gRqo4A-LVGJU4-2mYgnay-2mYY4L1
-G9F1fA-2aMobgB-2kLCyWS-NcsAUK
-FnyuTH-GhQ9ut-LVGnBe-LTGZAf
-MnWqtE-L7kd4X-NcsAop-2aNA7dM
-2aJ5Tu9-NcsA8z.

Balyeat's Coffee Shop Historic District. Photo
by and courtesy of Bill Badzo, Flickr,
https://www.flickr.com/photos/onasill
/25841901143/in/photolist-2jZ9ug6-FnyuTH
-8eYv1g-50NFmY-LZ9cW.

VERMILLION

Vermillion Lighthouse. Courtesy Lake Erie Shores & Islands.

Lake Erie. Courtesy Lake Erie Shores & Islands.

Nokomis Park. Courtesy Lake Erie Shores & Islands.

The Wine Vault. Courtesy Lake Erie Shores & Islands.

WALNUT CREEK

Coblentz Chocolates. Photo by author.

Coblentz Chocolates. Photo by author.

WAPAKONETA

Auglaize County Courthouse. Photo by Derek Jensen, Wikimedia Commons, https://commons.wikimedia.org/wiki/File:Wapakoneta-ohio-courthouse.jpg, released to public domain.

1937 mural. Photo by and courtesy of Jimmy Emerson, DVM, Flickr, https://www.flickr.com/photos/auvet/16896169737/in/photolist-NcszBz-2nxZzsH-2ny2XT7-2nxZzwq-Wvn3yu-2jEXMy2-2nxZzjX-2mxvYUM-2n3U7pW-cdEffQ-rK4hBk-rLNT7y-2nxUjVa-2mxuMaK-2mxysP6-8xjNna-M6Wi7w.

WASHINGTON COURT HOUSE

Fayette County Courthouse. Photo by and courtesy of Bill Badzo, Flickr, https://www.flickr.com/photos/onasill/8313183014/in/album-72157632355285117/.

Fayette County Museum. Photo by Aesopposea, Wikimedia Commons, https://commons.wikimedia.org/wiki/File:MorrisSharp.JPG, CC BY-SA 3.0.

WATERVILLE

Columbian House. Photo by Doug Kerr, Flickr, https://www.flickr.com/photos/dougtone/14514378683/in/photolist-o5GEF9-o5vzwn-o7zZ7k-o5NUNi-o5GHtd-nNjuA6-o5GfUJ-o7zWXa-nNkdwD-o5vxhx-o5GFFW-o3Ls5L-o3Lrd5-o5GfrQ-o5vxSa-nNjuq5-nNjgy5-dtUNnh-4HCaA1-qLuVmJ, CC BY-SA 2.0.

WAYNESVILLE

Caesar's Creek Pioneer Village. Photo by author.

Caesar's Creek Pioneer Village. Photo by author.

WHITEHOUSE

Whitehouse Inn. Photo by author.

Wabash caboose. Photo by author.

YELLOW SPRINGS

Birch Creek Falls. Photo by and courtesy of Thomas Dwyer, Flickr, https://www.flickr.com/photos/double_o_zero/24249463218/in/photolist-Z5cXnW-Z4PHUY-YSZYBX-2atTpHS-CWQQzq-G7cBzt-V1CDzA-vEV8UU.

Grinnell Mill. Photo by and courtesy of Thomas Dwyer, Flickr, https://www.flickr.com/photos/double_o_zero/34788532306/in/photolist-25NzoXs-V19jD9.

Old Union School. Photo by and courtesy of Thomas Dwyer, Flickr, https://www.flickr.com/photos/double_o_zero/34609586741/in/album-72157679235003112/.

Ye Olde Trail Tavern. Photo by author.

ZOAR

1800s log cabin home. Photo by author.

Zoar Museum. Photo by author.

Ever since she started her own newspaper at age eight, selling it to neighbors who had no choice but to subscribe, **JANE SIMON AMMESON** has loved to write. She's now upped her game, writing about travel, food, and history for newspapers, magazines, and websites and is author of fifteen books, including the recently released *Lincoln Road Trip: Back-Roads Guide to America's Favorite President*, winner of the Lowell Thomas Journalism Award for Best Travel Book, Bronze, as well as a finalist for the 2019 Foreword INDIES Book of the Year Awards. She is also author of *How to Murder Your Wealthy Love and Get Away with It: Murder and Money and Mayhem in the Gilded Age*, a historic true crime tale of an ultimate femme fatale; *Hauntings of the Underground Railroad: Ghosts of the Midwest*; and *Murders That Made Headlines: Crimes of Indiana*. She is also author of *A Jazz Age Murder in Northwest Indiana*, a true crime book about a murder that took place in her hometown. Jane writes a weekly food column for the *Herald Palladium* and Shelf Life and a travel column for the *Times of Northwest Indiana*, and she currently is getting her travel app for TouchScreenTravel ready to go live.

A member of the Society of American Travel Writers (SATW); International Food, Wine and Travel Writers Association (IFWTWA); and Midwest Travel Journalists Association (MTJA), Jane's home base is on the shores of Lake Michigan in Southwest Michigan. Follow Jane on instagram.com/janeammeson; facebook.com/janesimonammeson; twitter.com/janeammeson1; and on her blogs, janeammeson.com and shelflife.blog.